Contemporary Turkish Short Fiction: A Selection

Volume 2

Edited by
Suat Karantay

Çitlembik Publications 172

Contemporary Turkish Short Fiction:
A Selection

Volume 2

Suat Karantay earned a B.A. in comparative literature from Robert College (Istanbul), an M.A. in Comparative Literature from the University of Southern California, and a PhD in English and American Literature from Istanbul University. Since 1983 he has been a professor of Translation and Interpreting Studies at Bosphorus University, Istanbul. He has edited numerous books and literary journals in addition to translating works of Turkish literature into English.

© Çitlembik / Nettleberry Publications, 2010
© Suat Karantay, 2010

All rights reserved. No part of this publication may be reproduced in any form and by any means without the prior permission of Çitlembik.

Library of Congress Cataloging-in-Publication Data:

Contemporary Turkish short fiction: a selection, vol. 2 / ed. Suat Karantay
Istanbul: Çitlembik, 2010.
2 v.: photo; 16.5x23.5 cm

ISBN: 978-9944-424-54-7

1. Authors, Turkish—20th century
2. Turkish fiction—20th century   I. Karantay, Suat

LC: PL248   DC: 894.3533

Layout: Çiğdem Dilbaz

Printed at Ayhan Matbaası
Mahmutbey Mah. Deve Kaldırım Cad.
Gelincik Sokak No.: 6 Kat: 3 Bağcılar/İstanbul
Tel: (0212) 445 32 38

In Turkey:
Şehbender Sokak 18/4
Asmalımescit Tünel 34430 İstanbul
Tel: 0 212 292 30 32 / 252 31 63
Fax: 0 212 293 34 66
www.citlembik.com.tr
kitap@citlembik.com.tr

In the USA:
Nettleberry LLC
44030 123rd St.
Eden, South Dakota 57232
www.nettleberry.com

Contents

Note on the Translated Turkish Literature Series 9
Preface 11
A Look at Short Fiction in Turkey Today: Introduction by Feridun Andaç 13

FEYZA HEPÇİLİNGİRLER
Troksalila 17
Floods of the Day 21
Before Death and Birth 25

IŞIL ÖZGENTÜRK
On the Heels of a Blue Horse 28

SELİM İLERİ
The Last Day of a Friendship 31

HABİB BEKTAŞ
Panacea: A Story 39
Holiday 41

FERİDE ÇİÇEKOĞLU
The Coincidence 43
Some Get Clawed by Falcons 47
A 100-Asa Country 51

CEMİL KAVUKÇU
Into the Depths of the Forest 85
The Route of the Crows 102
Just Has to Be 107

MEHMET ÇETİN
    Does What We Call a Human Resemble a Cloud?..................109

MURATHAN MUNGAN
    Snow White Without the Seven Dwarfs...................117

MEHMET ZAMAN SAÇLIOĞLU
    The Big Eye 120

HÜR YUMER
    Just What I Had in Mind...................128
    The Best Sunday 135

SİBEL BİLGİN
    The Blue Dress 140

ÜMİT KIVANÇ
    A Crossing of Paths 146

HALİL İBRAHİM ÖZCAN
    While Rain Was Falling on the Hazar...................151
    Preparation for a Rendezvous...................154

CEZMİ ERSÖZ
    The Writer Unable to Write 157

PERİHAN MAĞDEN
    The Secret Meanings of Unappreciated Words 161
    Courage Does Not Reign 169

NALAN BARBAROSOĞLU
    The Daisies of My Spring Morning 178
    Teller of Tales...................182

HAKAN ŞENOCAK
    Ci Ci 187

SUZAN SAMANCI
    Click-Click...................191
    Two Mothers 194

GAYE BORALIOĞLU
  Subtle Calculation 197

AYFER TUNÇ
  A Small Well 203

ÖZEN YULA
  One Last Word for the Sake of Health: Treachery in the Near East 212

İNAN ÇETİN
  A Story of Separation 231

MÜGE İPLİKÇİ
  The Ramparts..237
  You Are Without Me 241

ASLI ERDOĞAN
  Wooden Birds..246

MURAT GÜLSOY
  My Life's a Lie...258

DENİZ SPATAR
  The Scar..267

MURAT SOHTORİK
  The Village Seen..273

KARİN KARAKAŞLI
  Days of the Flood in Zeugma 276

ŞEBNEM İŞİGÜZEL
  Fragments from Real Life for the Last Scene of a Movie.........................279

ALMİLA ÖZDEK
  The Goddess of Fertility...284

Biographical Notes 289

Note on the Translated Turkish Literature Series

This series of publications is being launched to help familiarize the world with contemporary Turkish literature through English translations of recent works by celebrated Turkish authors, poets, and playwrights. The focus is mainly on contemporary Turkish literature, and the target language is English, intended to reach the greatest possible international readership.

A broad range in both style and subject matter is represented among the outstanding writings—in all literary genres—appearing on the vibrant literary scene in Turkey today. The endeavor to present this literature to an international audience was begun in the virtual arena in the year 2001. A website with English translations of contemporary Turkish literature, may be accessed at <www.turkish-lit.boun.edu.tr>. We are now making such translations available in a printed format.

Suat Karantay
Editor-in-Chief

Editor's Preface

The amount of Turkish short fiction introduced to the West has been, until quite recently, not very impressive—having appeared in English translation only in a few anthologies and in collections of individual writers (e.g. those of Haldun Taner, Sait Faik and Osman Şahin, among a few others). Moreover, the anthologies have remained—as collective works tend to do—rather subjective and thus not fully representative. There are many Turkish short fiction writers who have been denied the attention they deserve.

These two new volumes of recent Turkish short fiction in translation are being launched to better familiarize the English-speaking world with contemporary Turkish short fiction. Several constraints, however, come to the fore. These volumes do not claim to represent all contemporary Turkish short fiction—nor to be an objective selection of the best contemporary Turkish writers who write short fiction. What is included here reflects the preferences of the translators rather than any canonical status of the short fiction. These volumes represent, therefore, a selection that "appeals to readers." Consequently, we anticipate neither polemics nor controversy. It must be stressed, however, that our "selection" is by no means haphazard, though we must admit that several masters (Nezihe Meriç, Pınar Kür, Buket Uzuner, to name a few) are missing due to lack of translation.

One great advantage of the selection in the present volumes is that not only established Turkish writers but also relative newcomers are represented. Also included is one specimen of short fiction written in English by a Turkish writer and three translated into English by the writers themselves.

There is no attempt at hierarchy in these volumes. That some writers are better represented than others reflects only the availability of translations. Nor can we claim that the short fiction included here is necessarily the finest of each individual

Contemporary Turkish Short Fiction: A Selection

writer; however, each and every one is a fine piece of short fiction in its own right, qualified to stimulate the imagination of the target reader.

A chronological organization has been chosen, beginning with Nazım Hikmet. Included are very short stories as well as longer ones. Form, content, and theme are reflected by a rich spectrum ranging from metropolitan to provincial, from individualistic to committed fiction, as well as satire and romances.

With a long and sustained tradition, Turkish short fiction underwent a period of disorientation in the twentieth century. To compose a well-balanced picture of contemporary Turkish fiction is no easy task. The historical surveys written are often sketchy. To provide the reader with some relevant background and to single out distinctive trends in contemporary Turkish fiction, an essay by Feridun Andaç has been included as the Introduction.

This modest collection will hopefully serve as an introduction to those interested in the short fiction of contemporary Turkey and in the Turkish sensibility. It certainly bears witness to a vibrant and rich tradition of short fiction.

Thanks are due to all of our translators / contributors, whose names appear below each selection. We are especially indebted to the late Jean Carpenter Efe for her invaluable assistance in the preparation of these volumes.

A Look at Short Fiction in Turkey Today: Introduction by Feridun Andaç

The launching of prose into Turkish literature—and its subsequent development as a literary genre—accompanied the rise of the Republic, beginning in the era known as the "Early Republican" period. This venturesome journey indeed reflects a historic process. Its continuation into a new phase with the coming of the Republic and its persevering development over a period of more than two centuries underlines its resolute spirit. With the first strides of the Ottoman-Turk into modernization, literature too gleaned its fair share from the concept known as Westernization. Moreover, we witness the early works of Turkish prose embracing this concept as if taking on a mission.

The 19th century represented a first step. During this period—in which the novel appeared in adaptation as well as translation—short texts based on legend and folktales began to appear in print. A search for the "new" was found in translation. Authors such as Ahmet Mithat and Emin Nihat, not to mention Şemsettin Sami, Namık Kemal, Samipaşazade Sezai, Recaizade Mahmut Ekrem, Nabizade Nazım and Ebubekir Hazım Tepeyran, produced the first examples of Turkish fiction.

It is in the following generation that we encounter samples of original modern prose. Writers such as Halit Ziya Uşaklıgil, Mehmet Rauf, Hüseyin Rahmi Gürpınar, Yakup Kadri Karaosmanoğlu, Halide Edip Adıvar and Reşat Nuri Güntekin are hailed as the founders of the Turkish novel.

In short fiction we see a similar initiative. The founders of the modern Turkish short story—in one sense—are Ömer Seyfettin, Memduh Şevket Esendal and F. Celâlettin, who created original works by rendering the fictional framework of the Turkish oral tradition in the "new prose" that reflected the molds of short fiction popular worldwide. These writers, espousing in their fiction a look-and-see attitude towards life and a define-and-describe approach towards the individual, were thus in a sense the "first"— the "heralds"—of the generations to come.

Contemporary Turkish Short Fiction: A Selection

When we come to the period of the actual Republic, we encounter the "new realists"—a group of outstanding writers now gifted with an inheritance from the preceding generation. Among them are certainly some—Refik Halit Karay, Sadri Ertem, Kenan Hulusi Koray, Bekir Sıtkı Kunt, Osman Cemal Kaygılı—whose short fiction addresses the new concept of "national literature" portraying the social realities existing among various populations within the nation. These authors may be regarded as pioneers. Then we have writers of short fiction such as Sait Faik Abasıyanık, Sabahattin Ali, Umran Nazif Yiğiter, İlhan Tarus, Samim Kocagöz, Orhan Kemal, Necati Cumalı, Oktay Akbal, Haldun Taner and Tarık Buğra, who take on a creative trailblazing role by emphasizing relationships between the individual and society in reference to the changing realities of the times.

In the 1940s and '50s, new tendencies mark the direction of short fiction. On the one hand, certain writers—reflecting the heritage of "national literature"—stress the realities of life within specific local-geographical contexts; they not only mirror the problems of such societies from the viewpoint of observe-and-define, but they take one step forward by adding a critical approach as well. Their prose also bears witness to variations in speech and language. In the fiction of Kemal Bilbaşar, the "Halicarnassos Fisherman" (Halikarnas Balıkçısı), Yaşar Kemal, Mehmet Seyda, Faik Baysal, Fakir Baykurt, Talip Apaydın and Mehmet Başaran, it is the realities of rural / backwoods populations that similarly support this theme. On the other hand, the stories of other writers present the plight of the "little man" caught up in the rural-urban dichotomy. The stories of Aziz Nesin, Tarık Dursun K., Muzaffer Buyrukçu, Demirtaş Ceyhun, Zeyyat Selimoğlu and Erhan Bener take on a new stance by portraying this theme not only in plot but in language register as well. A novelty in short fiction dealing with the realities of the urban population was the search for new linguistic form and expression; outstanding authors of this generation include Nezihe Meriç, Tahsin Yücel, Vüs'at O. Bener, Bilge Karasu, Orhan Duru, Ferit Edgü, Onat Kutlar, Erdal Öz, Demir Özlü, Adnan Özyalçıner and Leyla Erbil.

We might say that it was during these two decades in the mid-20th century that the characteristics establishing short prose as an esteemed element of modern Turkish literature were defined. The writers' handling of the language, their approaches to linguistic expression—their realistic interpretations of society and the individual—altered the form of the short story, rejuvenated it, bringing to it a breath of fresh air.

It is actually in the short fiction of the 1960s onward that a fine balance between traditional and modern expression and themes becomes apparent. This more recent phase represents a period most productive in all aspects. The democratization of Turkey had opened the way for this. The former East-West dichotomy found a common foothold; no longer a bone of contention, it now provided a ground for efforts aimed at comprehension and clarification. Modern literature in general and prose in particular—the novel as well as shorter fiction—now played a great role in developing awareness of the contemporary world; expression became original and creative.

Introduction

In this more recent period, the communicative role of the author allows, moreover, a sense of his or her own identity. One notes that women writers have assumed a significant role. Tomris Uyar, Füruzan, Sevgi Soysal, Adalet Ağaoğlu, Tezer Özlü, Selçuk Baran, Ayhan Bozfırat, Sevinç Çokum, Nazlı Eray, Pınar Kür and İnci Aral are among the names dominating the 1960s and '70s. The role of the woman, her problems and her personal relationships are reflected; the themes of many writers address a search for identity and the anxiety to justify one's own existence.

For short fiction this has proved a rich and varied phase. At one end of the spectrum we have writers such as Bekir Yıldız and Osman Şahin who have given a "new voice" to old traditional stories, widening their scope to encompass the realities of present-day society; at the other end, we have those such as Selim İleri, Nedim Gürsel, Hulki Aktunç, Necati Tosuner, Sulhi Dölek, Mustafa Kutlu and Burhan Günel, who emphasize newly constructed elements in their short fiction. In place of the urban-rural dichotomy earlier reflected, we may say that the question of personal / individual adjustment has come to the fore. As well as women's roles and challenges, basic themes include identity and sense-of-belonging, societal disintegration, migration, rejection, alienation, change, and the like.

In the 1980s an alternative development appears; the narration of "secret lives" leaves an imprint on many works. We might describe this as a journey into the human soul. As a trend it continued into the 1990s.

In the new millennium, the outstanding names among women writers of short fiction include Erendiz Atasü, Feyza Hepçilingirler, Oya Baydar, Ayşe Kulin, Feride Çiçekoğlu, Perihan Mağden, Nalan Barbarosoğlu, Suzan Samancı, Müge İplikci, Aslı Erdoğan and Şebnem İşigüzel. Men who have made their mark in short fiction include Murathan Mungan, Cemil Kavukçu, Mehmet Zaman Saçlıoğlu, Hür Yumer, Hakan Şenocak, Özen Yula and Murat Gülsoy; with their feet firmly planted on different shores, they have all displayed creative talent to make their own voices heard.

Short fiction, having found its own path into the widening field of Turkish literature, has become its most effective prose genre. It has brought literary considerations into question—placing them as it were under a microscope—to a great extent through the many literary journals focused upon short fiction that have sprung up on the market one after the other. This latter phenomenon in itself is perhaps the most significant witness to the development of the genre.

The collection in these volumes bears witness to this development; the selections included follow the course of short fiction in Turkey. They reveal the essence of Turkish story-telling as it developed day by day, blazing its own pathway into prose literature; they represent an accumulation of attributes embedded in this short fiction: meaning and expression, a nationwide recognition of the individual-within-society and the properties of perception / conception.

Translated by Jean Carpenter Efe

FEYZA HEPÇİLİNGİRLER

Troksalila

His arrival was like always. It was as ordinary as it was unusual. I could see.

As always, of the whole body and head, it was above all his eyes that came to the fore. It was the spell of love; it was the nectar of living that he presented me with his eyes—opening in a crown of leaves, the biggest of blue—that for twenty years had never tired of coming or loving. Neither was the sea too dark when he came; nor had the moon started to show her face—blushing with joy—in the embrace of the sea. It was still daytime, an ordinary evening under oblique rays. And he, my mate, was smiling with a smile that gave no hint of his falling asleep.

The wind of his coming, blowing with and after him cools my house when it's summer, and in winter warms every corner, softening the armchairs, even the floor.

Does love ever wear out?

The reason love wears out is that the heart has shriveled and slackened and just doesn't want to go on anymore. His was a giant's heart, so full and so deep. Neither to forget nor to be forgotten nor any such inclination could exist in his heart; weaving love with patience, he was a voluntary slave of the cage he'd woven for two.

Was tonight the right time for silence?

Just when my lover is sleeping next to me, as if smiling—his arm under his head like a pillow. He always slept as if smiling.

We have listened to its voice for years—sitting, talking, sipping tea at the marble table there in the garden, from china laid out on a tablecloth as if there were people around even when there were none, without depriving each other of the respect that would be shown to others. Why should we deprive each other of that, it's our love and ourselves that is more deserving of it than strangers we don't even know. But especially while lying in bed—haven't we listened to it for years from our bed, a devoted audience when there is silence everywhere, with the troksalila on the throne, having commanded silence from everyone for the concert?

Tonight is no different from the other nights. Why then has it deprived us of its invisible voice? Adding what is left from the previous day to the next, considering as well the following day, being careful not to leave any moment as a gap in love; it understands the experience of love. Nobody can understand better than the troksalila how to love and voice love in its song. Would the troksalila ever tire of its voice and chirping? Would it ever stop loving just because it was bored?

Tonight is like all other nights. He came back to the house quite early tonight, too. He warmed and lit up every corner with an ever-fresh beauty. Whoever doesn't believe me should have a look. If the troksalila doesn't believe me, it should have a look, too. He's lying right next to me. His head is so young and so lovely, like his heart. A bouquet of smiling flowers blossomed in his cheeks and will always blossom there. A bouquet of smiling flowers that is destined not to wilt. Loving is not a dream; it is the core of reality. If the garden is not constantly watered with love, and the flower not refreshed, it will die. But it hasn't even wilted. Could a flower that hasn't wilted in twenty years ever die?

This silence of the troksalila is just as ridiculous as a desire to exaggerate happiness with ringing laughter. It didn't have to be silent in order to make its presence conspicuous. Our hearts have become accustomed to warming to the sincerity of that smile—demonstrating the patience of a voice that rang out as if with no effort at all— that went far beyond the boundary of sound. Our hearts are accustomed to warming only to that warmth. If only it would smile in my imagination, not to my face, with its dreams, then it would be the warmth of a smile deep in my heart that could reach through the darkness.

If only a canary's ballad were heard now! If only his masculine voice singing *"Kaneri mou gliko"* would overflow his sleeping body, filling first my ears, then the room, then everyplace. My husband's voice, which takes its tenderness from his love and its depth from the breeze of the open sea... Perhaps that voice won't come because the troksalila is silent. It hasn't been silent for years. Why tonight? When that love song which never paused from dusk till dawn every night for years, for years, for long, long years—for some twenty years—suddenly stopped tonight... I don't know what has happened— what could have happened—I don't know what to think. Could the troksalila have died? How dare I say die? Our Troksalila was love. It was an everlasting love song that poured its soul into its love, and its love into its soul; it couldn't end. And why tonight—of all nights—would it end? Was love at an end, or life? If he weren't sleeping right next to me now, he would be very angry at such thoughts of mine. My thinking, I mean, that love could end like a roll of muslin at the end of the bolt.

The broom is covered with yellow blossoms at this season. There they are now with the very brightest and freshest of yellows showing off for those who await them with unbearable patience. The broom won't blossom again till this season next year. Tomorrow at dusk, I shall go out, and revel in that beauty. With him by my side. Nothing can be beautiful without him. Because there is nothing beautiful without love, nothing that has the power to be beautiful on its own. I can walk in the fields till dawn. My time is plenty and empty—how much time I will have—I may make my way through the scrub oak and dwarf junipers to climb the hills. This is my duty in the hours that welcome the night, just when the troksalila takes up its chirping once again. It's time to check the wild apples to see if they are ripe. It's time to pick wild strawberries to bring to my beloved in a white handkerchief, to inhale the smell of the chaste trees until my sinuses burn, to lose myself in the smell of the chaste trees.

Was that a chirp?

I thought what I heard was a short, broken, breath-like chirping. He will wake up once it sings, I know. That's why I'm begging, see? Please, sing for once, Troksalila. Once... Please! Make me believe nothing has ended. I don't have enough power to bear the end. But since you're silent like this... Please don't be silent. Tell me that my lover is next to me. Sing "*Samiotisa*," imitating his voice. Tell the love story of Samiotisa with the three moles "*Me tris elyes.*" Especially tonight I want to hear it. To fully experience her love, her sacrifice, and her death... To die with love is not really dying, Troksalila.

Why is it suddenly so bright everywhere? Is day breaking after my first lonely night?

It didn't sing tonight. *It won't sing.* I am putting out to the open sea. Feeling the water under me deepening at every stroke, and fearing it—so afraid—yet not turning back. One more, one more stroke. He will wake up, I know. He will get up and say "Good morning." Our good mornings will begin again.

In the pale, whitened sky of the aging night is a traveler cloud, pinkening on the side towards the day, with the side towards the night still persisting in its determined leaden gray. Behind the mottled gray is crimson. The sea is vast, like folds of silvery satin. He just has to see this. Why doesn't he stir? Why does he just lie there in a position to see me if he opens his eyes? He should wake up now.

Suddenly a wave breaks. With a roar and sound like the pang of a mother whose breathing has quickened. This is birth, too. The day will be born. Don't feel bad that we don't have a child, all right? Because we've given birth to each other. Now with the new day, you are being born, too. Look! You are reborn every day. You will be reborn every day.

Use your last chance now, Troksalila. Sing before the night exhales its final breath. Or else you won't be able to see the sunrise, the sunrise like a ball of fire. And you, my love, if you don't wake up, you will be too late for the day.

One final star remains in the sky, like a lusterless eye trying to shine. The waves no longer rise and fall. The day is breaking. The night is over.

So it will never sing again.

Thank god he is lying at my side like this. Thank god he is sleeping at my side. Otherwise I would believe he, too, had gone with the troksalila, and that he would never love me again, that he would never ever breathe again, that he simply didn't exist.

Thank god he is here. Thank god he is lying at my side like this. He would have awakened if the troksalila had sung, I know. He wouldn't be sleeping like this, as if dead. I won't let them take him away from me. I will never ever let them fill his blue eyes with earth. Let him sleep as if he would see me when he opens his eyes. And I will stay here with him. There is nothing to be afraid of: The broom can blossom by itself. The wild apples will ripen by themselves, too, without my watching them. As for the troksalila, who cares whether it sings or not? By myself, I can express my love to him. To my beloved.

Translated by İlke Deniz and Jean Carpenter Efe

"Troksalila," *Ürkek Kuşlar* (1999). Istanbul: Remzi Kitabevi, pp. 19-23.

FEYZA HEPÇİLİNGİRLER

Floods of the Day

I sold my camera last summer, he said. It was getting expensive, what with the cost of film development and other things. I'd taken photographs of you, remember? Upstairs; here; in the garden; with Siret Hanım; alone...

Was it last summer, or more recently, when was it?

–When do you mean? Recently?

–Recently? Recently what?

–The photographs, I mean. I know of some very old photographs.

I don't mention the net stockings and the roses.

–That's what I was talking about...

I understood. Does any reason remain to figure out when those photographs were taken? Nearly a lifetime has passed since then. The one who captures the instant, İhsan Bey—jumping from the armchairs to the couches, running, rearranging things, chasing and capturing... Dissolute, wild, rowdy İhsan Bey, can he be this man who is now trying to re-live the joy of his past as a photographer? With a noble, considerate, polite expression, he looks at this person he photographed so often in his youthful days. Indeed, as he himself said, there were so many pictures taken in the garden, here, upstairs—I used to think that he was taking photographs of my legs rather than of me. I was afraid. Of an unnamed evil. In a refined manner İhsan Bey used to pull my skirt above my knees, not touching my legs. (Did I think, at the time, that this was what refined manners ought to be?) Black net stockings, a handful, a very soft ball of silk. I had a blue woolen dress with a very wide collar, for the first time covering part of my knees, and, again for the first time, with darts in the bodice.

Net stockings came to Turkey much later than İhsan Bey had me wear them, and they became an inseparable part of women's legs. However, İhsan Bey was not obsessed with bare legs. What was it then? Later, in this same house, I saw legs in net stockings, looking more naked than the bare legs in some magazines. So many magazines! Newspapers, books, too: but most of all magazines. On the bedside table over there was an old-fashioned radio. At that time Siret Hanım never spilled any water when she filled a glass; decanters were elegantly made. And Siret Hanım had beautiful legs, long and shapely. In high-heeled slippers they looked even more striking, but she never got to wear net stockings. On a small, low, three-legged table were piled issues of a magazine, together with those others. Where is that table now? And Siret Hanım's high-heeled slippers? What slippers am I talking about? She never wore slippers; in the house she walked around in high-heeled shoes; she considered wearing slippers low-class; whenever visitors took off their shoes at the door she would act as if she were insulted. Except for her very special guests, she used to receive her visitors here. On the small, low tables were lace drapings with tassles that touched the floor. Once when I saw some cheap nylon covers on them I was terrified. (Was it because I considered it the beginning of a downfall?) It was the doings of Mehveş, who favored any sort of novelty. Mehveş, Siret Hanım's daughter, was a young girl at the time. She's been married for a long time now and has children as tall as she is. Whenever I came, I would find her sitting in a corner of the couch embroidering. On a frame. With one hand underneath and one on top, she embroidered birds, flowers and men with guitars serenading their sweethearts. Sometimes she would teach me how to dance: "So that you won't be embarrassed some day." I feel like "a poor girl being raised as a princess"—God knows under the influence of which film! I cannot tell this to anybody but I love learning to dance like a princess.

When I reached for Siret Hanım's doorbell (old fashioned, bow-shaped, the kind that you don't press but turn) I knew what I was searching for. Rather than these two old people, it was my childhood which ought to be lying somewhere around here. That's why I feel an uneasiness mixed with fear. I want to run away: What if I don't find it? How many years has it been since I was last here? The approaching footsteps take a long time. I am about to ask the hunchbacked old woman who opens the door if Siret Hanım is in: She used to live here. But she recognizes me as soon as she sees me. "Oh, my precious one..." she says. "My precious one... İhsan Bey, come and see who is here." It doesn't sound odd to me that Siret Hanım addresses her husband as İhsan Bey. Not in the least.

–You look fine, I say. How nice it is... To age together.

–Yes, we have aged, haven't we? says Siret Hanım.

İhsan Bey finds his wife's question very childish, and with a condescending smile, makes me excuse her: "Don't pay any attention to what she says." Still, I proceed:

–No. That's not what I meant. Your togetherness is so wonderful! To grow old together and keep on loving one another—that I find beautiful.

They smile like guilty children.

İhsan Bey seats me on a couch with curved arms and no back in the guest room upstairs, where Siret Hanım usually allowed no one to enter. But where is Siret Hanım? Perhaps downstairs, perhaps in the garden, or maybe she's not home, I don't know. İhsan Bey picks up my leg as though it were an independent part of my body, bends it, puts it in a certain position, doesn't like the location, picks it up again—I'm scared that he'll keep holding it forever. With my right leg stretched straight, he lifts the other leg over and crosses my ankles—no, this won't do either. My left leg is in his hand. He pushes it backwards and presses my foot against the couch at knee-level. This looks fine. He pulls the leg forward a little and widens the angle between the knees. Now he'll check things through the viewfinder. If it's OK, we're ready. Years later a man will pick up this same leg from where İhsan Bey has placed it, as if picking up a crystal pointer inlaid with silver (impossible, can crystal be inlaid with silver?) (but it was possible, and as if it were a pointer that would show mountains, desertions, liberations, infatuations on a world map) he'll take it to his lips. Then he will gently caress the pointer with his fingers.

"Let's pick out a name for you," says İhsan Bey. Let's call you Dilşad—a name of Persian origin, meaning "happy, contented." I can't say no. I can't ask who Dilşad is. My name is pretty, what's wrong with it, this I dare not ask. And I don't, as yet, know that I would like my name to be Günseli—a modern Turkish name that literally means "flood of the day."

"I used to call you Dilşad, do you remember" asks İhsan Bey.

I do. Siret Hanım does, too, nodding her head knowingly. Siret Hanım knows who the real Dilşad is. I don't, and I no longer want to find out.

I also remember him looking intently at my face as though he were searching for something under my skin. His straightening my eyebrows with one finger, lowering a lock of hair over one eye, then placing a rose between my lips. Where are those photographs? Where? I remember them all being taken, but I haven't seen a single one of them.

İhsan Bey still thinks I'm a little girl he can photograph. I feel his glance, the glance of a photographer (old and still amateurish) on my face. I hope he won't see my wrinkles, the sadness that pervades my face like a second skin.

—You look fine, says İhsan Bey. You look beautiful.

At that same instant another voice says, "You are very beautiful. I haven't told you this, have I?" Had he? I don't remember.

İhsan Bey used to have a motorbike. He used to take his camera and go up into the mountains. He would photograph slopes, gulfs, mountains, seaside mansions, bays, sunsets, pine and olive trees, pathways, straw baskets hanging from olive branches, children running after their donkeys, and women picking olives with half gloves that left their fingers bare. He would then come and photograph me, posing with a rose between my lips and a coquettish look on my face. He no longer has a motorbike. He is too old to ride a motorbike. He no longer gives me a rose to hold between my lips, nor teaches me how to look at the camera.

–Let's go out into the garden, he says. It's filled with sunshine.

I know that he means "light." He is obsessed with light, with sunshine, not with the garden. Let's go up into the mountains. Photograph me in the mountains so that those moments won't be lost. Take me and place me in the lap of a man with eyes full of light. Make my hair look longer, scatter it in the wind; but don't let my hair darken those eyes full of light.

–I have to go now, I say. But if you wish...

–There's no reason for us to sit in the garden, says one of them. But which one?

I had come here to find my childhood. I needed to do that. And did I find it! I stayed too long though. I had called on them just to see how they were doing. As I straighten my wrinkled skirt, I remember once again my first dress with the darts in the bodice. We had taken the material to a dressmaker who lived in the house on the corner and the woman had said, "She needs darts in the bodice." She and Mother had looked at one another and smiled. I had blushed. Actually there is nothing embarrassing about a girl's breasts growing. Now I know, but at the time I didn't. I am amazed at how much I know now, only now. At the time I also didn't know that İhsan Bey would become too old to ride a motorbike and that he wouldn't be able to take pictures even in the bright sunshine; nor that the man with the eyes full of light would take his eyes and light right out of my life and leave me. Now I know. And enough is enough; no more photographs.

Translated by Suat Karantay

"Gün Selleri," *Kırlangıçsız Geçti Yaz* (1990). Istanbul: Cem Yayınevi, pp. 61-64.

FEYZA HEPÇİLİNGİRLER

Before Death and Birth

I felt as if I were being dragged to the seaside. Some source of power always kept pulling me in that direction. I walked without any resistance. Till I saw her. I couldn't believe it; I would never have believed that I'd recognize her. I had no idea what she was like at that age, but I recognized her immediately when I saw her. Then it must have been clear how much I needed to see and talk to her, especially at that very age, at the very beginning of all that was going to happen, right before the marriage. So that's why I'd been sent.

She was sitting alone on a faded park bench that was about to collapse, looking out to sea. I suddenly remembered how much she'd liked it here and that this was the place we'd visited most often after I started walking, especially this point where the waves break and the sea suddenly deepens and turns dark blue, at the very top of the hill here where no one ever bothers to climb. Quietly I went and sat down beside her. I thought she hadn't noticed me, but she turned and smiled at me. To be sure, she didn't recognize me. I didn't exist when she was that age. She fixed her eyes on a point where the deep blue water crashed against the steep cliffs of the hill and whirled up in a white foam; she stared there most perniciously. I tried to see things through her eyes, but I couldn't. I wasn't permitted that, it seems.

Just to start a conversation I remarked, "You look a bit worried," and she didn't seem to mind my unnatural interest in sharing her worries. She turned her head slowly and smiled, then she hastened to find the same point she'd taken her eyes from; she kept on staring at it as if that were her task.

I couldn't say, "I'm the daughter whom you haven't yet born." I wasn't allowed to say that much or to change the stream of things. In fact there was nothing I could do, but I wanted to see her anyway. I couldn't prevent her from marrying my father or giving birth to me or committing suicide. That was actually what I most wanted to do, but no. Let everything happen as it is to be! It's not permitted that things happen any other way.

"I know you," I said suddenly.

"From the neighborhood?" she asked. If she hadn't said that I don't know what I would have said or how I would have explained how I knew her. I seized the opportunity. "Yes," I said. "You're Havva Hanım's daughter and your name is Emine." She didn't see anything extraordinary in what I said. She nodded her head. Something inside me spurred me on to tease her. "You're in love with Mustafa. Kamile Hanım's son. He's in love with you, too."

This time she glanced at me suspiciously. "How do you know all this?" Her voice seemed to be scolding me.

"You're about to marry him." I couldn't keep it back.

"Or are you a sooth-sayer?" she asked. The tone in her voice was teasing.

I couldn't say I wasn't; instead I warned, "But you won't be happy!" She didn't smile. "We love each other," she said.

"Perhaps," I said smiling.

"Who are you?" she asked. "You're not one of the girls in the neighborhood, I know all of them. You're not even from around here, and you're lying, aren't you?"

I couldn't take it any longer. Accepting all the consequences, "I am your daughter," I said. "The one that you haven't born yet."

I thought that the moment I said it everything would change, that there would be an incredible clap of thunder, the rain would pour down, the lightning would flash and rainbow-colored smoke would pervade the air; nothing of the sort happened. There was just an ordinary silence!

"Is that so?" asked the teasing voice of my mother. "I am very pleased to meet you." Standing up and walking away from me she added: "My dear daughter, my dear, dear daughter who hasn't even been born." I felt that if she had been in good spirits, she would even have laughed. However, she was too busy thinking about the petty problems and the disagreements that kept arising before the wedding.

Don't go, Mommy! I thought of telling her that she was proceeding towards her death, but that was of no use. Calculating the date, I knew that she was going to give birth to me exactly one year later—but she didn't know. I also knew she would commit suicide exactly fifteen years later. Moreover, she was going to throw herself into the sea from the very spot where this bench was—off the cliff into the swirling foam below my feet. I would be fourteen then. I also knew that after she was gone they would say, "She never loved her husband. She had a lover, and when he left her… That was it!" I knew too, that it wouldn't be my mother but my father who would fall in love with someone else, and my mother wouldn't be able to bear the pain of being betrayed by her Mustafa, that dear man.

"Don't go, Mommy!" I called after her. "Don't marry my father! He'll drag you to your death."

"Everybody is being dragged to his own death," she said. "You, whoever you may be! If you are my daughter you will realize that death by choice is not actually a death but a scream. A scream uttered with the very last remnant of your strength. If you don't realize that, then you don't deserve to be my daughter."

She walked away. Towards whose death, towards hers or mine? I didn't know whose life would be more deserving or whose death would be more meaningful.

Translated by Hande Özdemir and Jean Carpenter Efe
"Ölmeden ve Doğmadan Önce," *Öykünmece* (2000).
Istanbul: Remzi Kitabevi, pp. 107-109.

IŞIL ÖZGENTÜRK

On the Heels of a Blue Horse

I've taken two weeks off. For myself—it's not problems back home. It's not any fear of economic woe, depression or apprehension of what the future will bring. I now picture myself sitting in a courtyard— in the shade of a giant shelter of jasmine. Sitting here, I'm ready to tell you a story. A small fountain in the court is playing; it seems to be balancing a small—ping-pong sized—ball upon its jets. Other than this, silence reaches to infinity.

So I shall begin.

"It's that blue horse there, just lying there among the pearls and coral that overwhelm the vitrine. Ever since I've been frequenting the Covered Bazaar, I keep coming here to view it. I doubt that anyone's ever noticed it and suspect that it will remain here in the vaults of the Grand Bazaar for some time to come. It will remain my source of inspiration.

"An object that might have been crafted by a child, so simple, so sweet... I can't imagine anything that would better become turquoise. It is a pure blue horse.

"The longer I look at it, the more it reminds me of the long and carefree days of my childhood; together there begins a journey into the past.

"I was thirteen and we were living in Urfa. In this city of the prophets it was the most natural thing in the world to visit the sacred goldfish pond and feed the fish till they were ready to burst; all the children of the government employees did it. So did I, although I was a guest there, waiting to return to school in Antep in the fall.

"It had been a long hot summer that I had spent as a guest in a small room in one of the Urfa residences centered upon jasmine-scented courtyards. My room looked out onto a landscape that seemed to stretch into infinity.

"I'd look out the window, where I'd gaze at the colors of the landscape constantly in flux; what I liked most were these evenings when the sun so routinely and invariably set. I'd sit in the chair near the window, watching the scorched soil cool and awaiting the rise of the moon.

"It was then that a man on horseback would appear each evening without fail and pose, silhouetted against the sun. Who was he? Why should he appear every day at sunset to gaze into the setting sun? This became a secret of mine, something I did not want to share with anyone visiting the house—not even with my friends. Every evening, though, I'd hurry to my room and take my place in the chair to await him, and every day he'd appear at sunset to take his place before the setting sun.

"The summer had passed in joy, carefree, until one day there was a sudden change. First we heard a frightful shriek in the neighborhood, followed by the long, drawn-out and incomprehensible wailing of a female—the likes of which I have never ever heard again. One instant we kids were all splashing one another in the courtyard garden, the next we were all collected and trying to catch our breath in the room of Aunt Makber, the eldest in the house. She was sitting on the couch; her pleasant face—wrapped in her white scarf—looked rather pale. On our entry she summoned us all to her side, embraced us one by one, and tried to assuage our panic.

"The lament from outside continued, however, and I managed to summon up the courage to ask what was going on.

"Aunt Makber then began to explain.

"It seems that there was a man, a man famous for breeding the most outstanding Arabian stallions in the region—perhaps even in the whole world. It happened that this man had fallen in love with the striking young beauty named Esme who lived only three houses away. The girl Esme, however, had been promised in marriage to someone else; her father, furthermore, had no intention of letting her marry a horse-breeder.

"This explained why the man so famous for his Arab stallions had appeared at sunset every day before my window; looking into the setting sun, he had been professing his love for the girl. Just at the right time of day, therefore, the girl's father had laid a trap for the man; he'd gone and ambushed this man famed for his Arab stallions; with one round of fire he'd done him in. The Arab horse had thereupon dragged his master's body to the girl's doorstep to await the consequences.

"The girl noticed first the steed, and then the man; at this her grief had begun—a lament that knew no end.

"Upon hearing this I flew to my room to look out the window. That day at sunset no man on the back of an Arabic stallion arrived. Nor did he ever appear again."

Thus it was that the blue horse touched my memory, bringing back thoughts and voices from my past. Who created this horse, I wonder. Whose dreams once fashioned the creature? Who knows by what routes—overseas or overland—it has reached this shop window, and what adventures it experienced?

I look at it and smile.

Perhaps one evening it will see dreams of its own. Who knows?

Translated by Jean Carpenter Efe
"Mavi Bir Atın Peşinde," *Cumhuriyet*, 20 November 2001.

SELİM İLERİ

The Last Day of a Friendship

As if we wouldn't be happy. As if we wouldn't *ever* be. (The ruthless words of a fortune-teller.) In the ashtray, a half-burnt cigarette, never to be finished; on the wall, the childish prints of my dirty fingers; and in a vase, a bouquet of hyacinths still wrapped in raffia might remind them of me. For a short time, maybe for a couple of hours. It seems as though everything has come to an end. What was it that drew me to that house: the humanity and sincerity of Gülten, the irreplaceable friendship of Ali, but it's all killing my enthusiasm. I'm giving up my enthusiasms one by one. They'll forget. In a few hours, all my feelings, all my love will fade into silence. They'll live through miserable Sunday mornings. (Spring is on the way; they say these rains bring good tidings of spring. The seasons seem to pass in a monotonous, ordinary sequence with no effect on our lives). If only I could keep them from forgetting; if only I could. If only I'd cease to be this dull and shadowy Kemal in their lives. Maybe they'll remember that I drink my coffee black. Gülten will; Gülten is nice.

I didn't have the right to ruin a Sunday morning when they could have been reading books or lying in bed for hours. (The rain starts and then stops. That's how spring rains are supposed to be; fruitful. That's what they always used to tell me, saying that the countryside I've never seen or known would turn green with the rains. But they only bring dust and dirt to the narrow back streets of Kurtuluş). The armchair I've sat in for so many evenings. "It's the first time we've sat in here since we got married," Ali said. *Every night. Every night you come here without thinking that you might be bothering us. Even friendship has its limits...* A house where the parlor has never been used. A teeny-tiny apartment. I do feel the twinge of being the third person, being out of place each time I come here. Still I come. Because of my heart-breaking loneliness. "We're tired of your bourgeois loneliness," Ali once said later on. Quite a while later—when the polite uneasiness of beginnings started to fade away.

I was fooled by the summers. Relaxing and benumbing summertime.

It's over now. All of it. I have to put a dead end to my honor. I will ignore the silence of my heart, its insidious resistance. It's been years since I deciphered the alphabet of solitude. I'm going to carry on from where I left off. These are all cheap sensibilities.

The moment the rain stops I go into the store. I'm surrounded by masses of colorful and speckled flowers. (A bouquet of hyacinths still wrapped in raffia. For some reason hyacinths symbolize happiness.) It's one of those rootless flowers that you can pull up easily. They grow along the banks of brooks, on rocky cliffs and around fountainheads.

"Where would we find them at this time of year? It's impossible." That's what the flower girl said. She straightened her tasseled belt, played with her skirt and smiled at me. I can no longer insist. But I can ask them to arrange a basket. I wanted the flowers to have a basket of their own. Let them put the flowers in a straw basket. (Ali won't say "bourgeois loneliness" any more). It was one of those bad winter days when night falls early. Once I got home, I couldn't help but go out again.

My mother had said, "Don't go to anyone's house on a Sunday. One of these days they'll throw you out." Then she complained that I'd never grown up in the first place and that I really ought to come to my senses. I ignored her. The walls of my room keep closing in on me. I can't be content with a teddy bear clinging to my bedside. In those moments of weakness when we really need people, need friendship the most.

"Mother, I'm going out," I say. She looks me crossly in the face. "Forget-me-nots don't bloom at this time of the year anyway." I'd ripped the ears off my teddy bear. I gently stroke its matted fur and give it a fillip on the nose: "We're on our own, if you know what I mean." I notice the florist's. A store I have to pass by everyday. But I seem to be noticing it for the first time. Who could I send flowers to? The loves I've never had; I'm a stranger to orchids in cellophane.

"I'd like to send some flowers."

Doubtful looks from the girl. She examines me from head to toe. Wrinkled corduroy pants, a raincoat frayed at the collar and cuffs, unshined shoes and I still want to send flowers. No way she could have understood. "It blinded their eyes and hardened their hearts, so that they couldn't see with their eyes or understand with their hearts…"

"A basket? Or would you prefer a box?"

"A basket. A small basket."

"Let's put violets in it…"

"No, no violets or hyacinths."

Blue flowers would be blossoming. They'd pull up as soon as I touched them with my hand.

Those years when Ali started to earn his own bread. I can taste all the disgust and sickness of my childhood. I used to wander around aimlessly; I'd chew forget-me-nots. Ali is someone who has found everything he's longed for in life. I envy even his hard times, those when he felt hungry and made wishes from the bottom of his heart. "You're healthy. That's what matters the most." He will bring up my bourgeois traits again. My "loneliness" will return to slap me in the face. My jaws will clench; I'll have to hold back my tears. Gülten will intervene. A working husband and wife who've hardly ever sat in their parlor. The room came into use when I turned up all of a sudden. I adore this room. I can't tell you how much. It's a proud and peaceful room that gives you confidence.

"I'm happy only when I'm with you." My words fall like an unbearable weight on Ali's shoulders. His shoulders sag.

Suddenly he straightens up, "Don't talk rubbish." I didn't think I was speaking rubbish. I'd taken shelter with them like a stray cat, not minding a few kicks and shoves now and then. I felt that I was demeaning myself, losing my dignity, but somehow I couldn't run away.

This was the last door I could knock on in my love-forsaken days.

"You're selfish," says Ali. He won't be saying that any more. I won't be riding in the Kurtuluş *dolmuş*es any longer. I've lived through all four seasons in this house. I can't say, though, that the seasons bring any new meanings to our lives. (We'll meet again. The same arguments, misunderstandings and deadly silences in the middle of conversations... Don't they see that each time something more is broken and hurt? Gülten probably does. Or she pities me. She pities me. Finally, I've become a person to be pitied. And Gülten pities me.) One Sunday morning, I get up and go over to their house. After a Saturday night spent together and probably enjoyed. How sorry I felt that the night had to end. We'd been together till dawn. Gülten's potato salad. The coffee Gülten makes, her kind and loving hopeful words. Ali was nice, too. You shouldn't wear people out. Last night, Ali was nice too.

"Every evening you go to their house. You've forgotten what it's like to stay in. One day they'll throw you out." My hands tremble as I reach out for the doorbell. Slowly I go up the stairs. So that our confrontation will be delayed. Actually, I should turn back.

"You overwhelm people. You want us to talk to you and care for you twenty-four hours and seven days."

"It's not like that, Ali. I'm so lonely. I'm sorry, I know I'm making you uneasy. I can't help it"

"You really are making us uneasy. You left in the middle of the night and now we wake up to your face again."

"I'm so lonely. I forget it only when I'm with you."

"Your loneliness is your own problem."

He didn't really mean what he said. "You never should have said that. You shouldn't underestimate the pain and fear I feel when a night ends. You don't *really* underestimate it." Chaos weighs heavily in our lives. We all blame one another.

Gülten had not left the stairwell. "Goodbye, Ali," I'd said. He'd held out his hand. (I have to make these Sunday mornings the dead end of my honor.) I retreat down the steps as fast as I can. If I knew that I wouldn't fall, trip or look ridiculous, I'd take two or three steps at a time; I'd race from here. Gülten, standing in the stairwell and saddened by some constantly slamming and beating sounds she seemed to be hearing, was sending regards to whomever she could think of. They know I never forward those regards, they know I'm dead jealous of my friendships. But there was no need to waste words. I was on the steps; it was impossible to think clearly.

"Last night, I felt like the third person. We were talking about summer vacations. This summer, there just had to be a visit to the seaside: Bodrum. You two were talking. I was listening. You didn't invite me. You didn't have to.

The beaches, the sun and the fish of Bodrum... I've never gone to Bodrum and I probably never will. Not even this summer. Because you didn't invite me."

"Where are you coming from?"

"I was at Ali's."

"So early in the morning... Shame on you. They'll start to wonder if you don't have a house of your own."

"They didn't say anything."

Ali didn't like the dead silence that filled the room from time to time. The abrupt ending of conversations, the impossibility to continue should have suggested that I get up and head home. However, I liked even that silence. I felt quite content buried in the armchair, living in the recently unlived-in room. Gülten is different. She can always find topics that won't lose interest. Ali's world was not so rich. Then too, Ali was an introvert. (The rain is whipping my face. I need to find some people. People who will take my mind off Gülten and Ali. And now the rain's pouring harder than ever.) In his friendships Ali calculates what to say and what not to say. He doesn't make confessions like I do. I'm incredibly honest with them, as I can never be with anyone else. They listen to me for nights on end. They'll listen for a whole month, until the intoxication of their yearly holiday ends. "Let's finally go somewhere this summer, Ali. We miss the sea." Gülten's thick dark hair; her fine sense of style. They'll be going to seaside restaurants in the evenings. Summer nights are unbelievably hot. In Istanbul we literally bake. In Bodrum the breeze blows in from the sea. They'll be eating fish, shrimp, oysters, squid...

"Is everything all right, Kemal?"

"Like what?"

"I don't know; you look a little pale. You seem to be upset about something."

"No, I'm fine."

I lower my head. My eyes meet Ali's. "His bourgeois loneliness has probably reawakened," says Ali, smiling. I could break the window, the china ashtrays, the plates and glasses in the kitchen, the lamps in the bedroom... But I don't sense any bad intention in his teasing. He's joking in a friendly manner. I love their friendship.

I'm as lonely now as if I'd known them for years. Actually it's only been a year since our friendship began.

It was a dull and empty Sunday morning. I'd had nothing to do. I couldn't find the strength to lie down and read a book the way Ali would. I never could. I thought for sure they'd call. I was beside the telephone. It didn't ring. I'd gone through the papers. With every line I scanned I could feel desperation surrounding and enclosing me. As if besieging me. All the hurt and broken-heartedness between Gülten, Ali and me was transformed into the butchery in the papers. I have to make them understand how unprotected I'll be on my own, that I can't defend myself and will be defeated by this hopelessness. ("How fortunate are those in mourning, for they shall be consoled... because they shall be shown mercy." They haven't, though. Maybe because they don't believe in the fruitfulness of the rain.) They were having breakfast. "Would you like some tea?" Gülten had asked.

What I expected Ali to say was, "As if he'd say no; he'd even take water." He didn't say anything. He'd opened the papers I hadn't been able to read as if trying to hide his face. As if there were something he didn't want to see, something he despised. He wrinkled his forehead; his eyes had lost their sympathy. Gülten was spreading butter on the toast.

"I'm full, Gülten, thank you," I say. She insists. Our eyes meet. She looks at me with sensitive and understanding eyes. This moisture in the corners of my eyes. I've got to hold back my tears no matter what. (The rain hadn't started yet. We could have gone to the Bosphorus. All the restaurants along the shore. All the varieties of fish. "You didn't invite me to Bodrum but I'm inviting you for a fish dinner." I'd rehearsed what I was going to say on my way there. I'd try to act lively, carefree and relaxed. That's how I'd be. Only a fortune-teller could have known that the rain was on its way. It was a winter morning heralding an early summer.)

"Go to Bodrum. Wander along the beaches if you like. I won't speak to you again when you return. I shouldn't. Go to Bodrum by yourselves. Enjoy your togetherness. Let the sun show its compassion only to you. Let the sea's cooling waters be a treat only to you. Like I said, wander along all those beaches..."

Then Ali put the paper down. We'd spoken little. "Has something happened?" he'd asked. "Something must have happened for you to have turned up like this." Then he'd gone into the bedroom. Gülten and I were left alone in the kitchen. (The first drops of rain on the windows, forming ponds on the window panes.)

"I've changed my mind. I don't want a basket."

"Whatever you like." Her eyes still on my raincoat, on the muddy cuffs of my corduroy pants.

"How much are the violets?"
"Ten liras a bouquet."
"What are those?"
"I wouldn't recommend them, Sir. They've been here for two days now. The violets have just arrived."
I'd only wanted to ask the name. They reminded me of lilies. I liked lilies as well.
"The violets are expensive. I'd like to send a lot. In a huge box."
"You're right. It would cost quite a bit. What price do you have in mind?"
I want to send flowers to Gülten—standing at the top of the stairs waiting for me to descend. I want to send her all these flowers.
"Why don't we prepare a bouquet of carnations? Carnations are nice, too." She points to the carnations with their petals about to fall off. I don't like them. I have to decide. Her playing with the tassels has quickened.
I stumble as I put on my shoes. My laces are still untied. Ali is standing in the doorway. I lean against the wall. My handprint remains on the wall. "I've left a mark on the wall," I say.
"No harm, I'll wipe it off," she responds. Something seems to tear inside me as I leave. Each time, I think I'll never see them again. I can't ask, "When shall we meet again?" I've always said, "We'll speak on the phone, keep in touch." Today I didn't. I tied my shoelaces. I wiped my hand on the skirt of my raincoat and held it out to them: "Goodbye Gülten, Goodbye Ali." Ali doesn't come out into the stairwell. I had no right to ruin their Sunday morning.
"You're friendly people. I really like you."
"Thank you, Kemal."
"I really mean it. From time to time, I believe you and Ali are the only way out."
"Still, you must shake this loneliness thing off."
"Gülten, you're forgetting that Kemal is a bourgeois."
"Ali's only teasing you."
"I'm teasing you, too. I'm no bourgeois."
A youngster brings the cellophane box. One night I'd gone to Ali's house. I'd enjoyed happy moments at their small table. Friendships are the last shelter. The girl opens the lid of the cellophane box. Her hands seem facile. "Is there a blank card?" The youngster hands me the card. I reach for the pen on the table: "Dearest Gülten, I've never met anyone else who shares one's loneliness like you do. Thank you for this morning." I put the pen back on the table. I give the girl the address. She is no longer playing with her tassels. She writes the address down in her notebook. "Send it exactly at seven please."
She smiles and adds, "Don't worry."
It had been a summer I loved. It had passed between an unused parlor and a small

balcony. It was a summer when monotony was replaced by finesse, sensitivity and meaning. I'd felt the same enthusiasm each time I ran up the stairs.

"You've been like this since you were a kid. You haven't changed a bit. Always at other people's houses. You were just there yesterday."

I've been like this since I was a kid. I haven't changed a bit. I was always attracted to other people's houses. What was it about Ali's house that I liked so much? At first it was a game, it hadn't yet been spoiled by the idea of having to give it up... Gülten, by no means ill at ease, seemed to enjoy preparing dinner even after an exhausting day at work. Ali's reliability and his attitude without contempt. We'd quickly found solidarity in each other. Ali would draw sharp lines across his life: born in poverty in Üsküdar—the years he studied and worked—falling in love with Gülten—getting married... Üsküdar is a neighborhood where we used to pick forget-me-nots in my childhood. It's a place we used to visit often. I can't seem to shake off this Üsküdar—as if it were my destiny. It's taking revenge for a sin I've never committed. I long for the health that Ali's found and experienced. It's not jealousy. I respect their happiness. "How fortunate are those in mourning…"

(I have to find others. Acquaintances I haven't seen for a long time. People who should be happy when they open the door. "We were together last night, and we wake up to your bell in the morning. You're so selfish." The dust and earth that the rain couldn't wash away. It's all mud now.) They'll send the flowers at seven. That youngster will deliver them. He'll curse at me deep inside. "In this rain…" he'll say. But they aren't being sent to celebrate or repair anything. I'm putting an end to this emotion; I've reached the end. I'll reminisce about so many things from that summer. Ali is not a man in his thirties. He is constantly rejuvenating, becoming more like a child. This rejuvenation of his is magical. He buys soda for Gülten and me. We're watching a bad movie at the outdoor summer cinema. Gülten's laughter, Ali's laughter. I join in; I laugh loudly. Tears start to run down my face, I'm still laughing. I'm dying of laughter. The crowd in the outdoor summer cinema begins to thin out. Gülten is telling me something. She is telling me something nice. I feel like wrapping my arms around both of them. A strange kind of insolence. An insolence that doesn't suit me. I should be humble. That's how I was brought up. My eyes are now fixed on the paving stones, on the cracks and crevices.

"Call again, Kemal."

Gülten knows that I won't call. Otherwise, she wouldn't have stood in the stairwell for so long. I feel sorry for her. (My dignity is bruised.)

"I was bored, that's why I stopped by."

"Have you eaten, Kemal?"

"I give you a lot of trouble, Gülten."

"Come off it, now. I'm cooking anyhow."

It's a stupid gesture, my sending flowers. I'll go back and tell them I've changed my mind. "I'll deliver them myself; give me the box," I'll say. I'll throw them down in some secluded place; if I drop them at a run nobody will notice. Ali will be absolutely furious. I couldn't stand Gülten's pity. The girl at the florist's will shake her tassels. The cuffs of my pants are muddier than ever.

I should go home and wait for Gülten's call.

Translated by Sevinç Ener and Jean Carpenter Efe
"Dostlukların Son Günü," *Dostlukların Son Günü* (1975).
Ankara: Bilgi Yayınevi, pp. 155-165.

HABİB BEKTAŞ

Panacea: A Story

For A. Dörfler

The doctor comes out of the operating room. Then a nurse. The other assistants are still inside. My grandson is inside as well; he must be lying there unconscious. The doctor says nothing. He just smiles as he passes us. We feel slightly relieved. But!

"There! You've seen the doctor. Don't worry," says my son as if somehow speaking to himself as well.

My voice sounds like that of a stranger.

"He didn't say anything!"

"He smiled, you see."

"If only he had spoken and said the operation went well and that we shouldn't worry…"

"Maybe he didn't have the time."

"Time, yeah, time!" Saying that, I must have been looking very cross.

On the couch against the wall is my son sitting next to my daughter-in-law. He's staring at the floor. It seems to me that he's looking at his shoes. An irrepressible fury wells up in me.

I realize that I won't feel any relief until I've seen my little friend and spoken to him. *These doctors who have no time,* I mutter to myself but can't complete the sentence. Only bad things come to mind. Just at that moment the doors of the operating room open again. Two nurses wheel out the bed my little friend is lying on. The masks they're still wearing make my hair stand on end. They stop right in front of me. (I may perhaps have forced them to a stop by stepping into their path.) The nurse in front turns to me and says, "It's over! It went very well. He'll be coming round in a few minutes." I smile. I have a notion to cry, but I smile. I can't take my eyes off the serum bottle hanging above my grandson's head. I ask, "May I stay with him—as he's waking up?" "Sure," she says, "Come with us." I'm as happy as a little kid. If it weren't an impropriety, I'd hug and kiss the nurse. I follow them. They hand me a sterilized smock before I enter the large room at the end of the corridor. I put nylon booties on over my shoes. I go inside. The nurse who spoke to me also stays in the room.

    I squat beside his bed. I hear little moans escaping from my little friend's pale lips. I am anxious. My friend's tiny sparrow-wing of a hand beside him on the bed says *hold me*. Reaching out, I take his sparrow-wing between my big calloused hands, careful not to injure it. With his tiny hand in my palm, I start to tell my little friend his favorite story. As I start the tale, his moans cease. An infinite happiness replaces the anxiety and uncertainty in my heart. I come eye to eye with the nurse. We share this happiness without a single word.

    My little friend must be hearing me even though he's unconscious. Just at that moment the doctor responsible for the operation enters the room. I continue with the story. When he sees me telling a tale, he calls out, "Grandpa, he can't hear you, he can't!" I could care less. He thinks I didn't hear him. He shouts, "Gramps, he's still unconscious; he won't hear you!" I want to cry. Staring at the floor, the nurse speaks,

    "But—but it isn't doing any harm!"

Translated by Fatma İdin and Jean Carpenter Efe
"Her Derde Deva Masal," *Ben Öykülere İnanırım*.
Istanbul: Can Yayınları, pp. 80-81.

HABİB BEKTAŞ

Holiday

The woman couldn't help smiling, "You are a man of lilac," she said. Then she dropped her head forward. She paused for a while, staring at the floor. Only if the man would smile, or say something! When she next spoke, she was not smiling as before.

"Lilac and melancholy!"

As the man had no idea what his face looked like under the purple light cast by the lamp over his head, he could not perceive what the woman meant; he had no desire to return her smile. From the rainbow of colorful lamps over the bar, it was the orange one that reflected upon her face.

While lighting the woman's cigarette, the man gazed at her bony oversized nose, her thin lips, and her small close-set eyes. It was as if his glance were locked upon the woman. How homely she was! For no reason at all, without knowing whom or what he pitied, he felt a great pity. And he noticed a scent that he could not describe. This must be the smell of tears —cold, dark and distant as it were, he thought to himself.

His eyes moved to the woman's glass. It was empty again. He waved to the big-mouthed woman behind the bar. In the wink of an eye the glass was filled.

The woman placed both her hands on the man's knees as if to say *hold my hand*.

The man looked at the woman's hands. The stubby-fingered hands on his knees reminded him of two dead doves. He closed his eyes.

"You aren't from Hamburg!" said the woman as if she meant *you're not the one I'm looking for*.

The man smiled deep purple.

"Yes, you're right," he replied. "I'm not."

He looked at the woman's bitter orange, rather indifferent smile. He didn't think he wanted to say anything. Nevertheless he spoke. His voice sounded to him like someone else's, distant.

"It's a holiday today where I come from!"

"So why aren't you smiling, then?"

"Who knows," said the man, "even if I were there, I might not be smiling!"

Translated by Fatma İdin and Jean Carpenter Efe
"Bayram," *Ben Öykülere İnanırım* (2001).
Istanbul: Can Yayınları, pp. 52-53.

FERİDE ÇİÇEKOĞLU

The Coincidence

Walking is not very enjoyable these days either.
The weather is suffocating; it must be the southwest wind. My varicose veins are aching, my feet are swollen. I walk without knowing where I'm going. Where should I go? I have so much to do though. Files, bills, phone calls, hellos, cigarette smoke, goodbyes, buttons to sew on, books, magazines... I couldn't balance the accounts again. I'll have to redo a whole week's accounts. Letters waiting to be answered. I was never like this before. Especially with letters sent from prison. It's no fun writing letters when one doesn't feel up to it.

A vendor passes by, stepping on my foot. He has plastic plants, taller than a man, stuck in huge, bright-colored pots. Resembling frightening fairy-tale giants tossing their green hair in bewilderment amongst the crowd, the plants move away. Who would buy such ugly stuff? Especially when you see it right in the middle of the street...

Perhaps I, too, should acquire some artificial plants. Is it that I can't keep things alive or something? Flowers, love... My ivy was drooping this morning. My umbrella plant has turned yellow. Even my geraniums have dried up. In the past my flowers didn't wilt, though. The crowd is overpowering me. The air is exhaust fumes. The noise is tank sirens. You are still to call me.

The USA has bombed Libya. Just yesterday. I wonder how many people were killed... How many lost their limbs. There is a twinge in my arms. Sakarya Street looks the same as on any other day. That woman, with layers of fat, trying to decide what fish to buy, couldn't care less about the bombing or anything else. She's going to cook fish for dinner. All that matters is her children, no mistake there. Her own children only; even the neighbor's children can go to hell. What does she care if babies keep dying of hunger in Africa! If she gets on a bus, she'll block the aisle like a stopper. Why, she got on, and that's all that matters! She won't move an inch unless you push her. She won't even stand sideways but will face forward like a bulldozer. She'll buy her fish and get on her bus. She'll prepare the salad and wait for her children with her selfish love. Her husband will come, with no love. Every home needs a husband; he is that sort of a husband. That woman doesn't even love her daughters. She adores her son though. "My son!" she always says. "My son has no equal." She sacrificed so much for his sake. She toiled day and night; she put up with the husband...

"My son will take care of me!"

Her love is going to oppress her son like the southwest wind.

Those two there must be newly married; it definitely shows. The heels of the woman's shoes are twisted out of shape, her stockings have run. They'll have boiled beans and rice for dinner and will be content. They'll turn on the news simply not to miss the TV series that follows. They don't buy meat but they have a complete set of furniture, cheap replicas of luxury furniture. By the time the installments are paid, the backs of the chairs and the legs of the tables will have fallen off. By that time the woman won't lean on her husband's arm anymore. They'll eat eggplant with rice and have fights. I should have put the culture in the yogurt this morning. Then there would be something to look forward to when I got home, some change. A feeling that life has gone on while I was away. Especially since my flowers have wilted...

I hurry away from Sakarya Street. I walk rapidly to the main intersection in Kızılay. I could take refuge in my office. Shut myself up in my room, someplace where I wouldn't see anyone.

People are crowding in on me. They grin mindlessly. The women have dark polish on their nails, half of which has peeled off. Their little toes fall over the sides of their cheap sandals. The men smell of sweat and have nicotine stains on their teeth. The children have buck teeth. I look at the people. I look at each and every one of them.

You're not among them.

I dismiss them all with the back of my hand. This does not suffice. I carve the stones, the concrete, the asphalt. I dig the city with my fingernails. I dig the city just as I scrape the whitewash stains from the windows, the grease from the oven, the wrinkles from my face, the centuries from a prehistoric vase. The street disappears under my feet. The sewage comes up to my ankles. The water is bubbling. It rises to my knees as if trying to swallow me. A child falls in the sticky mud. With a shrill voice the mother cries out. Her eyes are two very sharp screams. They jump out from their sockets. They are rolling. Sewer rats fall upon the eyes. They're gnawing at them. Other screams intermingle with those of the woman. The voices get louder, they reverberate, and they cover the whole sky.

Then, suddenly, a rainbow appears. I hear your voice. Is this reality or am I dreaming? It can't be you. What business would you have right at the center of Kızılay, in the middle of a crowded crosswalk? I prepare myself not to find you there when I turn back to look. Very slowly. Taking it easy. Delaying the heartbreak of not seeing you there.

I turn back.

You're there.

What's more, with all the colors of the rainbow in your eyes. A rainbow, which recedes as one approaches it, an evasive rainbow. It becomes cross if you try to catch it, and simply vanishes.

One mustn't feel overjoyed. Mustn't show it. Just a simple hello. As if you've run across an acquaintance on the street. Someone you'd totally forgotten about and now suddenly remember.

You ask me some questions. I mumble something or other. I ask you a question or two. You say something or other. Let there be no silence! If we start running out of words, we'll both try to be the first to bid farewell, I know. Let the words not cease and let the conversation continue without it seeming that we're trying to prolong it. Beware. When words start dripping rather than streaming, you'll be the first one to leave. Don't be fooled. There's no gold at the end of the rainbow. That's what you'd like to see. You bid farewell first.

Clouds everywhere. Where have all the people gone? We're in a soundproof air bubble for two, being tossed about under the sea. The sun is reflected on the coral reefs. Outside our bubble. Because even the sun cannot penetrate our bell jar. Only the seven hues of the rainbow. Around us are fish of myriad colors. They simply touch our jar with their noses. And turn back and swim away, swishing their tails. Swish, swish...

Watch out, they're going to hit us! Oh, it's the red light and the traffic is moving. All this lasted, then, simply half the time that pedestrians are allowed to cross the street. Where was I going? To the market on Sakarya Street. So you were headed in that direction also... What a coincidence! Well, yes, I certainly am going in the wrong direction... I was overwhelmed by the crowds. I guess I was going back. I had given up shopping. What was I going to buy? What should it be, I wonder... Something urgent. It must be believable and important. Spices! Why spices? At this hour of the day, in the middle of a work day... I said it with such certainty that I myself believed it. Well, I had run out of cinnamon. And mint, black pepper, even dill... I'll be rolling grape leaves, it seems. I didn't know it but that's what I'll be doing, it seems. I know that fresh grape leaves haven't come out yet. I could use salted grape leaves, why not?

So you're coming to the spice shop with me? I really am surprised! What a lovely red these peppers are, did cinnamon always smell so nice? No, I wasn't talking to you. How much do I want? I'm not sure. How much would fifty grams cost? Half of that paper bag is just fine. I'm glad I've bought these—for days now I haven't had the time.

We go out. An ordinary goodbye. No, I shouldn't turn around. I shouldn't be watching you walk away. Well, I can't control myself. My head turns involuntarily. You're gone! But this is impossible in such a short time. The hem of your jacket... Or does it just look like your jacket? Slowly I raise my eyes. I don't see your hair, just your eyes. For a second I catch your glance. We're like guilty children. We smile shyly. We have caught one another in the act. I can go now. I know that we won't call each other again. But your eyes are in my hands, and I am attaching your smile to my lips.

Is it the northeast wind or what? It feels fresh. On a corner a boy is selling marigolds. I can hear the newspaper man: "All over the world anti-American demonstrations are being held."

I should go and write a few letters. And... And I should roll the grape leaves. A huge pan of them. Without thinking who'll eat them, without putting it off. I know I cannot send them. But if I could, perhaps there would be enough to feed all the children in Ethiopia.

I must water the plants tonight.

Translated by Suat Karantay
"Rastlantı," *Sizin Hiç Babanız Öldü Mü?* (1991).
Istanbul: Can Yayınları, pp. 69-74.

FERİDE ÇİÇEKOĞLU

Some Get Clawed by Falcons

From the deck I am looking at the pier. The white boat is struggling to link the two shores of the city. Is this reality or just a dream? I had dreamt of this moment so often in the past! When the water puddle in the prison courtyard reflected the rays of the sun on the iron gate, when a faint smell of mold struck our noses as we paced back and forth...

"Nermin, look, it smells of seaweed when we cross that spot over there."

"I don't smell it."

"Take a deep breath on our way back, OK, now!"

"You're right, I guess somebody's sheets must be moldy."

"Whose sheets, girls?"

"Must be filthy Ayşe, who else? She spends all her time writing to her lover and has no time to wash her smelly underwear... These adulteresses should be..."

"Don't start that again, Döndü... How many times have I told you, whatever brings one here is her own business."

The sea we searched for in the smell of damp sheets is now at arm's length. All foam and garbage. Fish caught in the garbage; on the pier, imported mackerel fried in burnt oil, popular songs blasting at full volume, lahmacun with lots of onion, pickle juice, boiled corn, plastic slippers, cheap shirts.

And then, crowds crushing one another in order to get to the boat-landing fast. They can't all be in a rush, for as soon as they step on the landing they slow down. Pushing to get to the front is considered street-smart, so a sideways glance is thrown back—serves them right, those who lag behind!

"Ice-cold water, no money charged if it doesn't freeze your teeth..."

The water-seller's container is decorated. Horse carriages, trucks, shoeshine boxes, water containers... They all have decorations that speak the same language. Stylized flowers, gazelles at ponds, bright green eyes somewhat asquint, plus all those maxims. The identity and demands of the waterseller all around his container: "Can't Be Tamed", "Don't Be Coy, Girls", "Fate, Let Me Be"... He has no expectations from the future; he simply doesn't want to be bothered.

"Don't keep looking at the ground, dear; you seem to be lost in thought again. You were so eager to come here... Look, there is the New Mosque."

Anadolukavağı, Kalamış, Emirgân, the New Mosque... Have they changed or did I grow considerably while serving time in prison? At Anadolukavağı there used to be a Turkish toilet, next to the pier, facing the square. Across the square was a bakery shop; a huge plane tree used to shade the whole square. A Turkish toilet—the sea would ebb in and out caressing the floor. Each time my folks came from Istanbul on visiting days I'd ask after it like after an old friend.

"Is the toilet at Anadolukavağı still there?"

"Yes, just the way you left it."

When I was released, I went there and didn't find a trace of it; they'd kept it a secret like the death of a family member.

"You used to miss the pigeons, there they are, hordes of them..."

In the courtyard of the mosque the pigeons are wing to wing. On their necks the sunshine is red and green.

Pigeons flapping their wings, wandering about with tiny steps, gobbling up the grains of wheat on the ground.

"Throw them a large plate of seeds and you'll be blessed... May God never separate you two!"

The woman selling wheat grains is calling to a young girl and boy who approach hand in hand. They are quick to secure what they think will be lifelong happiness with a plate of wheat grains. To guarantee things even better, they buy a large plate. The girl tosses the grains to the empty corner of the courtyard.

The sun shines through dozens of flapping wings in that corner of the courtyard. The pigeons go for the grains, crushing one another. They even obliterate the sunshine squeezed between their bodies. To snatch a grain of wheat, to be the first one to jump onto the boat landing.

In this huge courtyard, in the wings of hundreds of pigeons, one cannot even find a tiny portion of the joy which the wings of a single pigeon bring to a prison courtyard thirteen steps long.

"Fadik, come quick, it perched on the roof."

"Oh, my! A white pigeon for the first time."

"What's more, it doesn't fly away."

"Especially on a visiting day... Someone will receive good news today."

"A letter, a letter..."

"That goes for those who expect letters."

For a moment one gets the feeling that the white pigeon carrying the sun on its wings cannot be of the same kind as this horde trampling the light.

"You were so anxious to see the pigeons, are you satisfied, is this all?"

Next to the mosque, a row of shops. In them, all kinds of animals. Fish behind the glass, birds behind wire netting, rabbits in cages. Plants, seeds, animal feed.

And then a pair of dark eyes. Scintillating, flickering. Lightning bolting in them. Filled with pain, or is this only my impression? Cuffed at the ankle. A small crowd around it. Turning its head to the left and right, as though wishing to go beyond, past the gaze of the onlookers.

As it turns its head, the feathers on its neck glide over one another. The sorrow of the sun on the lean feathers with edges tinged in black. I feel the urge to buy it and set it free.

"How much does this falcon cost?"

"Twenty-five thousand."

Its cuffs are tied to a pigeon cage with a chain. Seems like they did not want to confine it in a cage. If you didn't see the cuffs you might wonder why it didn't just fly away. With its gaze and stance it looks so free. What about the pigeons idling in the cages? They occasionally move their wings and exchange places. Then they pull their heads in again and fall asleep. Packed in like sardines in a can. One cannot tell whose wings are where or whose legs are under whom. Watching them is very boring. They've got no personality. They're resigned to living in a cage; they have the eyes of dead fish.

This phrase was the creation of an officer at the military prison; it must have stuck in my memory.

"In the past your eyes used to glitter, whereas my privates seemed to have the eyes of dead fish. From now on the tables will be turned—you will be the ones who'll look like dead fish."

That boy poking the falcon from a distance with the stick in his hand... He has rotten, gaping teeth. The evil inside him is reflected in his face. Take the cuffs off and fight with it bravely, if you dare! Or see if you can get closer to it... No way! An ugly sneer on his face, his eyes measuring the length of the chain that connects the cuffs to the cage. Standing in a safe spot at a distance beyond the full length of the chain, he pokes the falcon with his stick.

"Hey... Look this way, buster!"

The falcon takes no heed. Keeps looking into the distance. This indifference drives the boy with the stick crazy. I think the falcon is disgusted with such daring before cuffs, with cowardice that turns into heroism before a captive. Or is it my imagination? No, I can't be wrong—this is a falcon after all!

"Look this way... Hey, look this way, buster!"

The boy next to him gives his opinion.

"It's not scared of the stick. Let's throw a piece of bread, maybe that'll make it look our way."

A hunger strike at the military prison. It must be the ninth day. During the headcount one of the officers licks a piece of lemon, another slurps his tea noisily. His hair is turning gray. He should be a bit more considerate, one thinks. The one in charge has a very red face: In the corridors of the wards he has meatballs fried, then chews them in an exaggerated manner and swallows his morsels with a great show.

"Why don't you leave the animal in peace! Aren't you ashamed of yourselves?"
"It's none of your business."
"It has an owner, lady. Why do you meddle?"
"Never mind, dear. One cannot reason with such kinds. Let's go."

I have no intention of leaving. I look into the eyes of the falcon… I wish I could shrink enough to fit under those eyelids. I wish it would close its eyes then so that the people crushing one another, the street-vendors, that awful music, the sea filled with garbage, the boy with the stick would all be left out and I would be inside. I look at the falcon as if piercing it, as if I am melting and flowing into its eyes.

And all of a sudden I am violently smitten by something. A burning sensation on my face; on my cheek and chin a sharp pain. A fluttering above my head, the sound of wings in my ears.

People yelling and screaming all around me. Before one could tell what had happened, the falcon had flown back and was perched in its original place.

"My goodness, it's never done such a thing before. Are you OK, Miss? Would you like some water or something?"

"Your face is bleeding, dear. Why did you keep staring at the falcon for so long? Take this handkerchief. Does it hurt badly?"

"See, you tried to protect it from us, and it clawed you instead!"

"Come on, let's split buddy. With our luck only a cat would scratch us. See how lucky that broad is; she got clawed by a falcon."

Translated by Suat Karantay
"Kimini Şahin Tırmalar," *Sizin Hiç Babanız Öldü Mü?* (1990).
Istanbul: Can Yayınları, pp. 27-32.

FERİDE ÇİÇEKOĞLU

A 100-Asa Country

"Mrs. Tunsevich!
This is the last call for Mrs. Tunsevich, leaving for Moscow.
Mrs. Tunsevich to Gate Number..."

This is how I first met you in Zurich Airport. It was the last call for you. You were supposed to be at the departure gate. You were going to fly to Moscow.

While trying to guess why you might be late, I began with the most natural, innocent possibilities.

Last-minute shopping, a late check in a restaurant, that last glass of wine at the bar, a make-up case that you couldn't remember where you'd put, a rest-room door that was stuck...

No.

You were waiting quietly, not far at all from the departure gate. Your eyes were seeing the Moscow passengers off and avoiding even a glance at the ground stewardesses; their anxiety shouldn't change your mind.

I left you like that there in Zurich Airport.
Without knowing whether you'd fly to Moscow or not.
On my way to Dublin from Istanbul.
It was September 20, 1993, a Monday. It was 13:50, Zurich time.

* * *

THURSDAY, September 16, 1993

Homeland... Home... Land... Country...
What was the sub-title? "Changing relations between the citizen and the state"? "Changing relations..." Are they really changing? Have they changed? For better or for worse? Where? In countries... In my country... that's good, but... Where? Where is this 26/A? Have I passed it?

"Excuse me! Could you tell me where 26/A is, please?"

"You must have passed it; you'll have to go back. Not that one, the next one. Entrance is from the side."

"Thank you."

You'd better stop playing around with words. Especially on the road like this. If the woman on the phone was right, you won't even have the problem of presenting a paper. Because you won't be able to go. Between four to six weeks, they say. It's unbelievable. I hope this isn't true. Here's 26/A.

"Sorry to disturb you... Am I going the right way for the Honorary Irish Consulate?"
....

"May I disturb you with a question? For the Honorary Irish Consulate, the man at the entrance..."
....

"Excuse me, the woman at that table... This line? Of course I'll wait."
....
....
....

"Yes, I'm the one who tired you with questions on the phone yesterday. I wanted to bring the fax message that came from Dublin yesterday evening to you in person. Here it is. That I've been invited to the International Writers Festival, that all my expenses will be paid, that my round-trip ticket has already been paid for... it's all explained here... And there's a fax number, too. They told me that if you forwarded my visa application directly to this number at the Irish Ministry of Foreign Affairs, there wouldn't be any problem and that by tomorrow—maybe even today—I could be granted the visa..."

"Like I told you on the phone, it's impossible for you to get a visa any sooner than four weeks. And that's only if you're lucky. It normally takes six weeks."

"But the officials in Dublin said that..."

"Look, how many times have I told you... If you want, you can go ahead with your application, but it's impossible for you to get the visa..."

"I'd better give it a go... Here's my application... If you would please call this number right away..."

"You're not the only person here with business. You see the crowd, one by one..."

"But mine is urgent, and it's only a fax..."

"Everybody's is urgent because of the match."

"Match? Sorry, I don't understand."

"The match between Galatasaray and Cork. You don't know about it?"

"I'm sorry. I had no idea. When is it?"

"On the 29th..."

"But mine's even more urgent. I'm supposed to be there on the 20th. Anyway... there aren't any four weeks to the 29th, either. How is it that those applying for a visa for the match..."

"Listen, you've been keeping me busy for a long while! Within this time..."

"Yes, within this time you could easily have faxed my application to this number, there wouldn't have been any problem, and I wouldn't have had to keep you busy!"

"Do we have to send a fax for anybody who wants one? Whenever there's a match, they get really finicky; I think they're right... Using matches as an excuse, people seek refugee status in streams. What else can they do? Well, next please!"

My voice, with the increasingly quarrelsome tone you might expect from somebody preparing for a fight—something you'd hardly expect from me when you see my glasses—is interrupted by this incredible response. I freeze in surprise. The next person takes my turn. He says that he wants to go Cork via Dublin for the match. His application is processed immediately and then it's the next person's turn. I just stand there to one side. A young man in the middle of the line calls out to me:

"Ma'am, could you step over here for a moment?"

I turn back, taking the risk of being chided with keeping the official busy. He's summoning me to his side. I'm in such a state of shock that I go over to him to be scolded. But I'm not. He whispers into my ear:

"Why don't you just say you're going to the match? That way you don't have to pay the fee to leave the country."

I repeat the same meaningless sentence that I've had to repeat over and over this morning: "Sorry, I don't understand."

The young man with glasses gazes at me in pity.

"Don't you know that people who go abroad for a football match don't have to pay?"

"No, I'm not aware of that. How on earth has it happened that I—who hate this fee, this tax for the so-called "housing fund," which I see only as a sign of our being far behind the times—haven't heard of this chauvinistic exception, which serves only to multiply my hatred of it!

Inspecting the people in line, I now try to guess which of these people are potential refugees intent on escaping on the pretext of a match, and which of them are writers trying to avoid paying tax to the housing fund under the mask of a football fanatic!

Yet I must acknowledge Turkey's creativity in its own right. I wonder whether there's any other country that doesn't collect departure tax from those going to matches abroad. This means that anywhere on the face of the earth where there's a football match, there's a Little Turkey for a Turkish football fanatic! I must add this to my paper on the mother-country concept.

What paper? You're not writing anything. Have you forgotten? You can't go. You're left stranded in your mother country. If you were going to the match, maybe you could, but you're not allowed to go to the writers' conference.

I rush back to the office and call Dublin. Because of the time difference, I get a hold of a drowsy Aileen at the breakfast table, a woman with whom I've become friends because of this visa problem. Aileen and I know not only each other's office numbers but also all sorts of other phone numbers: home, mothers', lovers', car- and cell-phones.

"Aileen, hello! Sorry for calling you at this time of the morning.
Unfortunately, I won't be able to come.
I got it. Thank you very much.
I took it there myself this morning.
No, the answer's the same.
They told me that it's impossible within four weeks.
I know: "There are always exceptions."
But unfortunately I'm not one of them.
Really?
You think they might consider me an exception?
But I'm not a football fanatic!
Forget it, it was just a joke.
No, I haven't finished it yet. If you want the truth, I haven't even begun. I can't begin to write without knowing whether or not I'll be coming.
Okay, I'll make a start.
You really think so?
I'm not so optimistic.
Okay, Aileen. Thanks...
I hope so, I hope to see you soon."

"There are always exceptions..."
Art is an exception. So is love.
I think Aileen is, too.
Maybe her name is "Alien"? She does seem a most unusual woman. Strangers, exceptions...
What about the football fans?
In some countries they might be considered exceptions, but they're certainly not unusual.

Okay then, I'll continue with my paper.

What was the sub-title: "The changing relationship between the citizen and the state."

Let's see what the dictionary says: "state: condition, situation; quality; elegance, exuberance, magnificence; nation, administrative district, country."

In lower case, the condition, position or situation of anything at a given moment; obviously, not very promising in terms of transition. Capitalized, it's a subject on which you can't expect much positive input from me. If you ask me, I'd say that all those who were, have been or may be put in prison because of thinking aloud should automatically be excluded from optimism there.

When we come to the word "citizen": a member, native or naturalized, of a state or nation (as distinguished from "alien").

So that's the way it is!

If we're only "members" of a state or a nation, not citizens, then we're called aliens. If a citizen is *yurttaş*, what is an alien? "Alien: someone who belongs to a different country, race or group; not yet settled in; someone not yet assimilated." A stranger!

Now this is familiar...

It has been forever since I read Camus' *The Stranger* in middle school.

It's dangerous not to assimilate. If you remain too much of an individual, you'll ask too many questions. You may even end up in prison.

Art doesn't assimilate. Nor does love.

Oh! What am I going to write in this paper?

Hello!
Yes, of course I remember.
My dental appointment at two o'clock.
Okay, I'm on my way.

14:00

No, my face doesn't look like this because of my tooth. You know that filling that's always falling out? No, no, it hasn't fallen out... I just want to have it recapped before I set off. What if it should fall out... But now I can't go. I mean I probably won't be able to go. And I still have to write a paper that I don't know whether I'll be able to present or not just in case I can go. At least I have to pretend to be writing it...

No, my dear, how can you possibly say that my face looks this way because I'm here? This is one of the few places where I do feel I "belong." I know which boxes at the entrance are for the clean booties and which are for the dirty ones, which of the flowers on the back balcony are new, and at which point you'll scold me because of the tartar on my teeth, I know it all... Here I feel myself a citizen, not an alien...

No, I certainly didn't say it to make fun of you. No dear, it's nothing like that; I've never ever pictured you as a prison warden or a torturer. I swear I didn't use "citizen" with that connotation. Look, it's just what I'm writing about in my paper.

Okay, I'll shut up and open my mouth!

14:10

The phone, for me?
What could it be that's so urgent?
Oh no, something's happened to my daughter! Down the stairs...

Hello!
Hello, Aileen?
How did you possibly find me?
I don't believe it...
Of course... Of course I'm going, going at full speed... You can trust me to be there in half an hour!
No, Aileen, I don't have almost three hours; I have only fifty minutes.
Don't forget the time difference...
No, no! On the contrary, it's as cute as can be... I'm pleased you feel that close.
Actually, the fact that there are two hours' difference between us seems weird to me, too. Your voice seems so close! You know, Aileen, any place I have friends seems like home to me... Coming to Dublin I'm on my way to my own country... Once again, thanks a lot.

14:12

Ali, I'm off...
Forget it. We'll cap it when I get back.
Yes, I'm going.
They've called me from Dublin and said they'd taken care of my visa.

Can you imagine? Here—face to face—you can't even explain your problem to a fellow countryman who speaks your own language, but a complete stranger—thousands of kilometers away...
Sorry. I'm always such a crybaby like this... Don't worry, I'll get over it. Good-bye... What do you want from Dublin? You can be sure of that—I'll have a drink for both of you. Give my regards to Hülya.
Good-bye... No, it's not finished yet. I'm going to Dublin. If I return, I'll make another appointment.
Aaa! Yes, the plastic booties. I was about to go off with the booties on... Which box do we put the used ones in?

14:45

    Good morning, Sir... I have a request...
    For Dublin...
    Do you remember me?
    Hmm, thank you.
    Do I pick up my passport inside?
    Well, that was nice of him!

    Hello.
    Not at all.
    Never mind.
    Yes, you were very busy with applicants.
    Never mind.
    I tried to tell you...
    Anyway, let's forget it.
    Yes, I'm leaving on Monday.
    Good-bye.

FRIDAY, September 17, 1993

06:00

    Good morning, sweetheart!
    How nice of you to wake up so early... I adore building towers with colored blocks at six in the morning.
    All right, I'm getting up.
    ....
    No, I can't get up.
    I can't get up because I went to bed at 4 a.m.
    How will I ever get through the day?
    My paper still to write, the dirty dishes piled up, and so much work to be done at the office... Fortunately, I did do the laundry yesterday evening...
    Oh, darling, have you wet your bed again?
    It's no problem, don't worry, I won't shout at you for it, we'll have it cleaned up in no time.
    Do you want me to tune in a cartoon for you? And I'll warm up your milk right away...
    Your pacifier? Don't you remember—we threw it onto the next-door roof and the birds took it away? We weren't going to suck anymore, were we?
    You're right; I have lit a cigarette at this hour in the morning.
    I shouldn't have. I'm sorry. But last night when I tried to write something, I couldn't;

that's why I'm a bit nervous.
No, darling, I'm not angry with you.
Look what a nice cartoon: The Tazmanian Monster!

08:30

No, sweetheart, you shouldn't put that on; that's for the winter... It's too heavy, you'll sweat.
I've gotten this outfit all ready for you, look. And you can wear your red shoes, too; Okay?
No, no you can't put that on, either. We don't wear sundresses in this weather, you'll catch cold, that's for the summer...
I don't say "no" to everything. In spring we should wear spring clothes, not winter or summer clothes.
It's autumn now.
Yes, there are two in-between seasons.
Now it's autumn.
Autumn... September...
September isn't a season, it's a month...
No, not those shoes... those are boots. You can't wear them now.
Okay, I'll bring you some water...

09:00

Sweetheart, I told you not to put that on.
Come on, let's take it off now.
No, darling, you won't be able to watch *Maya the Bee* today. Because I have to go to the office early today. I mean, your friends will be waiting for you at kindergarten. I wonder what kind of games you'll play today! Maybe it's someone's birthday today...
No, sweetheart... No... That's a birthday dress, but it's for summer; look how nice this is. I've gotten it all ready for you!
NO!
PUT THIS ON!

10:30

Zehra, dearie, let's write the executive board meeting invitations. That way I can sign them; you can send them next week. Today, bring me only the most pressing matters; and one more thing: Don't put through any phone calls unless they're urgent. I really must finish this paper.

10:35

Okay, Zehra, my dear, connect me if it's urgent.

10:45

Do they say it's urgent? Then put it through...

11:10

Hello, yes...

11:30

Hello...

11:40

Okay, I'll sign them if they're ready. No, I haven't been able to write a word... You see, the phone hasn't stopped ringing. What meeting? Didn't we postpone it? When?

17:30

Hey folks, I'm off! Today at least she shouldn't be the last to be picked up from kindergarten... Every day she nags me: "Why am I the last one here?" Next week I'll be back—that is, if I haven't applied for refugee status...

I have been thinking about it. My mother could look after her, maybe better than I do. Don't forget to phone mother every day. In case of an emergency, call me. Aaa... the phone number! I'm writing it down here, in Zehra's notebook. For Ireland 00353, for Dublin 1, and for the Shelbourne Hotel... No, I haven't written it down. I wish I had; I haven't even been able to start... On the weekend I'll ask Anush to come over. If she keeps the kid busy maybe I can...

SATURDAY, September 18, 1993

09:30

Anush, good to see you... Today she's a little bit out of sorts. She heard me talking to my mother last night. She learned the news while I was on the phone with my mother... She realizes I'm going, maybe it's because of that... Could you take her to the park, please? I need to write and I need some tranquility. Tranquility! I'll disconnect the telephone... The refrigerator, too. I've even been thinking of stopping my watch. Get the picture? Yes, I must complete a paper... Yes, I'm leaving on Monday. Yes, Anush, everything is settled... Okay, I'll get the phone. No, she hasn't had her milk yet. Can you fix it? Hello! Not in that pan! No, I wasn't talking to you. Of course... Anush, the milk's about to boil over! Yes, I'm going on Monday... No, dear, I'm here, I'm not going anywhere today... You know, my daughter asked about it... I'm coming back a week from Monday. Anush, the milk!

09:45
How come she isn't drinking it? Then tell her a fairy tale... All right, I'm coming... Okay... But you're going to the park right after that... First to the swings, then to the slide, and then to the sandbox; after that again to the swings, to the slides, and to the sandbox... until you're both exhausted and feel sleepy! Is that clear, Anush?

10:15
Would it kill her to wash out the pan and put it away... If only she didn't remind me so much of my childhood! The Istanbul of my childhood... Perhaps that's why I just can't part with her... Even the sound of the name YerAnush is reminiscent of those days. Her black stockings... The typical smell that permeates her clothes... and invariably, the damp smell of the kitchen, tainted with that of the wood-pile... Grandma's kitchen... in Kireçburnu... Tepebaşı, the Hotel Bristol... The Greek and Armenian women always passing by the hotel, the sound of their words—incomprehensible to me—falling on my ears; this sound was an essential part of the city... The Greeks really shouldn't have left; Istanbul has been left stammering... "My homeland, my childhood..." What Latin American writer said that and where? Was he from Latin America, or have I just imagined it? My homeland, my childhood... I've lost the sounds of my childhood... It's as if I've been aging far away from home... Home... Homeland... Country... If only I could write the first sentence, then I could go on. "My Homeland: My Childhood..."

10:45
You're back so soon?
Anush, you couldn't keep her occupied, could you? My dear, she never keeps quiet when she knows I'm at home.
Where can I go at this hour? My dictionaries, my notes and papers...
How long can you look after her? What sorts of prayers do you have on this very Saturday? Then please, after you put her to sleep... Feed her, put her to bed, then I'll show up... Maybe I can write for a few hours longer while she's sleeping... I mean, try to write... Thank you very much. I'll be back by one at the latest. I'll be at Uncle Süleyman's café.

11:00
Uncle Süleyman, would you bring me a tea? No, I'll sit inside, don't worry about me... It's lovely out there under the trellis, too, but I have a little work to do. I have to write something, and my daughter won't let me concentrate. Of course she's right, it's me who's wrong. I know.

11:10

Uncle Süleyman, could we turn the radio down a little bit, please?
That's very nice of you, thank you very much. No, thank you, not right now. I had a lot this morning.

11:20

Fine, thank you, Mehmet Bey. And you?
Don't even ask, I've been trying to write something... My daughter won't leave me alone at home... It's no reflection on the girl, I know. Thank you, that's nice of you; she's fond of you, too. Yes, I'm leaving on Monday. To Ireland. Ireland... On the other side of England. An island on the ocean side.
I don't know, it must be a member. How many countries are there in the European Union? I do remember, it is a member. I've just read it in the brochure that I got from the Honorary Irish Consulate... What's more, ever since the 70s. No, Ireland isn't a part of Britain, it's an independent country. Yes, it's in the Commonwealth, but so are Canada and Australia. No, it's Northern Ireland that's a part of Britain. The capital is Belfast. I'm going to Dublin. And before leaving I have to finish this paper... So if you'll pardon me...

11:35

Of course, go right ahead... In the European Union? How should I know... Of course I do talk, but those I see where I go are in no better condition than I am here in Turkey... If it were up to them, they'd probably accept Turkey into the Union; however, I don't think they have any say in the political decisions made. Referendum... Yes, in Switzerland one was held, I think; the majority didn't want to... They themselves didn't want to join the Union. If they'd wanted to be a member, they would've been admitted. If we hold a referendum... these days... I just don't know. I can never figure out what the majority wants. What good would it do if I could... If you ask me, I'm for it... I know very little about the Customs Union; money and economic issues I don't know a thing about... as for art and culture... I don't know... Thanks to my favorite authors, the music I listen to, and the movies most of all... If there is something called Europe, in other words an international culture, actually, I don't feel myself outside it.
So you're saying they'll refuse to admit Turkey?
Why?
Ohh, this is so funny... Yes, you're right, we're just like the guest with nine children... No, I don't want that, either. Who wants a guest with nine children? Take a look at Istanbul's present condition.
Why do you say so, Kadir Efendi? What's the use of such a large population? The Muslim world? Hmm... So that's what you have in mind... You mean we'll rule the

world if our population reaches a hundred million? I really don't know what to say... Good luck with that... Actually, I have no intention whatsoever of wearing a veil... What's more, such enormous crowds would irritate me.
Who knows, if there weren't any other way out, I'd probably leave the country... That's how it is... In this country that's like the guest with nine children, maybe I'm the guest myself with only one child...

I wonder what my daughter's been up to? The time's flown by so fast. Anyway, it's time to go. Good-bye, Mehmet Bey. It doesn't matter. It's already been several days that I haven't been able to write. You're asking what I am going to write about? I don't know. I think probably the kind of things we've been talking about...

12:30
Anush, hasn't she gone to sleep yet?
What am I going to do now?
Okay, you can go.
Can you come tomorrow? I know you go to church. Take her along to church. That'd be better. She likes to go to church. Listen. I want to ask you something: What country are you from? Of course, dear, I know it's here, but... I mean, I wonder if you would feel happier in Armenia? Or, I don't know, in the US? Huh... So you're happy only in church? Sure, I see. No, I won't. No, not because of that. Of course I love Jesus. And I like churches—mosques and synagogues, too... Though I've never seen one, I suppose I'd like the Buddhist temples. All temples are beautiful, the light, the smell... Except for the Kocatepe Mosque! How on earth could they put a mosque above a supermarket? Sure, I might find peace there, but who wants peace? I'm happy being discontented. No, I won't influence her. Yes, she can become a Christian if she likes. Jewish or Muslim, or Buddhist or atheist. If she'd only go to sleep!
Anush, I definitely want you to come tomorrow... Good-bye...

17:30
Hello!
No, Mom, she hasn't slept yet.
I'm about to go mad.
Tomorrow morning Anush is going to come and take her to church.
What should I do, then?
I know you're busy; I can't hold that against you!
We're already taking all of next week away from you...
She's coughing a bit.
Mom, does it make any sense to turn the central heating on in this weather?
Besides, we haven't bought a   fuel yet.

You know that.
Mom, I know... I've married all the wrong men and lived in all the wrong houses...
Maybe I was born the wrong way round, in the wrong country, at the wrong time, to the wrong mother and father.

18:00
Hello!
Mom, I'm sorry.
I'm just a nervous wreck.
I still haven't been able to write the paper.
Forgive me.
Okay, don't worry.
I'll get her to sleep soon and get down to work.
On Monday Anush is taking her to kindergarten, in the afternoon you'll pick her up, okay; after that she's all yours.
I left the phone number in the office; the girls will call you every day.
Of course. See you tomorrow.
Bye.

SUNDAY, September 19, 1993

16:00
Hello!
Mom, dear.
Mom, who said "On Sundays, don't even let God take my life!"
Sadberk Hanım from Keçiören?
Is that Koç's wife, Sadberk Hanım?
Someone different?
Was the name Sadberk common in those days?
What did she say?
"On Sundays, don't ever let God take my life!"
A Yugoslavian emigrant...
Do they use "ever" instead of "even"?
Her daughter Sulhiye, her son Hamdi...
No, I'm not crying... I mean...
Today even the name is gone. I'm crying for Yugoslavia.
Now they call it "ex-Yugoslavia"—that means "the Yugoslavia of the past..." If she were alive now, she wouldn't know what country she emigrated from.
No, I haven't been able to write.
Maybe that's why I don't feel very good now.

Or maybe because it's Sunday.
On Sundays, don't ever let God take my life!

MONDAY, September 20, 1993

07:15

Anush, welcome!
Fortunately she's asleep... If she'd awakened, what state would I be in now... We'd never have been able to shut her up. Seeing these suitcases she'd know for sure that I'm going far away. Of course, I told her... Never would I lie to her! I told her I wouldn't be around for a while and her grandma would be staying with her... Whatever it is, children just can't bear the moment of parting.

Maybe this explains the panic they feel just before falling asleep. Perhaps we're all alike. I never tell anyone a lie... Maybe that's why... Look now, just before leaving... Anush, just a second. I'll go quietly and give her a kiss. I won't wake her up; very quietly!
Oh no, these days my eyes are always filling with tears. Don't worry.
Okay, good-bye.
Yes, I called for it. It's waiting outside.
Remember Ahmet Bey? He's the cab driver. I glanced out the window, he's already here.
Don't worry.
Yes, I did; I've got everything.
My passport's here, and I'll pick up the ticket at the airport... Okay.
Good-bye.
No, I haven't been able to finish it.
I have lots of notes. We'll see; I'll complete it on board. There won't be any phone ringing and no little sweetie crying.
No excuses.
Okay, I won't drink, I promise. Why am I promising? I'll drink if I feel like it! I'll drink to your health, too, Anush, my dear. All right, you pray for me. I hope God won't answer your prayers.
Good-bye. I'm only kidding, don't be sore.

07:20

Hi. How are you, Ahmet Bey?
Sorry I kept you waiting.
We'll be at the airport by eight o'clock, won't we?
International departures... to Ireland.

I have never been there, either.
I'm very pleased to be going there.
Often? You might say so...
You're right, when I left for Essen, it was you who took me to the airport.
Huh! You took me to the airport on my way to Hamburg, too?
What a coincidence, you've hit all my journeys to Germany... After all, you're half-German yourself!
Thirty years is no short time!
Do you miss Germany?
Of course you do.
You miss it there when you're here, and miss it here when you're there.
You're lucky, then, if you're still missing it...
Maybe I'll miss Ireland, too...
Match? What match?
Ohh, I do know.
Galatasaray's match against Cork, on the 29th.
No, I'm not a Galatasaray fan. But If I supported any team, it'd probably be Galatasaray.
I like French, therefore I like the Galatasaray School, and because of that I like the team... I never managed to learn French; I can understand it but I can't speak it. I have; for twenty-five years now I've been to almost every course there is. I want my daughter to learn it. It is so strange. I never thought I'd be one of those mothers who expect their children to do what they couldn't do.
I know your children stayed in Germany.
But you're a Beşiktaş fan, I think...
That's natural, you live in Beşiktaş...
My daughter says so, too; she'll always be a Beşiktaş fan. What if she doesn't want to go to the Galatasaray School... even if she passes the entrance exam? Why should she? Did I become a doctor? Or a lawyer as my father wanted me to? I haven't even practiced architecture. Even though I was the one who wanted to become an architect... Just the other day my mother pouted because I didn't write architect as my profession on a form I was filling out...
Ahmet Bey, what's all this traffic?
They've picked the perfect time for an accident!
This is what the new bridge over the Golden Horn is always like...
Why didn't we take the other road?
It's my fault... That's right, I'm the one who said so. Sorry.
Because it's shorter this way... I don't know, I'm worse than a stranger about finding my way around. I can't predict anything in advance in this city, in this country, even.

08:15

    We have about two hours until take-off, but my ticket...
    I'm going to pick it up at the airport.
    We should be at the airport by now.
    But here we are stranded.
    I wonder when the jam will clear up...
    We haven't moved an inch!
    Yes, you're right, if this were Germany...
    You miss Germany, don't you?
    Would you mind if I asked you something? Where do you feel more at home? And now that your children are there, too...
    So you say you like it here, isn't that strange?
    They say one always misses his hometown as he gets older...
    Why should you be approaching death; you're still young...

08:30

    Don't be afraid, there's no way now you could come even close to death; look at this, we can't even move.

08:57

    Good-bye. Say hi to the neighborhood from me...

09:00

    TK 107. Yes, it's at 10:10.
    Istanbul-Zurich. I'm changing planes in Zurich. Zurich-Dublin, Air Lingus. Yes, that's today, also: transit. I'm supposed to get my ticket from you... Of course it was paid for—in Dublin. I'm late because there was an accident on the road. I know that doesn't have anything to do with you, but... What do you mean it doesn't show up on the screen? How can that possibly not show up if you can see the reservation? Look, here in this fax... Fine, but why should I pay for a ticket that's already paid for? Yes, I am shouting, because I'm a nervous wreck. What kind of a jam is this? How come only one half of the computer jams? Why does everything in this country jam up, will somebody please tell me? The traffic jams, computers jam, because our minds are jammed! Go ahead, call the security officials... call the gendarmes, too, and the police and the army...

    Ohm! Hi... How nice it is to see you here... Of course, even if you'd forgotten, you'd have come when you heard my voice...
    Was I shouting all that loudly? Very rude, isn't it? Yes, there is a problem. Is there anything without a problem in this country? Fortunately, your daughter is leaving...

I'm sorry; I'm so preoccupied with my own problems. Has she left yet? Her flight was at nine o'clock, wasn't it? And, it took off without any delay? That's great. Her first separation, huh? That's very normal. It was clever of her to go away. I hope she doesn't come back after she graduates... Tell her to go on for an MA, then a PhD... and then find a job. Whatever she does, she shouldn't come back! Look at this mess, everything's jammed. I know we don't say it; we say, "May God reunite you." But not here, there. You should go to Vienna, too. What're you doing here? If I ever get off, I'll never come back. There's just an hour to departure and I still can't get my hands on my ticket. They're trying to check with the head-office of Turkish Airlines, but the computers are jammed and they can't ask. Yes, that's the most ridiculous side to it! My ticket reads "confirmed," but not paid. You know I don't know a thing about computers. All I know is that in no other country on earth could a computer manage to jam so strangely. They say I can't have the ticket unless I pay for it again in cash. What would I be doing with that much on me? Really? But how can you do that? Let me check... No, I don't even have that much... Well, then... No, that's impossible! Then you won't even have money left for a cab. How will you get back to town? What if they don't come to pick you up? That's right, what are friends for... I'm sorry... These days I cry easily. Maybe that's because I've parted ways with all my friends. I don't know if I have any friends here...

11:02

Local time at origin: 11:02
Distance from departure: 560 km.

"Could you bring me another glass of wine, please?"

Temperature outside: -52°C
Distance from departure: 573 km.
Local time at origin: 11:03

Your prayer hasn't been answered, Anush! At this hour in the morning I'm drinking my second glass. And in honor of your prayers... Actually, we're drinking together. With whom? With my own god... If there does exist a god, I'm sure his name must be simply the God of Coincidence, and he must be laughing at a lot of Muslims and Christians; Protestants and Catholics; Hindus and Muslims; Sunnis and Alawites; believers and nonbelievers all slaying one another in his name and on his behalf; the moment when I feel the closest to him is when the plane takes off. The moment I isolate myself from everybody killing each other down below and from all my identities; only at that moment does my god speak to me and say, "C'mon, light your cigarette as soon as the 'No Smoking' notice goes off and order our wine so that I can feel you beside me in this dimension without time or space."

Altitude: 10,667 m.
Distance from departure...
Distance to destination...

Sadberk Hanım!
Not Koç's wife, the other one...
Your husband was supposed to be a colonel, and rather ugly...
Maybe just because of that you hated Sundays.
Look, according to the red arrow on the monitor we're passing high over *Kragujevac* to *Belgrade*; in other words, we're flying over your land. Not even the name has survived, what do they say now: Yugoslavia / the once-upon-a-time country!
I hope you didn't ever die on a Sunday...
At this very moment a child who was perhaps pointing out our plane may have been shot to death, just as we disappeared behind a cloud.
You won't see him on the map or in the statistics.
How many children have been killed and how many more have been born to mothers who were raped?
Does the killing of the children conceived with enemy sperm then deserve a hearty "Serves you right!"?
What do you make of this, Sadberk Hanım, or is the answer still blowing in the wind?
Or were the answers left in the songs Joan Baez and Bob Dylan sang twenty years ago?

Time to destination: 2:01
Local time at destination: 10:29
Local time at origin: 11:29

11:29
"*Welcome on board, ladies and gentlemen...*
This is your captain speaking
We'll be landing in Zurich at 12:30 local time..."

Oh no, if we're arriving at 12:30, how will I ever catch the 13:10 flight out?
We were supposed to be in Zurich at 12:10. We took off after a twenty-minute delay, of course; that explains everything.
I wonder if anyone could show me one single thing that's punctual in Turkey?

"*The weather is cloudy and the temperature is 12°C in Zurich.*
Local time in Zurich is 10:30 at the moment."

10:30

I'm setting my watch back now. It must feel right at home. After all, it's from Zurich. Not just in origin—it came from Zurich with memories. The hour hand, the minute hand, the second hand and the crystal; the inscription on it reads: *Zurich für den Film*. The watch was a gift from Xavier Koller, the Swiss director of *Journey of Hope*. A sort of peace pipe after our quarrels, which went far beyond the usual director-script writer squabbles. I remember Zurich and the quarrels I had with Xavier.

The plot of the movie is based on a real-life story about a refugee family from Maraş who lose their child in the mountains while trying to reach Switzerland. An eight-year-old child frozen to death in the snow... A child forced to leave his home on a "journey of hope." Was it because of oppression or hunger, or merely in the expectation of a better life?
Does it matter?
Did leaving home pay off? What did they leave? Their land! Was it really their land?
"Home is not where you're born but where you can make a living..."
Which is your land?

"The flower's most beautiful on the branch..."
So where does it belong?

What about me... Why did I squabble so with Koller? The cast must be well dressed; they have to carry decent suitcases... No, their suitcases won't be tied with rope! What? A typical Westerner's eye! A commercial exotic that turns the East into a commodity! No, you mustn't humiliate our people... The women should take off those baggy pants they wear under their skirts... what's more these people are escapees; it shouldn't look like a costume party! And take the ropes off the suitcases... It's as though everybody from Turkey drags a suitcase bursting at the seams into the hub of Europe!

What happened afterwards? Wouldn't you know, the lock of my suitcase broke. And this right in the middle of Zurich Airport! Ah, Xavier! Your spell must have been effective... We didn't let you shoot the movie the way you wanted... That's the most unfair thing that can happen to a director. But you got your revenge. The glee on your face as you eyed that suitcase of mine all tied up with a rope! That's why I speak of my "God of Coincidences!"

Anyhow, the watch was our peace pipe...
Look! The watch is home again. And here's Zurich Airport... The watch is at home, but what about me? By the way, where is my home? If I don't belong anywhere, then why did I wrangle with Xavier?

12:40
> Excuse me... I have to catch the 13:10 flight.
> Dublin... Yes, Air Lingus...
> No, I haven't looked at the departure board.
> Really? Do delays occur very often? In Zurich? In the Land of Clocks?

13:00
> You see, Xavier... We're even now, 1-1.
> Even if my suitcase was tied with a rope then, now I hear there are often delays at Zurich Airport.
> My flight scheduled to take off at 13:10 has been delayed to 14:15...
> I don't mind. I love airports. Especially airport bars... They are the world's most nondescript corners. You can write the most melancholy letters—filled with longing. In fact, everyone writing, whatever they write, are actually writing letters. In an hour my notes on homelands...

13:15
> "He must be a queen; he's had his bum turned to me the whole time!"
> Homeland, motherland, mother tongue... I turn around to look, startled by these words in my mother tongue.
> A pilot!
> He's on the phone... There's another man beside him also speaking Turkish, and also with a huge mustache.
> They're laughing. In the mother tongue we share, they call out to a stewardess in the distance.
> "Look what he wants; he wants some bonito!"
> The screech of the stewardess who's running towards them mingles with the sound of her high heels:
> "He can have as much of whatever fish he wants!"
> The pilot's yelling into the phone.
> He's reporting her words: "'He can have all the bonito he wants,' she says. It'd be a sin and shame if I didn't send you some bonito."
> The other man snatches the receiver before the stewardess can get to it: "Don't believe the queen! Of course I had him call you... You thought he called you? Buddy, he's a bastard... If he hadn't bumped into me..."
> The stewardess keeps reaching for the receiver; when she can't get hold of it she raises her voice to be heard by the person on the other end of the line:
> "Believe me, we were going to call you!"
> The receiver's then handed back to the pilot.
> "What kind do you want? To boil or fry?"

The pilot chuckles.

"That's what happens when you marry an infidel! Good for her, pal... She seems to have brought you into line. God only knows if she hasn't probably weaned you from the bottle, too..."

The pilot announces to his buddies next to him:

"He says his missus won't have it cooked in the house because the smell lingers so."

The homesick countryman who seems to have run into the pilot at the airport pats his chest:

"Let's cook it at my place so the smell will linger... I could live for six months on that smell..."

Those passing by, those sitting, those standing, those sipping their drinks, those doing shopping, the cab drivers, the controllers in the control tower, and those all over the airport and all over Zurich—and of course Xavier Koller—are staring at the three people by the phone:

"*What language* are *they speaking?*"

The smell of bonito permeates my clothes... The smell of fish... The homeland... The oil is bubbling... Notes on the homeland... I really must go to the departure gate... To Dublin... I glance at my watch: 13.49... I get up... Will I ever get away from the smell of bubbling oil?

13:50

"*Mrs. Tunsevich!*
This is the last call for Mrs. Tunsevich, leaving for Moscow.
Mrs. Tunsevich to Gate Number..."

Can you really run away from your flight, Mrs. Tunsevich?
From your flight and from Moscow?
I'd like to have a chat with you.
I'd like to ask you some questions. What does homeland mean to you, and what changes have occurred in the state-citizen relationships in your homeland over the last century?
One of my friends who just came from Moscow said your people were surprised to see a water meter being installed at their door. Yes, Mrs. Tunsevich, I'm afraid the number of meters in your life will keep increasing from now on. I think you'll soon be billed for education and health, too. Please don't think I'm a bigoted socialist; no, not at all! But do forgive me when I say that Lenin's *Subbotnics* still thrills me. Of course, I agree with you; it's sheer utopia that on a Saturday, without pay, workers voluntarily set right the enormous locomotive that couldn't be budged during the week, and after that they had bread and rum, and sang in the shanty... Perhaps for this reason *Subbotnics* became my land for a long time.

Mrs. Tunsevich, can you imagine a more perfect homeland than Utopia? From the eternal youth of the Gilgamesh legend to Majnun's Leila, and from *Subbotnics* to Lennon's "Imagine." How young we were when we sang that song, remember? Yes, Mrs. Tunsevich, unfortunately I can imagine; I would imagine, too, that in those days "imagination" and its song might have been forbidden in your country.
And now, Mrs. Tunsevich?
Are you going back?
Shall we return, Mrs. Tunsevich, what d'you say?

14:30

"Good afternoon, ladies and gentlemen...
Welcome on board...
Air Lingus and our crew wish you a pleasant flight...
We'll be landing in Dublin at 15:35 p.m. local time...
Local time in Dublin is 13:30 p.m. at the moment..."

13:30

And now my watch is on Dublin time...
The time difference between home and here has gone up to two hours. Home? Country? Homeland?
My little one must be about to wake up from her midday nap.
Will she cry for me?

14:00

We—my seat-mate and I, who've become friends thanks to the first cigarettes we both lit the moment the *"No Smoking"* sign was turned off—are now puffing away at the second cigarettes we offered each other. I'm finding out that he's a musician from Dublin; that he plays the harmonica and holds that wind instruments best reflect the soul. We tell each other where we're coming from and where we're going in life and on the plane. We laugh at the fact that both of us have arrived at our current occupations thanks to past imprisonments. He says he's coming from the dubbing of a movie in Germany. "Which movie?" I ask. *"In the Name of the Father,"* he answers. He says the film is making its debut at the Berlin Film Festival. I wonder who the director might be. Jim Sheridan, he replies. Though the name sounds familiar, it escapes me. I'm told that Sheridan has also directed *My Left Foot.* He adds that Daniel Day Lewis is again playing the lead in *In the Name of the Father.* Of course, now I recall Sheridan. And *My Left Foot,* and Lewis, too... I tell him that I've seen the movie, but wasn't much impressed by it. I also say pedantically that I don't like exaggerated Hollywood-style characters and happy endings. He keeps silent. Little by little, one question after another, I learn that he's a childhood friend of Jim Sheridan—from the same neighborhood—and that he's accepted the offer because the story is about Ireland; and it's his first film role. "What kind of role?" I ask. "A small part," he replies. "Well, but what exactly? "An IRA militant..."

Then he makes a request: "Sheridan wants to film my life. Would you write the scenario?"
I think he's kidding.
He says he's serious.
"It's no coincidence that we're sitting together," he says.
Why do I say "No"?
Aren't I really an "alien"?
Why am I obsessed with the fear that I can write only stories that "belong" to me?
How much of *Journey of Hope* belonged to me?
Maybe our sitting together isn't really a coincidence after all.
I feel as though one part of me has been living in Dublin and the only coincidence is that we haven't met until now.
How many friends do we have that we've never met?
And how many cities are there that might be our home, even though we've never been to them?
Is the answer still blowing in the wind?
If you play your harmonica, will the answer reach me?

15:30

The last cigarettes are being extinguished. We fasten our seat belts. He's jotting down his phone number at the last moment and handing it to me.
He must have sensed from my expression that I'd be shy of calling him up; therefore he wants to know where I'll be staying.
"The Shelbourne," I say.

15:40

Dublin Airport
We're headed towards different gates.
I realize that I'm parting not only from him but from everyone else as well.
Those carrying EC passports and those of the Commonwealth countries disappear as if through unseen doors.
I am the only one from the plane—I alone—who's headed towards the visa desk.
Alone, all alone.
I turn around. He signals to me, "I'll call you."
I don't believe it.
He disappears.

I can't find my passport.
The official at the visa desk is a rather mature, bespectacled man.
"Calm down," he says in a gentle voice.
He wants to know why I'm here.
"The writers' conference," I answer.
"Are you a writer?" he asks with respect.
"I'm rather doubtful whether I deserve that title, but I've been invited here on the assumption that I am," I reply while rummaging through my bag for the passport.
"We're very fond of writers here," he pronounces and then he gets up to shake my hand, reaching under the glass at the front of the counter. Suddenly I find my passport and feel pleased that I've come to his window, that I'm able to be here at all, that I am a writer instead of a soccer fan—pleased with everything. I'm even convinced that the meeting on board wasn't a coincidence and—why not—that I'll be getting a phone call.

16:00

As I walk out the gate, a sweet, short, gray-haired man with veins protruding on his face snatches my suitcase. I insist on holding onto it.
"I'm the cab driver who's been sent to pick you up," he says.
"How do you know who I am?" I ask him, employing some cleverness, which seemed to have been lagging behind because of the time difference.
He takes a placard from under his arm and tries to pronounce my name; he has difficulty with the surname and asks for help.
While he's still struggling with the *c cedillas* and the *g* with the little mark over it, "Okay," I announce, "but how did you understand it's me?"
He points at the exit gate, and it finally occurs to me I am the last from the plane to leave the airport so that there is no possibility of his mistaking me.
I shake his hand in pure astonishment; and this time it's out of respect for his age that I won't let him carry my suitcase. "You have the Irish stubbornness," he says. We burst out laughing. Now I feel myself more like a Dubliner.

We chat continuously during the drive. From time to time I doubt that this much laughter becomes me.
While driving along the River Liffey, I try to impress upon my mind the pubs where we can drink beer if we have time; The Customs House on the Liffey; the O'Connell Bridge; the courtesy of the English who compensated for their rudeness in bricking up the windows of the Parliament House in the 1820s by the kindness they showed the injured O'Connell, letting him sit during his execution though they shot the other rebels one by one on their feet; the bricks blocking the windows of the Bank of Ireland (preserved intact not for the protection of the money in the

building but as a reminder of the building's past as the former house of parliament); the traditional and lovely stubbornness of the Irish who still dry their clothes in the sweet-smelling breeze despite all the automatic washer-dryers; and again another famous bar at this corner; "The Bailey" that we can't actually see from the road; and finally Grafton Street, where I really must come if I want to do some shopping. The names of most of the streets and squares call to mind associations—be they explicit or vague. I feel as if I had stepped into Joyce's *The Dead* or was wandering through the sets of John Huston's movie based on the same story. I've always found my real identity in such feelings. I'm melting into Dublin.

As we come nearer to the Shelbourne Hotel, my companion speeds up the sentences of his discourse in order to complete the entire history of Ireland before the drive ends. I thus learn that the Irish Constitution was drafted in one of the halls in this very hotel in 1922.

"Our republics are the same age," I comment when saying good-bye to him.
The feeling of "belonging" in my sentence doesn't bother me.
On the contrary, I get the feeling that the two countries' being the same age has reinforced my kinship with Ireland.

No sooner have I given my name to the reception to learn my room number than I hear a shriek behind me.
Immediately I know: This has to be Aileen!
We throw our arms around each other.
Speaking both at the same time, we try to fill in details missing from the images created over the phone.
Aileen introduces me to the festival director and then comes what I have been dreading most. "Your paper! We haven't received it yet... I hope you can hand it over right away. We need to duplicate and distribute it..."

I suddenly realize that I haven't once thought about the paper since I lit the first cigarette on the Dublin plane. Before I can decide what to say, I hear my own voice: "If I can find a "home" before nightfall, I'll be able to finish it up. I'm quite optimistic about Dublin."

They laugh; they think I'm kidding.

21:00

We're at a table for three in a Georgian style hall in the hotel. Nadine Gordimer, Nasim Khaksar and myself. In the candlelight with our wine, the black chadors of

Iran; with our lamb chops, the apartheid in South Africa; with out fruit salad, the Kurdish situation in Turkey. An ordinary international table. Over coffee, I then ask Nadine Gordimer how she copes with the difficulty of writing and raising a child at the same time. I can read the answer in the lightning that flashes in her eyes before I even hear her words. Our table is soon literally a "mother"land. Perhaps "home" is a concept valid only for mothers, or perhaps the whole world is a home to mothers. I find myself thinking that there is no subject more universal than motherhood.

22:00

It's tomorrow there. How deep asleep are you by now, my little doll, my sweetheart?

TUESDAY, September 21, 1993

According to the program, I'm supposed to deliver my paper at three o'clock tomorrow. Now it's no joke any longer. I have to complete my paper today. That's fine, but what am I going to say?
I go downstairs, leaving my jumbled notes on the desk and promising myself that a marvelous breakfast will bring me to my senses.
I find myself sitting next to Ivan Klima, a Czech author whose short stories, novels, plays and essays have been translated into many different languages.
I manage to keep silent for a long time. Just as we're about to leave, I suddenly feel compelled to tell him about my encounter with Mrs. Tunsevich at Zurich Airport, perhaps in order to avoid going back and sitting down to write.
"What do you think?" I ask Klima. "Has Mrs. Tunsevich returned to Moscow despite all the meters that have already been and are still to be installed at the doors?"
"Before we had meters," Klima says, "Prague's heating system used to be switched on in the middle of September and off again in the middle of May, no matter what the weather was. And Prague was one of those cities where air pollution had reached critical levels because most residents were leaving the radiators turned up high when they went on holiday at the weekends."
"But why?" I ask in a sorrowful voice.
"Which why?" he asks. "The flipping of the switches on the 15th of September and May regardless of the weather, or the mad heating of the empty houses?"
Of course, both... Although I know the answer lies in the reply, I keep on thrashing it over:
"But in his *Subbotnics*... Lenin says that... Where each worker sees every bit of the iron, wheat and coal as his own... Sorry, I think I am being pedantic... Well, I don't know, my eyes fill with tears every time I read it. Utopia, all right; maybe that's why... Who knows, perhaps the tears well up because then I was naive and young enough to believe in it but now all kinds of belief avoid me; and perhaps because I

am so selfish as to believe that humanity is aging along with me... Yes, I still get emotional when I read *Subbotnics*. You know, you must have read it..."
Ivan Klima looks into my face with an expression suggesting a difference in maturity even greater than the twenty-year difference in our ages, and with a certain pity: "Of course I have," he says. "It was compulsory reading for us at school."

When the last call for Utopia is made, I've decided I'll wait calmly near the departure gate. I'm adding utopia—above love, even—to the top of the ever-growing list of things whose magic disappears when they become reality.
Let's wait like this near all departure gates, Mrs. Tunsevich... Let all the planes give up waiting for us and take off without us. Let's keep yearning for the destinations of all the planes we haven't boarded... There should always be places to long for; we mustn't ever attempt to actually arrive!

I part with Ivan Klima.
I walk through the lobby and head toward the elevator, my feet shuffling. I was sure I was set with "My Homeland, Utopia"... Now it occurs to me that this, too, has slipped through my fingers... And tomorrow at 3.00, I...
Aileen calls out:
"They want to interview you for TV; can you spare a moment now?"
I'm dying to! There couldn't be any better excuse to shirk.
There's a new spring in my steps; there's a smile on my face... As it occurs to me that this enthusiasm might be attributed to my excitement at appearing on TV, I pull myself together; I subdue myself somewhat.

"What do I think of "homelands"?
Yes, I know this is the theme of the festival this year..."

How could I not be aware of the theme? For days, I've been living with it...

"Homeland is no land, or homeland is all lands if you are alien. Maybe because of all the nationalism and chauvinism and fanaticism surrounding us, one can sometimes feel at home only when together with other aliens. So, I guess Dublin is my home this week, for one week..."

The interviewer seems to like my remarks. I don't know whether my words sound more important and impressive in English, or if it's because they are simply foreign to me, but they do sound fine, even to me. I'm trying to "save" my remarks in my head, so I can use them later in my paper.

If you're an alien—or should I say "stranger"?—homeland is either nowhere or everywhere. Perhaps because of all the nationalism, chauvinism and fanaticism—conservatism, bigotry, and radicalism?—surrounding us, one sometimes feels at home only when together with other aliens. So, I guess it's true that Dublin is my home this week, for one week...

As the same remarks flow through my head in Turkish, I change my mind about liking them and forget about "saving" them... What is the Turkish equivalent of "alien," anyway? *Yaban, yabancı, aidiyetsiz?* Then, what is it?

The interviewer, taken with the idea that the festival itself creates a homeland, then asks:

"Wouldn't you like such a homeland to be permanent?"

"That's impossible! Then aliens would be non-aliens and aliens would be citizens: the citizens of "Aliens' Land"... Then we'd have to change the name of the country and it wouldn't be a homeland any more..."

"Sure," the interviewer says, expressing agreement, "in that case aliens would be citizens..."

The interview ends with the speaker inviting me to feel at home during my week as a guest at the festival.

Jotting the interview down on a piece of paper and heading toward the elevators on my way towards tackling the problem of my speech, a tall, short-haired woman nearly the same age as myself approaches me. We introduce ourselves to one another. I learn that she's a poet from Dublin. She says she's overheard the interview and liked my idea of the one-week homeland. She asks whether I wouldn't like to drop into a pub with her to get to know our one-week homeland better?

Why wouldn't I?

She asks if I've tasted the famous *Guinness* beer.

No, not yet.

Then what are we waiting for?

We set off immediately...

We go to Ryans Pub near the Guinness factory. Said to be one of Dublin's oldest pubs, it's from the Victorian period. Having learned long ago that the city's history is reflected in its pubs, I begin to contemplate who might have sat in these small, wood-scented booths called snugs—built for privacy, but not insulated from the chat outside—as if just made for writing: Going back in time, Samuel Beckett, James Joyce, Bernard Shaw, Oscar Wilde, Yeats... how about Jonathan Swift?

"Now you've gone too far," Jocelyn says.

I'm a bit ashamed to find out that Swift lived a century before Queen Victoria. "Not too bad, considering it's only a one-week homeland," I say.

"This is only your second day," Jocelyn consoles me. "You should wait till the weekend!"

That's right, it hasn't been even two days yet. How strange that I feel as if I'd spent half my life here!
While making our way towards one of the snugs at the back, I ask the bartender: "Is smoking permitted?"
"*It's compulsory!*" he says, without lifting his head from the glasses he's drying.
I burst out with a loud guffaw and feel that I must have lived most of my life in Dublin and might spend the rest here as well.

Do you smoke, Mrs. Tunsevich?
Even if you don't... Isn't it nice to live with such a sense of humor?
Forget the Moscow flight... Catch the first plane to Dublin and...
The Guinness beer with a head as thick as cream is usually drunk from huge glasses; it doesn't last long enough, however. It seems to vanish of itself. When I highly approve of the beer, Jocelyn says: "The beer at this pub is special. There are those who claim that it's not brought in kegs, but pumped directly under the road." Over the first glass, we compare our writing experiences; and over the second, Turkish and Celtic vocabulary. We feel enthused by the occurrence of the word *Ocak* in both languages. During our third round, we invite Mrs. Tunsevich to the table. Thereafter, we stop counting.
Upon seeing Aileen's anxiety I realize I've arrived late for dinner. They'd been worried that something had happened to me. "Your paper..." she tries to say. "Okay," I cut her off, "it's almost finished!" She's happy to hear that. We decide to have dinner after I make a quick stop in my room. We're in front of the reception desk.
"Number 430, please..."
There's a bustle at the reception which puzzles me.
"There's a note for you," says the girl at the reception. And the other young girl approaches me.
Oh no, my daughter! No matter where on earth I am, every ambulance siren, every phone call and every note...
"Don Baker," the receptionist begins. Now everyone is staring at me. "He's left a note for you, and wants you to call him."
Aileen is too confused even to let out one of her shrieks. "You can't possibly know Don Baker," she says, looking as if she were seeing me for the very first time.
Just as I start to say, "On the plane we..."
"You're kidding," she interrupts. "You sat next to Don Baker?"
I forget about the paper, my intention of going up to the room and just about everything else. Aileen is tugging at me and wants to hear all the details at once. We

head towards the dining room. Meanwhile, I begin to describe the episode on the plane. As soon as we've sat down at the last empty table, we draw out our cigarettes. While I'm wondering how on earth we were lucky enough to find this lovely table for two by the window, a youngish waiter politely points out the quite elegant "No smoking" notice on the table.

Then, a table where smoking *is* permitted...

No. All the tables are full.

We decide not to eat and prepare to leave the table. Our intention is to go into the bar. We've agreed to get by with a snack.

The maitre d'hôtel approaches us and asks: "Is there some problem?"

Showing him the sign, I say:

"No problem except for this."

Very seriously, he picks up the notice and slips it into his pocket, commenting:

"What notice? I don't see any notice."

Oh my goodness! I begin to cry.

At this Aileen freezes.

"It's because of happiness," I say.

WEDNESDAY, September 22, 1993

Good morning, Mrs. Tunsevich!

I've been up all night last night for the first time in a good while. This shows that I must be in fine fettle.

It's widely acknowledged that people's biological clocks classify them into two groups: night-owls and early-birds. I don't know if this has been scientifically confirmed or is simply voiced by the media, but my observations would confirm that this distinction is most prevalent in times of depression, when the night-owls suffer from sleeplessness, and the early-birds from oversleep.

I'm most pleased that I've been able to stay awake till dawn and greet the first gleams of the day at my desk!

I've finished my paper: "*A One-Week Homeland.*"

You can guess the content. At first that may seem rather melancholy, but in fact it isn't. One week isn't really that short a time, now, is it?

Now I can hand the paper in to be duplicated (at last!) and go out to take photographs. The more memories and the more of this life I can capture in my shots, the better... Isn't being able to say, "In that week of my life I had an identity," something of no little importance?

Are you coming to breakfast, Mrs. Tunsevich?

When I saw her, I first thought that you'd accepted my invitation. She was someone I'd never met but knew very well. After all, that could have been you!

But it wasn't you. Because it seemed to me that I'd seen her some time in the past. Not herself, but maybe a photograph; not her photograph, but a painting of her... Her picture... Modigliani!

Modigliani's tall long-necked women with short hair and long memories...

I start after her and catch up with her in front of the orange juice. We greet each other, balancing plates—on which we've put various tidbits—in one hand, and our orange juice in the other; we look for a place to sit down. Actually, she's the one looking for a place, I'm just following her because she is—insistently and with disgust—running away from the tables where people are smoking. That's okay; we sit down.

I can't help staring at her face with admiration. At her face, her gray hair, her straight posture and most especially her long neck...

"You remind me of Modigliani's paintings," I say to her.

For a moment we find ourselves exchanging glances.

I find out that her mother had been acquainted with Modigliani, and had even posed for him.

Before I even learn her name.

When I do find out who she is, I recall her as the poet with unforgettable lines on why we can't kill a spider at the water's edge: the first time because we hate seeing a dead spider in the water; the second time because we hadn't killed it the first time; and the third time because by now we feel we know the spider.

This is my third day in Dublin.

It's our third day, Mrs. Tunsevich, isn't it?

If even a spider at the water's edge becomes an acquaintance the third time we see it, then why shouldn't this city, on whose horizon we've witnessed the sun set three times, be "ours" by now?

Let's take some photographs, Mrs. Tunsevich!

Because, as a photographer friend of mine once very aptly said, "All photographs depict the past," and once this city and this week during which we've "belonged" here has become the past, every moment we can seize from our common past should remain as tangible as possible.

I head downstairs to the hotel shop to buy a roll of film. I ask an old woman—surrounded by Aran sweaters, plaid skirts, pure woolen shawls, maps of Dublin and souvenirs featuring pictures of Irish writers—for film.

"What number?"

"36 exposures."

"36-exposure is all we have. That's not what I meant. The ASA number?"
"100!"
"Where are you from?"

In my distraction I don't understand why she's asked. Supposing she's a bored and lonely clerk, "Turkey," I say. "I'm from Istanbul."

I flash her a smile in line with a series of recollections which might start with, "When my husband and I went to Greece on holiday twenty years ago, we'd planned to visit Istanbul, too but..." and climax in the tragedy of her husband's death, or with what she'd been told about Istanbul by her daughter, who'd dropped in briefly on her way to India, and I wait.

However, the woman behind the counter doesn't look twice at my face. She's running her finger from top to bottom down the price-list hanging beside the film shelf.

"100 ASA is for the Mediterranean," she says. "To take pictures in your country, it's fine. But if you want to take pictures here, you need 200 or 300. For overcast weather 300, for sunny weather..."

Is a change of light advisable for a person over the age of 40, Mrs. Tunsevich? Mrs. Tunsevich... Where are you?

* * *

You've deserted me like this—in the Mediterranean light.
Just when we thought we'd found a place to take refuge.

On September 23, 1993, a Wednesday.
At 10:37, Dublin time.

Because I had to deliver my paper on one's "homeland" at three that afternoon, I had just under four hours to rewrite it.

After I'd bought the 100-ASA film, I went back to my room and wrote a new title down on a clean sheet of paper: *"A 100-ASA Country."*

* * *

The next day I received a letter, Mrs. Tunsevich.
It had been left at the hotel reception in a long thin elegant envelope. On it was my name, written in a lovely hand, and below that was a note saying "personal."

I used to think that I had no fellow countrymen, but you see, Mrs. Tunsevich, one of them found me, and what's more, there in Dublin. The letter was from Marta, an Italian, claiming, "I too am from a 100-ASA country."

Marta had begun to live in Dublin after she'd come for a week's stay. In her letter, she wrote how close she'd felt towards me while listening to my seven-day diary. When she arrived back at her small apartment, the words "home", "homeland", "exile", "passport", and "border" were echoing in her ears and she sat down on the floor and thought hard and long about her Aliens' Office days while staring at the four walls. She wrote: "The only bridge between this country and myself is English; I realize that my mother tongue's been slipping away from me. *Patria* is becoming "homeland"; *sole*, "the sun," and *ricordi*, my "memories." This scares me."

When Marta and I first met, we embraced in a seizure of hugs, laughs, and tears typical of those coming from 100-ASA countries. Then we chatted.

We spoke of you, too, Mrs. Tunsevich.

I told Marta how you'd deserted me; she said that I was actually the one who deserted you.

Did it happen that way, Mrs. Tunsevich?

I always think that I'm the one who's been deserted; then later I'm told that I'm the one who's walked off... Has it happened that way again? I didn't mean to leave you; if it was I who left first, I do apologize to you.

Afterwards, I don't remember exactly how, but somehow, we began to talk about Joyce. Actually, in Dublin it isn't so astounding to talk about Joyce; it would be more amazing if one didn't mention Joyce. Rather than the fact that Joyce had exiled himself from Dublin to Italy at the beginning of this century, our focus was on Marta's having re-lived the mirror image of this adventure at the end of the century. At that moment it occurred to us that the aim of Joyce's continuing to write—beyond his taking shelter in words—and of course his writing in English—was to prevent the transformation of "homeland" into *patria*, of "sun" into *sole* and of "memories" into *ricordi*. Who knows, maybe Joyce had left himself in Dublin and taken only Stephen Dedalus to Trieste with him. Stephen Dedalus had become more Joycean than he had been in Dublin because now Dedalus was living in Joyce's dreams and words...

Marta and I think that there are only words, melodies and colors in the invisible passport of the strange intangible homeland which shelters all aliens... Do you agree with us, Mrs. Tunsevich?

It's that passport which protects and forgives those existing beyond the dimensions of time and space...

On the way home I cast my eyes about for you in Zurich Airport, but you weren't there, Mrs. Tunsevich.

There was only one person who resembled you; she was drinking wine at the bar. In her hand was a poetry book with a line from William Blake highlighted: "Never seek to tell thy love / Love that never told can be."

What about you? If it had been you, would you have recognized me?

That lonely woman, however, had no intention of recognizing anyone. She looked as if she had been waiting for her flight, but knew that all the planes would take off without her.

When I got back to foggy Istanbul and found my daughter down with the flu, and when it rained during the fall of 1993 and raindrops were falling on my desk, and later in February 1995 when my house burnt down and I was left without a roof to leak, I thought of you. And also in November of 1993 when I received the news of Naime's death, and each time I remembered her hunger strikes and how she was left stranded with cancer at the age of 35 because England wouldn't grant her a visa, and how her smiles never vanished during her endless pacing. And again when Onat Kutlar's spine was shattered by a bomb, and whenever the milk boiled over or a sty developed on my eyelid or even when my stockings ran, I thought of you. When Marta sent me a silver bookmark along with the poems that she's now been writing in Italian and I sent her a dried olive branch in return; when I cried watching *In the Name of My Father*; and these days—approaching the end of July 1996—tallying fatalities in the hunger strikes in my 100-ASA country, when the number of my notches has actually doubled the number of IRA militants who died during their hunger strikes (each notch reminding me of the statue of that giant worker getting soaked by the rain there on Karl Liebnicht Avenue in front of the thin red lights on the billboard behind it) I've always been thinking of you.

Ever since that day, whenever I find myself in an airport, I listen for the calls of flights to Moscow and my eyes search of you. Not only in the departure lounges of Moscow flights, but in those leaving for Montreal, Johannesburg, Rio, Tokyo and Oslo as well. I keep looking for you. I've avoided only the New York flights because I'm wary of encountering my own youth there.

Have you found a place of refuge, Mrs. Tunsevich?
If you have, please let me know...
Let me know so that I can feel myself at home...
Has anyone ever told you which film I should take to the land of words?

Translated by Mustafa Bağcı and Jean Carpenter Efe
"100'lük Ülke," *100'lük Ülkeden Mektuplar* (1996).
Istanbul: Can Yayınları, pp. 94-140.

CEMİL KAVUKÇU

Into the Depths of the Forest

I'm in a truck; a Volvo that runs only on a miracle. We are proceeding along on a rough steep mountain road with hairpin bends. The lorry is groaning so much that I say, alright, now it's about to fall to pieces or go up in flames and we'll never make it through alive. At the bend of every curve we catch a fleeting glimpse of the plain scorching under the hot September sun and the village spreading out like a colorful bandana; then we immediately lose them behind a veil of trees with thick trunks and dense foliage. We are way above the plain and the village. Although my elbow leaning out the open window is being teased by the sunshine, the cool breeze gives me goose bumps.

How much the driver suffers changing the gears! It's due to the gearshift, that's what he says. Since I'm not at all familiar with such matters (I had always felt a resistance approaching obstinacy against the social pressure on me to get a driver's license) I'm content just to nod my head. Had I learned anything at all, we could at least talk about the motor. Recep (the driver) is not very talkative. It's better for me, but on the other hand I'm worried that he might get bored. Then he may regret that he's given me a lift. He might put on the brakes and ask me to get out. Too long a silence is no good. There's no danger for the moment. Recep speaks whenever he wants and keeps silent whenever he wants. That's a sign that he's not bored. The lorry slept all winter long. Suddenly I'm stuck on that expression; how, I wonder—on two wheels on its side, or on its back, with all four wheels pointing to the sky? Perhaps kneeling down, its eyes half-closed—like an exhausted cow chewing her foamy slaver... No work, nothing to do. (Actually the truck isn't in any state to move. Years ago I saw an old horse harnessed to a carriage. It was so tired that it didn't feel even the slightest pain from the whip cracking on its flanks.) During the winter Recep spent his days (and nights) in the coffee house (he even told me the name of the coffee house keeper: Yakup); take the queen and hand over the king.

Just as the weather was about to break—but didn't let up very much, that is, as soon as Recep could handle things, it gave him a lot of trouble. (What? The Volvo, of course!) Never mind, I said. (This isn't my own voice; I hardly recognize it when I haven't spoken for a long time. Actually, you've disappointed me, Captain Recep. This should have been an Austin running on real gasoline and not a Volvo, and you should've removed the doors so that the heat of the motor wouldn't be so stifling. And you should've propped up the hood by an inch or so. And the chassis shouldn't have wings; it reminds me of a junker I once knew. The driver, a cigarette always dangling from the corner of his mouth, wore a cap pushed way back on his head. He'd drive like mad down the cobbled streets of the village, and everyone would know that Rattletrap Seyfi was going logging. Time and technology have upset the apple cart, Captain Recep. Like the fossils of ancient creatures only seen in museums of natural history, those Austin trucks running on gasoline have disappeared; I see them only in some local black-and-white films and my heart overflows. I don't know whether this is love for the trucks or for the child in love with them—for Rattletrap Seyfi was my father.)

You saw the snake? asked Recep.

Where? I said, this time it was my voice.

We passed it, he said, it was at the side of the ditch and looked like a stovepipe.

He's making it up, I thought to myself, is this Africa…

The motor's screaming as loudly as it can, and so is Recep, just to make himself heard. I asked the model of the truck. He doesn't know. He doesn't care, as long as it works, it can be an ancient motherfucker, that's not important. Nothing on it is original, it's all second-hand parts.

Recep has a long thin face with very pronounced cheek-bones. He hasn't shaved for a couple of days. A cigarette's always dangling from the corner of his mouth; that's why one of his eyes is always squinting, like Rattletrap Seyfi's. When he first offered me a cigarette I told him I didn't smoke. How nice, he said. However, a couple of nights ago when I decided to take this trip, I'd been smoking like a chimney on the balcony of home, miles and miles from here. Recep has no idea how I struggled to get rid of this enemy. We don't really know each other. We're just two people sharing the same space and time because of the situation at this moment in our lives; that's all! Later on he won't remember me, and I won't remember him. If, however, I'd hopped into his truck before I'd made the decision to come on this trip, what ridiculous questions I would have asked him, and what traps I'd have set to pry into his private life. First I'd have asked about him and his truck; did he own it or was he only the driver? His marital status, his outlook on life, his character… That is to say a heap of nonsense. Then one day I'd have sat down to write a story in which Recep wouldn't even be Recep. I'd "dramatize" him. I'd put all my sensitivity, together with my strong impressions, into an event to shock and manipulate the reader. Recep would never find out. In a bar, a group of three or four of us, convinced that the world and art revolved around us, would discuss it. Even from the way we'd be sitting one would recognize how proud of ourselves we were and how much we exaggerated. We'd be chain-smoking. Once I was done with him, I would have to run after some other Receps.

I grinned a lop-sided smile (a smile I know by heart, rehearsed in front of the mirror, crooked and sad. "Pardon?" said Recep—because with the smile I'd let out a humiliating "hah." I turned and looked. He didn't repeat his question, so the blankness on my face must have suggested to him that my exclamation was related neither to him nor to the truck. I can ask him just one question: Was your father's name Seyfi, that is, Rattletrap Seyfi? This time he looks at me with his eyes wide open in surprise (questioning and a little frightened), saying yes, how do you know? I know someone called Seyfi who named his son Recep. And I had a friend called Recep, whose father's name was Seyfi. What I'm doing is not making a generalization; it's only a "maybe" brought up by those coincidences. Interesting, said Recep, as he stretched his mouth and bowed his neck. This is not the first time I've lied to him, I lied when he first gave me a lift. He hadn't asked, but I was sure that he was curious, so I told him that I was a natural scientist, that we'd hit the road from the capital two days ago with our research team and that due to the breakdown of our vehicle my teammates (who were two, one driving the vehicle) were staying in the village until it was repaired and would then come to find me; that I'd come to where he picked me up on a village minibus (because I was standing exactly at the fork). He believed me. Why shouldn't he; the scenario was great. With my backpack, tent, boots, short hair and dark glasses I looked more like a foreign hitchhiker than a scientist. Recep had thought the same: Man, I looked and said, probably a tourist. You're right, Recep, but what would a tourist be doing here, huh? Don't say that, man, our country's a paradise, we just don't appreciate it, but that's another story. Those giaours travel all over the country. They might be after treasure or ancient works of art, no? Recep is a shrewd one; I'd better be careful.

Okay, man, he said while lighting another cigarette, but how're your friends gonna find you on the mountain?

Means he's picked up on that. Things I've said must have seemed unreal to him. No going back! (No.)

We arranged beforehand the place we'd meet, I said, and we marked it on our maps. It's easy so long as we have maps. A new tack from Recep: Suppose that the vehicle can't be fixed and they don't come. What are you gonna do then?

I laughed. (Bless you!) My eyes straight ahead, I say I'll pitch my tent and sleep.

Alone?

Of course!

Don't say that, man, the forest's full of creatures. Not for the world would I stay here.

Of course you wouldn't, I say to myself, I wouldn't either; then I turn to him and say we're used to it.

We fell silent again. After a curve, the roofs of the village houses, scattered here and there, appeared. The roofs were quite steep. It must be because of heavy winter snowfall in this region.

This is a Bosnian village, said Recep, and its original name's Polena.

I didn't say I knew. Because Recep doesn't think I know much at all. To say something, I asked the present name of the village.

İhsaniye, he said.

Nonsense, I said.

We both remained silent for some time. We hadn't seen any residences along the way; why did they—the Polenas—choose to settle up this high?

Recep shrugged his shoulders; apparently this had never crossed his mind.

I'd guess, I said, it might have been in order to isolate themselves and continue their traditions more freely. Good for you, said Recep, and placed another cigarette between his lips. What I understood from his "good for you" is: Although I haven't understood a word of what you've just said, I want to please you.

The entrance to the village is up a steep hill. We see the minaret of an old mosque. There's a coffee house in the square. The village is nearly empty, with only a couple of people sitting on chairs beneath a hundred-year-old chestnut tree. These look like figures straight out of a surrealistic painting. Recep stuck his hand out the window and waved. They just nodded their heads. They seem very lazy. There are hedgerows along either side of the road where it leaves the village and a round thicket of blackberry bushes. Neither the plain nor the village is any longer within eyeshot.

Is it a long way to the log yard?

It'll take an hour, says Recep.

***

I'm looking in the mirror, my eyes squinted; how expressionless my face is. The Emperor of Blanks is what I'd call the face in the mirror. Now, right behind my face, I see the slim longhaired boy in a white smock. He's a scamp and expressionless, too. His shaking out a blue cloth, flip-flop—he surely could have been more silent—is just an empty show. Knowing that he's obliged to do that makes everything more difficult for me. A moment ago he folded my shirt-collar inside and carefully placed a sea-blue towel (everything is blue here) around my neck, before turning on the tap to check if the water was warm or not and said, "Yessir?" and touched my shoulder gently, indicating that I should lean back into the sink. Everything was like a dream. My head in the sink, my eyes open, looking very closely at the white tiles. Hot water flows through my hair and over my scalp, dirty water and shampoo suds running off. My eyes always open. Wrapping the towel around my head he helps me sit up straight in the chair. Now I shut my eyes. Some kind of smuggled peace in me shivers as if it might be spoiled at any second. I know it's going to end when I open my eyes.

I saw myself when I looked in the mirror. I'd changed. How much I'd changed.

You look like you're about to die, brother, said the boy.

Die? I said. No, I must not have said it, but only thought it, for he keeps on shaking the blue cloth as if he hasn't heard a thing.

How d'ya want it, brother?

This isn't the voice I heard a minute ago, I thought.

Short, I said, very short.

The comb went into the hair over my ear and the scissors started snip-snapping. Locks of hair fall onto my lap and the cloth.

He's right, I'm dying.

* * *

There's a level clearing at the end of this slope where Recep's going to stop and let the motor cool down. With a fountain, too, called Bitterwater, that tastes like mineral water. Yes, I've heard of it, I said, being a natural scientist. There I'll part ways with Recep.

The climb is over. The Volvo is groaning as if it had expended its very last effort—and that, too, only for Recep's sake. "Whew!" said Recep and hit the steering wheel. We're both soaked in sweat because of the heat from the motor. Before the bridge of thick logs he turned left onto a path formed by wheel-ruts. There's a green field surrounded by trees with massive trunks. Not far off, there's a stream flowing enthusiastically, splashing over large stones and spewing white foam. Both banks are covered with plants sporting wide dark green leaves. On the other side of the stream, rises a steep hill lined with trees growing straight as pens. He stopped and pulled on the handbrake. The Volvo's groaning like a wounded animal.

The fountain's further on, we'll have to walk a bit.

We got out of the truck. My body, bathed in sweat, bristled at the cool air. I stopped for a moment and scratched my head.

Is there anything wrong? asked Recep.

No, I said, this is the very spot where I'm supposed to meet my friends, what a coincidence!

For the first time, I saw traces of suspicion in Recep's eyes. How could I possibly know that this was the place we'd decided on without consulting my map? Immediately I changed the subject and asked why he had a plastic container with him. He said he was going to fill it with the bitter water. He'd also fill his stomach with water here, but after only a short while he'd feel as if he hadn't drunk any at all, and then he'd fill his stomach again by drinking the water in the plastic container. And that too would finish before he reached the log yard. So why don't you take two containers and drink the second on the way back here, I suggested. That, it seems, was not possible. This water spoils a short while after it's taken from the source. It loses its special quality if you don't drink it immediately. It gives you an appetite. Recep and three of his friends ate a sheep here and drank four big bottles of *rakı*. By the time they reached the plain they were again as hungry as if they hadn't stuffed themselves.

We walked along a narrow path and went around a rather large boulder. Water was leaking from a crack. There was a wooden gutter to make it easier to drink (the Polenas must have made that). The flowing water forms a little pond and then dribbles through a narrow channel towards the stream. The stones at the bottom of the pond are deep red.

A wooden gutter and red stones. Two clues that help me make a connection with long ago. Then I strain my memory and the bridge fits in. But I can't seem to place this joyfully flowing stream. The level clearing where we left the truck isn't the same in my memory, either. All are blurred and fragmented.

Why are these stones red?

I was on the verge of saying that I didn't know, when suddenly I remembered that I'd introduced myself to Recep as a natural scientist. As a result of the minerals in its composition; the iron content must be high.

Good for you, said Recep; you become hard as iron when you drink it.

Now we're sitting in the shade of a tree. His socks were off and his trousers were rolled up to the knee. Do the same, you'll relax, he said. However, I didn't even take off my shades. The Volvo is letting its motor cool like an old crocodile. That's it, he said as if we'd been talking about something and he were returning to some point. I didn't have to ask what, for Recep was pointing to the Volvo with his eyebrows cocked. So I turned and looked at the truck with its hood raised. And this is our life! He was speaking of the Volvo as if it were a living thing. This ship of death and I have become comrades; we jus' keep on rollin'. Nothing comes easy, I said. I didn't say it, I thought it. Recep lay on his back and went on with his story, meanwhile he's stuck a reed in his mouth. He must have wedged it between his teeth, he was speaking so comfortably: At one point I was so bored, fuck such a life I said. Well, it was winter and those were the days I was unemployed. The Volvo fell into a long, deep sleep in front of the house. Who knew what he was gonna cry for when he awoke—like a hungry kid who doesn't know which end's up... How could I make ends meet! I was dozing off in Yakup's Coffee House, thinking stupid things. I saw Ercü sitting like a prophet, reclining at his table in the corner. No grief, no anxiety. Even though his situation is much worse than mine. He's a driver, too. But one with neither a car, nor a house, nor a wife and children. There's only Ercü and his driver's license. He has a driver's license but no job. He has various vices: drugs, hash, alcohol; he can't even count the accidents he's had. Of course, since he's acquired such a bad reputation no one wants to hand over any goods to him. But he sits with such poise that you'd say he ruled the world... I stood up and went over to him. Tell me your secret; I'm about to go crazy, I said. There's only one way: You gotta shift into neutral! How? I asked. He acted as if he were taking the truck out of gear with his hand—like this—he said. Just then I didn't understand what he meant. Later on I thought about it quite often. One day I decided to try, just for fun. I couldn't be like Ercü, I knew that, but I could shift into neutral. And I've halfway succeeded. Whenever I'm bored, shift into neutral, I say. I take it out of gear and coast.

Shifting into neutral!

Recep told me a lot more. His words flowed over me like the murmur of a stream; I didn't even listen. I was stuck on those couple of words. What did this mean? To suddenly shift into neutral while going down a hill in low gear? What happens then: Out of gear, the mechanism goes freewheeling, the vehicle accelerates and there's nothing you can do. But what's it like in real life "shifting into neutral"? My getting a lift with Recep must be more than a coincidence; it's one of the bricks this structure is built of. Just as we were parting ways he'd given me the key: Shifting into neutral!

***

As I leave the barbershop, I take my shades out of my shirt-pocket and put them on. This time I'm determined, I know exactly what I'm going to do. I've prepared for trips a couple of times before, but somehow never found the energy in me to go through with them.

I'm walking towards a shop I've picked out. I came across that shop during my earlier attempts at traveling, but couldn't bring myself to go in, so I've only looked in the shop-window. The sign reads EXPLORER. They sell equipment for various sports, from mountaineering to cycling. Most of the goods are imported. I guess that's why the shop is so busy. Not that I care much about it.

The friendly youngster who greets me asks how he could help me (he has an American haircut and his faded jeans must be imports) and I tell him how he might help me. You're exactly in the right place, he says and snaps his fingers. Whereas I'm very serious. Are you a mountaineer? he asks. Because he cannot see my eyes (my face is stony, I'm making him nervous, I haven't even taken off my shades), he now has a more temperate smile on his face. Because the customer is "a character." Yes, I say, I'm a mountaineer. I could have left him without an answer. Maybe that would have been better. Because this way the tone of my voice conflicts with my appearance. It's made him relax. Look, he said, this is the ideal one. Ideal for what? The very thing you're looking for. How does this fellow know what I'm looking for... I gazed at the tent package indifferently. It's very strong, he continued, absolutely waterproof, and you don't need to fear the wind. This time I can't help laughing: As if I were afraid of the wind or anything else!

While the young man (I think I was wrong to regard him as a yuppie) is struggling to pitch the tent right in the middle of the shop, I light a cigarette, sitting on the chair the shopkeeper's offered me. Would you like anything to drink? he asks. No, thank you. I pat my chest to show my appreciation. Really... Really, I say. What I first said was real, too, but he didn't get it. This time the shopkeeper speaks up, it's exactly what you're looking for, just big enough for one, small, light and useful. I've sold many of these. We import them, first class... What a wonder, I haven't even told them what I'm looking for. But they know. It is exactly what I'm looking for. I nod my head to show that I like it. With every word that comes out of my mouth, I know I'll lose a bit more self-confidence.

Okay, I said to the shopkeeper's assistant, never mind setting up the tent, I'll take it.

What about the sleeping bag and the backpack?

Of course I'll take them, too. I also need a strong pair of trekking boots that will keep my feet warm.

You're probably a novice.

This time I don't reply but stare at the patron from behind my sunglasses for a while. He's disturbed. Rising from his comfortable armchair, he reproaches his assistant: Just a minute... just a minute, not like that! He goes to his side and shows him how to do it.

My packages are ready. I pay the bill. The boss smiles and thanks me, saying he'll be happy to be of assistance (the crook) should I have any other needs. Are you driving, sir (he's sure that I have a car; he knows his job, if he asks whether you have a car, he might lose a touchy customer who doesn't have a car and who's ashamed of it) or shall I call a taxi? The youngster with the American haircut is ready for action. He looks first at me and then at the door. He's going to start running like a faithful dog once the word "taxi" comes out of my mouth. I just say no. I leave the shop and walk slowly on my way.

* * *

I can't decide whether I should tell Recep that when I was a child, my father owned a truck and that he, too, would transport timber from the woods in the summer and rest during the winter. Rattletrap Seyfi would be unemployed during the winter, too (well, he was my father, but behind his back I called him Rattletrap Seyfi like everyone else). He spent his days playing cards in the coffee house. I'd go up to the coffee house (I wasn't allowed to go in) and using my hands as a shield, I'd look in through the window. He had a special table where he always sat. Cupping my hands I'd blow onto the window pane and write a 25 on the frosted pane with my finger. Rattletrap Seyfi, that is to say my father, would push up the brim of his cap, which he never bothered to take off, and—even with the whole of his attention focused on the hand of cards he held like a fan—with one of his eyes squinted because of the cigarette dangling from one side of his mouth, without even glancing towards the window, with his fingers he'd fish two-bits out of his pocket and toss it towards the door of the coffee house. He wouldn't even turn and look; his eyes never left his cards. Although I wasn't allowed to go in, I was permitted one step inside to pick up the money. I'd turn and run as soon as I had the money.

Recep stood up.

Little by little, I'd better be on my way.

I rose to my feet, too, to say good-bye to him.

If you like, I'll take you up the yard, he said, we can have tea and then I'll drop you off on the way back.

Thanks, I said, but my friends might be along at any time. If they don't find me here they'll be worried.

He lowered his head as if saying you know best.

I shook his hand and thanked him.

You're the last person I'll ever lie to, I thought; I'll shift into neutral if I can.

My eyes followed the Volvo till it was out of sight.

Now I'm alone. For some time I didn't move, just stood where I was. Then I took off my shades and put them in the pocket of my backpack. I no longer need to hide from anyone. In what direction I'm going to walk now is indeterminate. I'm at the point where for years I've wanted to be. I left the level clearing where Recep and I'd been resting and walked to the road we'd come up in the Volvo. I stopped at the wooden bridge for a while and gazed down at the stream. Except for the peculiar howling of the woods and the splashing of the water, I'm engulfed by a harmonious silence. I'm being cleansed. I cheered up and started whistling. It's been thirty-four years, I thought. I'm gazing at this water again, at the tired planks of the bridge, at the road Recep went up. I wandered slowly into the forest. The earth is carpeted with the dead leaves of earlier years. It sinks down lightly at every step. I feel like I'm treading on a ground cushioned with springs; from time to time I hear the crackle of a snapping branch. The trees are dense here. I've lost the sky now; there's a dome of autumn leaves above me. After all, it's September. As the slope becomes steeper and steeper, I proceed very carefully. The splashing of the water that I haven't heard for some time again reaches my ear. Is it the same stream? It might be anything. Because this forest is a safe haven for web-like streams that cross one another. The city and city life are far away now. With every step I take into the depths of the forest everything is distancing itself from me while I come closer to myself.

I've reached the water. Like a playful child, it leaps from one stone to the other, first foaming and then calming, limpid. Its joyfulness and my tranquility have coincided in such a way that it convinces me to pitch my tent temporarily somewhere nearby. I mustn't be taken in by the childlike appearance of the water; the rock masses it's dragged and left along its course show that from time to time it raves and rages, thundering angrily. However, it's a child now, a very small child. Thank God I found you, I said. I lay face down and drank deeply and desperately. You'll have to get used to me; I will neither disturb you nor ask you any questions. Here, I'll let my hair and beard grow; I'll change. Maybe then you'll like me.

It didn't take me long to pitch my tent. When I was done, I sat down and leaned back against a tree. A bird with a song I've never heard before was singing. A cigarette. There aren't any. I forgot, there won't be any cigarettes. I have to gather some wood; I'll be lighting a fire when it gets dark. The forest will be frightening. But I won't be afraid, for there won't be any fear, either. I'll sit and watch the fire. In my backpack I have canned food, zwieback, cookies and instant soup. I'll have to use them very carefully. I shut my eyes. I'm very much at peace. I could stay like this for hours.

Now I think back to that summer day. Rumors soon turned into joyful anticipation among us children. My father Rattletrap Seyfi—we'd often seen my mom cursing that "wild fellow" behind his back—for once in forty years had somehow come up with the idea of loading, instead of timber, the whole neighborhood into the back of his Austin and taking us all to a surprise destination for a Sunday-morning "outing." There is great to-do in the houses, thin pastry is rolled out, vegetables are stuffed and cookies and rolls are baked. And Mom, with a forced smile on her face, goes around inviting the whole neighborhood (not everyone of course, she's already made some elimination on her own) to join us in the back of the truck for an outing. Well, she says, I'm not sure, probably to Bitterwater. Nobody asks why it's only probably. In fear of some last-minute hitch, she hasn't asked her old man where they're going.

With visions of the great adventure of the following day dancing in our heads, we're enjoying a very special summer night and (even after the call to evening prayer) running and playing in the streets. None of us could possibly sleep, we know that. Because we have to get up very early in the morning. Rattletrap has said that we'd better make it there before it gets too hot. He didn't specify any exact time, but Mom, going around the neighborhood (my sister on her apron-strings) says, we'd better get up with the morning call to prayer or thereabouts. As all the preparations are being made tonight, we're having an exceptional evening.

I remember waking up a couple of times, pricking up my ears to the silence, and pulling back the curtain just enough to peep at the magnificent truck standing sadly under the glow of the street lamp as if it would never go anywhere again.

Like all other nights, that night the next morning came suddenly. I woke up at my mom's prodding. I was late; a joyful rush had already begun in the street. *Kilim*s in all colors decorated the back of the truck, and comfortable corners with cushions and bedding had been arranged for the elderly passengers. The women and young girls were carrying baskets, bags, and watermelons to the truck. As for us kids, we were scolded, pushed and kicked around even though our only intention was to get the show on the road, to hit the road as soon as possible. Never mind, that was a day no one would mind about anything. Dad pushed his cap back as he did when he was playing cards, and with his cigarette in the corner of his mouth, opened the hood of the truck to check the oil with a long thin iron rod. Some of the neighbors having no idea what to do at the moment are staring at the motor their hands folded behind their backs. I'm proud of Dad; he's a hero today. While the women are climbing into the back of the truck one by one, young girls are warming up the drum with a piece of newspaper they've lit; from time to time they stroke the leather with their hands and tap it with their fingers. The leather must be taut and firm. Mom's still running around like a chicken with its head cut off.

Then that mysterious and magnificent trip begins. Disregarding Mom's objections, I sit with the older children on the baggage rack, right above Rattletrap Seyfi. The girls have already started; one's playing the drum, and the others sing: Are the cornels yet ripe... I, however, gaze down at the nose of the Austin—at its hood cracked open with a stick—as it snakes around the curves like a docile tiger. Leaving an incredible cloud of dust behind us.

The steep and winding dusty roads take us to Bitterwater. The voices fade out, the image blurs, but the rhythmic drum-beat continues. The drum turns into the stream, and the stream into the drum. Then I realize that the forest has amazingly fallen into a deep silence. There's neither the song of a bird nor the buzzing of a bug. Only the rhythmic beating of my heart and the stream (that is to say, the child-like stream) speaking with the stones.

I light a fire. Because it's twilight. I want to have some light. This is my first night—maybe I won't need it later. My tent looks like a huge coffin.

The city, the lights of which I was watching, sitting on the balcony of my apartment a couple of nights ago is still gleaming tonight; in the houses where orderly or disorderly or seeming orderly but in fact disorderly lives are led, dinner is being prepared; white tablecloths are being spread on the tables in the pubs, the waiters are lying in ambush, a woman is singing a melancholy song in a high voice, some are discussing life and art, toasting with and drowning in their frosty beer glasses; nothing's clear because of the smoke, and everyone becomes the sun of his own solar system and fixes life in orbit. However, none of them can imagine what it's like in such a forest on such a night. Like a little kid tired and spoiled all day long and about to fall asleep, I'm trying to find a different face of life here by the side of the stream.

Groves of trees, the details of which have been erased, are now sharply outlined, turned to a shade between green and black. Night birds with huge round eyes are calling to each other because secretive preparations are underway in the forest. A tired bear, unaware of all this, is stretched out sleeping in the natural bedding and sliding quickly into a dream world full of bees. I feel as if I'm sitting at the bottom of a well, and when I raise my face I see the sky with stars sparkling through the limbs of the dreadful trees. It's as though I were not alone, but at a Saturday festival in the city's busiest street, flooded with humanity and light—as though I were immersed in the humming of people on a square. Trees are talking, quarreling, chatting, and singing as people do. Certain maxims, certain screams and the rat-ta-tat-tat of automatic weapons echo in my ears. I hear children crying, a casualty moaning, and street vendors, laughter, applause, songs, ballads and the Voice of the Country on the radio, horns, sirens, a train passing by and shaking the rails, the whistle of a watchman, a rakı bottle shattering on the stones, a dog barking and a drunk pissing on the yellow walls of a school. A full moon is rising above the trees. No breeze, yet the forest's humming. Night birds are once again warning: Secret preparations are underway. Bowing, gigantic trees are whispering to one another to say that they're aware of all. The joyful flames that were dancing on the fire a while ago have turned to embers. The still light of the moon that's just risen is reflected on the water that's leapt from a high stone into a little pond; the water reminds me of a girl's head with her fair hair blowing free in the wind. Reptiles, the noble creatures of the forest, are sleeping in their moist and dark but secure shelters for a new—unplanned—day. I'm going to sleep, too, my dear creatures, trees and stream. I'll crawl into my tent and wriggle into my sleeping bag. A miserable fellow who has scant chance of coming here sold them to me. Miserable yuppie, I said again. I really do think that's the truth. There's so much noise to frighten me and keep me from falling asleep. I feel that a four-legged creature is proceeding towards my little tent with cautious steps that still make crackling and rustling sounds. It doesn't resemble any animal I've ever seen in pictures or in a cage. It's a completely different creature. I don't know what it's after, but the most rational guess is that it's a curious beast. I'm not afraid. It keeps on coming but it can't get to me, anyway. Its eyes are bright and its long sharp teeth are gleaming from its half-open mouth. I shudder as some object (a piece of branch or a stone cast from far away) falls to the ground. A noise like a whistle and then the warning call of the night bird with a weird hoot: You're in an unfamiliar place that has laws you don't know about.

Closing my eyes I say, you'll shift into neutral!

I must have died, I say, on the other hand how could a corpse understand that he's died, I ask myself. All of a sudden I realize that this thing surrounding my body is my sleeping bag and this small place suffocating me is my tent and that one-syllable scream is the voice of a bird. I'm in the forest... The night is over. The sun's rays are filtering through the trees like long wide lances. The dense layer of mist is slowly rising. The joyful little stream and I greet one another: Good morning. I wash my face and I graze my wet fingers over my short hair. Because I haven't brought my watch, it's impossible for me to tell the time. With the help of some dry sticks I light another fire on the ashes from the previous night. I've filled my coffeepot from the stream and placed it on the fire, I'm going to make myself some soup. I count what's left in my bag, twenty-nine packets of instant soup.

On the swing hung from a tree branch, there's a girl with long plaited hair. She's shrieking continuously. When the swing has completed its swing and come back, they push her so hard that she flies up again; this time her feet touch the leaves. Enough, for God's sake, enough, she screams—in a mixture of fear and pleasure. Another group is skipping rope. A group of women are down by the stream. Each has buttocks as big as a leviathan's mother. They're squatting down to wash the dishes. However we, as children, have flocked into the forest in gangs—with long sticks and little pocket-knives in our hands. Some have even taken off their tops to play Indians. But, scaring each other, after a few steps we turned back. "The feast" of the men grouped around a separate table is still going on. Only Rattletrap Seyfi is on his own, sleeping under a tree—he's taken his shirt off and is now in his holey undershirt, his cap fallen down onto his nose. The Austin, on the other hand, neglected—as if abandoned, is standing in the clearing where it was left. I separate from the children who are trying to find the nerve to go into the forest again, and approach the truck. Once I'm beside it, I look at my dad again. He's sound asleep. I open the door and get into the cab. I grasp the steering wheel and although my feet don't properly reach them, I can feel the pedals when I slide down a bit. The keys aren't in the ignition; Rattletrap has taken the necessary precautions. Gripping the black knob of the gearshift and moving the stick from right to left gives me a great satisfaction. Then suddenly my heart leaps into my throat at that high shrill whistle. I jump down out of the cab. Dad—still under the tree where he was sleeping—has suddenly straightened up like a lion awakened to some unexpected danger; he is glaring straight at me, his cap now pushed up to his forehead from his nose. Come, he motions to me with his hand. I walk towards him in deep guilt. Two lightening-fast slaps strike my cheeks. Then, pulling his cap down onto his nose, Rattletrap Seyfi lies down again and falls asleep. My cheeks are flaming. The boys are looking at me. The girls skipping rope have seen me, too. The adventurous "outing" I'd stayed up all night looking forward to has turned out to be a disillusionment—a catastrophe. I run into the forest, deep into the forest, into the depths where they won't find me... Crouching behind a tree, I weep. I swear that I'll never ever again get into that Austin.

Someone reclining in his chair with eyes shrunk from drink was about to take a drag on his cigarette, and while exhaling through his nose, offer a psychological explanation for this. The subject would pass from Freud to Reich and then to Marcuse (Fromm? C'mon, little kids are reading him now). At the end there'd be a quarrel. Someone else who was convinced that he wrote poetry (his writing is new, of course, that's why no one likes it) would throw an ashtray at the one sitting opposite him. (Eh, instead of criticizing him for his terrible writing and making fun of him behind his back, why don't you simply tell him to his face...) Still another, holding his pipe as if he were holding the balls of his organ and scratching his white eyebrows with the tip of the pipe would say, my dear friend, the subject's a perfect narrative; why don't you just write it down?

I didn't tell Recep about my dad and the truck.

It's good I didn't.

There's a sound, the sound of a motor. Neither like that of a truck nor of any other vehicle. It's a chain saw. I can't tell how far away it is. A person or persons are felling trees in the forest. They might even be contraband lumberjacks. After a while they may find me here. I'll have to say good-bye to the little stream—that child-like water. I take down the tent and pack it. My backpack is ready, too. I step on the stones to get across the stream. I look at my friend the water for the last time and walk up the opposite slope. I know that forest is full of little streams crossing each other like a web.

Having climbed up a very steep hill, I'm terribly sweaty. I've stopped to have a little rest. From this point, I can no longer ascertain where Bitterwater is, or the stream by which I spent the night. If the thesis that for every uphill there's a downhill is right—and it is right—I'll relax soon. I have to walk till I find a new stream. But for the moment I'm sitting here leaning against a tree because I'm out of breath and my heart is pounding pit-a-pat. The thick cracked bark of the tree is partially covered by velvety moss, and in and out of the cracks puzzled bugs are scurrying. I've become aware that the days are getting short and that nature is preparing for a long winter. How wonderful, I say, no cigarettes, no alcohol (why, there was a time I was almost addicted), no nightmares, no quarrels, no fights. TV programs, frowning newspapers, nations thirsting after the blood of one another, faiths going bankrupt, disillusionments, murders, disasters, water cuts and electrical shortages, traffic jams, underpasses, overpasses, red-yellow-green lights, jealousies, insomnia… none of these, none at all exists.

Is this shifting into neutral, Ercü?

A film. I don't remember the title, nor the name of the director nor the cast. Type: Western. The only part I recall is this. A group of people—the leading actor among them—are traveling in a mail coach. At some juncture on this long and difficult trip they halt to rest and feed the horses at a place very typical of this type of film. The passengers (among whom there's a lady with her hair in ringlets, slim-waisted in a gown with a wide skirt falling to her feet—she must have had some reason to take this trip), tired of sitting, are having a break. Everything happens at that point. A rowdy gang of five to six is there, too. They smirk while watching the newcomers for a while and then try to cause trouble, mocking and humiliating them. As if this isn't enough, they take the passengers' money and valuables. So what does the leading actor do? Nothing. He just sits there with a face dull as stone and does No-thing. This is something we were totally unprepared for; we were expecting him to do something. The gangsters are done with the robbery and have had their fun; they're satisfied now. Smiling with their mouths full of straight white teeth (but as horribly groomed as they are, how do they keep their teeth like that) they mount their horses—as restless as they—and ride off in a cloud of dust. At that moment the lead stands up, slowly exits and strolls towards the mail coach with the same dull face. He stands on the door-step and stretches up to the luggage on the roof to pull out a long-barreled rifle. There's no doubt it's his own gun that he's put with his backpack—thinking that he won't need it—to be loaded on the roof. One hand on the barrel, the other on the handle, he opens and closes the rifle; squinting, he takes aim at the quickly distancing riders. His face remains the same, not a line moves. With the self-confidence of one who knows exactly what he's doing, he pulls the trigger. From a wound on the back of one of the gangsters, blood spurts out, and he rolls off onto his back... With one foot stuck in the stirrup, he's dragged along for a while. Then the hero puts another cartridge in the barrel and pulls the trigger once again. This hits the target, too, and another rider goes down. The others, recovering from their first astonishment, spread out across the landscape (they're minimizing the target, of course) and head back rather than escape. They must be thinking: Who would be fool enough to undertake such madness! They not only outnumber the group, but each is a professional musketeer... This group is no more than a handful of disorganized people. There's only one challenging us (they've figured it out from the gunshots). The best thing is to do that mother-fucker in. It's a matter of honor now. Our hero—aware of what kind of trouble he's in (he needn't have done anything because they didn't do anything to him)—grabs his gun and cartridges and dashes towards a secure place where he can fight with them: What happens then? A bloody fight. They all die; including him? Or does he survive, only wounded? I've forgotten. That's all I can recall.

So, Ercü, why is it, do you think, I haven't forgotten or couldn't forget this part of the film?

A warm night. The heavy odor of the trees spreads through the air. I'm by the fire, talking to myself so I won't forget how to talk. Because my voice seems unfamiliar to me, it's like two people's. I have a couple packets of soup left; I don't count them any more. I've run out of cookies. If I look carefully through the bag I might even find a can left. I don't know how long it's been since I left Recep's truck in Bitterwater. What day of the week it is, isn't important. It must have been quite a long time since people (who?) have begun to look for me. I haven't seen my face for days. I rub my chin; I've grown a beard. I must smell bad because I've sweated a lot during those long and tiring walks, but I don't sense it. I only wash my face. My hair's like felt. The stars are not that bright and relatively scarce because the sky is covered by ever-changing clouds.

Doppio Rum hits the road to deliver some really important news to Couver Castle. While he's proceeding quickly through the forest, from time to time glancing back to see whether or not he's being chased, something awful happens. This is something that happens frequently; not only to Doppio Rum, but to almost all heroes, gangsters—even the Indians. Shouldn't they be more careful? Because in the wild, there are many trees with branches parallel to the ground and at the same level with the head of a horseman.

Riding so fast (especially if they're escaping or thinking that they're being chased) they hit their heads on stove-pipe-like branches as they glance back for a moment. With the force of the blow they are knocked to the ground—some have time to murmur Fuck; some don't—before they pass out. Now in this forest I've lost my way, I'm under such a tree. Soon Doppio Rum on the way to Couver Castle will hit his forehead on the branch above me while he's passing under this tree and fall off at my feet. I've held my breath since I heard the sound of the horseshoes. I'm excited—he's one of my childhood heroes. Yes, there he is, I recognize him by his plaid pants. I can't see his face 'cause he's looking back. He falls right in front of me. I touch his white hair and look at his bruises. He reeks of alcohol. I've read your adventures for years; I never dreamed we'd meet in this forest under such circumstances one day. I know nothing bad's gonna happen 'cause you're immortal. In your world you've gotta look at the coincidences—like everything else—through a magnifying glass. Therefore Captain Miki or Dr. Salasso will soon be here. The best is to hide. I'll go behind this bush. Instead of Miki and Dr. Salasso, Sam Boyle—scalped by the Indians—and his son Silver—kidnapped and brought up by the Indians—pass by. Of course they don't see Doppio Rum because they're not in the same adventure or in the same dimension. I shout with all my strength: KINOVA. They don't hear.

When I woke up it was raining. The autumn leaves lay under the trees, and as they became wet their colors kept changing. After a while the sky cleared up again. I feel weak today. I'll try to warm up in my sleeping bag. I can see the trees through the half-open door of the tent. This is another stream bank. It looks very much like the other stream banks, which from time to time makes me think I'm going in circles and camping at the same point each time. However, this forest shelters web-like streams in all its dark hollows. Ercü's told me that. No, not Ercü, Recep. Drops have begun to tap again. It can't be the rain, the wind must have shaken the trees, and the drops clinging to the ends of the branches couldn't take it and have let themselves fall. A bear sticks his head in through the open door of the tent and looks around. Curiosity. Or he's looking for food. Or he thought it was his den. I know him; I've come across him in the forest a couple times before. He moans and goes away. I suppose he'll come back. I wish he'd bring some honey. Actually, I don't have much appetite. Perhaps I've caught a cold. It's quite cold here. I can't light a fire. If I see Tex Willer again, I'll ask for some matches; he always has some. To bring round the fellows he's knocked out with a punch, he always puts an unlit match between their toes and lights it.

It rained all day long. It turned to hail for some time. I feared that the tent might be torn apart. It was cold in the evening. I was cold.

The bear came again. This time he stuck his two front feet inside. Then somehow I realized that it wasn't a bear, but Ercü. I guess I was feverish.

Ercü: Look, Master, he said, you hafta shift into neutral, but if the truck is loaded that's very dangerous.

I: Why?

Ercü: You can't control the speed.

I: And then?

Ercü: Then no one can save you.

I left the tent. I can hardly walk even with the support of the stick I'm leaning on. How cold it is now! Maybe I'll go to the bear's den and go into hibernation. What was his name? Recep. No, the bear's name. He told me but I've forgotten.

I'm walking along a path; if what I'm doing can be called walking, of course. After every few little steps I stop and rest. I'm very weak. I've passed by here a couple of times before; pretty soon I'll arrive at a level.

When I arrived at the level clearing, I was rooted to the ground. There was a truck in front of me: an Austin running on real gasoline. Throwing all my weight onto the stick, I dragged myself towards the truck. There didn't seem to be anybody around. I opened the door on the driver's side. The cab was empty. I climbed in and sat down. I turned on the wipers because it was raining. I turned on the headlights, too, because it was night. In the two conical beams of light hatched by the rain, I could see someone standing under a large tree, looking at me. He'd pushed the brim of his cap back. Father, I murmured. He was younger than I, though. The dead stay young, I'd forgotten. In the cone of light, he was walking toward the truck; he was wearing a crooked as well as a sad smile. Opening the other door, he climbed in next to me.

How ya doin' son? he asked.

I'm lost, I answered.

Start it up and let's go, he said.

I couldn't bring myself to tell him that I had no driver's license and didn't know how to drive. I started up the truck. A sweet smell of gas wafted about.

Where we goin', Dad?

Into the depths of the forest, son.

OK, Dad.

The truck began to move. What a surprise, I'm driving. A sweet numbness spread throughout my body. That was the inebriation from the gas and the truck.

In a minute we'll come to the slope, he said.

We will, Dad.

Then you'll shift into neutral!

I will, Dad...

Translated by Sezen Kaya and Jean Carpenter Efe
"Ormanın İçlerine Doğru," *Uzak Noktalara Doğru* (1995).
Istanbul: Can Yayınları, pp. 57-88.

CEMİL KAVUKÇU

The Route of the Crows

I am drinking soup from a steel bowl at the portable kitchen table covered with checkered oilcloth—an object which has born witness to most stages of my life. Its surface has grown old and resembles a wavy sea. The oilcloth with numerous cuts and scratches has resisted time. How many of them are my doings, I do not know. I see ants moving around the thickly sliced bread. It looks as if they are on an aimless trip.

Ziynet turned on the light a short while ago. The bulb is covered with dots of fly feces and emits a yellow and raw light. In the dreadful silence my own slurping disturbs me. Ziynet is sitting across from me. Her big hands are resting on her lap; she looks dejected and is staring at me uncomfortably. Then she talks to me in a whisper: I could not understand her at all today.

When did you ever understand her? I ask myself. I play around with the spoon in the soup. She has all my movements under control and waits anxiously for my response. The spoon is still in the soup and she is expecting me to talk. I speak without taking my eyes off the plate; she is in a different mood every day—sometimes her mind is blurred, I don't understand her when she is like that.

Slowly I raise the spoon to my mouth. Ziynet, now, looks at her hands resting on her lap. That same silence again in the kitchen. I continue drinking my soup with an even louder noise.

But today she was really restless, she was anxious to say something, says Ziynet.

Forget it, I say, I'll find out.

Do you want another bowl of soup?

I shake my head: No, I don't. I light up a cigarette. Now I'll have a cup of coffee with Ziynet. She got me into this habit. If she's in a good mood, she'll tell me to turn the cup over and will read my fortune without moving a single line in her plump face. I always find it amazing that she sees so much in the patterns formed by the coffee grains. She keeps talking about "kismet." She says it is blocked again. Tell me, why haven't you married? I don't know, I reply, aren't you the one who tells me my fortune is blocked?

She is not in a good mood today, so no fortune telling, nothing! We drink our coffee in silence. I don't ask her any other questions; I have learnt not to be curious in matters that may turn out to be annoying.

I stand up after finishing my coffee. Now I can go to her. I feel uneasy whenever I enter the room with its rotten air smelling of excrement and human skin not washed for a long time. I can almost feel death waiting patiently in a corner.

No matter how long Ziynet ventilates the room the smell remains. She is in her bed as defenseless and lonely as a kitten. She senses that I am inside but she cannot turn her head to look nor open her eyelids. She, too, is an object just like the table and the chair. A live, breathing object. I am the only one to understand her silent, motionless language. Ziynet just thinks she does.

Her white hair is spread on the pillow; her tiny face reflects the absolute tranquillity of death. A twitch of the mouth. She is glad to see me, she is trying to say. I sit on the side of the bed. I see you are a little restless today, I say, is something bothering you? A small twitch of the forehead. She is indicating the window. I stand up and open the curtain slightly.

There's nothing there!

There is.

What? I say, the darkness?

No, that isn't it.

The crows?

Her eyelids quiver.

But there are no crows, I say, it's night-time.

A small twitch of the lower lip. Is she hurt? She doesn't think I believe her.

They have clearly annoyed you during the day, but I will take my gun and wait for them in the backyard; they will never annoy you again...

The twitching of the lower lip continues.

Are you trying to tell me they've been talking to you?

Her eyelids quiver again.

* * *

I am smoking beside the window, gazing at the dark and frightening silence of the stone yard. I hear the door close quietly. I do not turn around to look; I know it is Ziynet. She is probably waiting, her back leaning against the wall. She is silent for some time and, then, whispers warily: What happened?

Nothing, I say, keeping my eyes fixed on the yard.

What was worrying her, did you find out?

It was the crows!

Well, they do make a fuss the whole day long, as if there was a wedding or something.

It isn't that, the crows are talking to her. She used to talk to the crows when I was young. When I was naughty and tried to cover something up, she would come and tell me what I had done. If I tried to deny it, she'd say the crows had told her.

And you would believe it.

And I would believe it.

So what have they told her this time?

The creaking of the bed.

How can that be possible, Ziynet says, she can't talk, she can't even open her eyes. She is a dead person, don't you see? She can only breathe and feed from the spoon at the corner of her mouth, spilling things all over. She is aware neither of her bottom nor of her top. She isn't aware of anything; how on earth do you draw such conclusions?

How do you manage to draw all those conclusions when you look at the coffee cup?

I make it up.

So do I.

Ohh, she says.

She's relieved.

There is no light but the room is not all dark. I look at the nightgown which makes her look plumper and shorter than she really is. She's let her hair fall onto her shoulders. The springs of the bed creak when she sits on the bed.

These sounds... She can hear them... Even if she is in a vegetative state she can understand that...

Not tonight, I whisper, because I was sure that there was a black crow hiding somewhere in the room.

Ziynet shrugs her shoulders. No one can hear, she says, and lies down on the bed.

I light a new cigarette and listen more cautiously to the frightening silence of the garden. There were secret preparations, I knew it.

* * *

I woke up early in the morning. The sun had just risen. I opened the curtain and looked out. A crow was lying flat on its back in the yard. Its upright beak seemed to indicate a point in the sky. Its wings resembled a musketeer who had pulled both guns but became stiff before he could fire them—they were also pointed towards the sky. It was quiet. Normally if a crow was in trouble, the rest of them would gather and make a great fuss. What had happened to these creatures of perfect solidarity?

When I heard Ziynet's footsteps, I went back to bed. I closed my eyes and pretended to sleep. She came and shook the base of my neck. She was rather careless this morning, the way she opened the door, the way she walked clicking her heels, the way she shouted hey! all because of her fury.

What, I said angrily, what's the matter?

Nothing, she said lowering her voice, it's morning...

So what!

Why is she obsessed with the crows? she asked.

Maybe I misunderstood, I said, I don't know.

Of course you did. How can the crows know what is going on here in this room! It's just something made up to scare the kids...

There is a crow in the yard, I said, I guess it's dead.

She looked hollowly. The one who watched us and told her all about it?

I looked down; maybe, maybe not.

She walked to the window. She was plumper and shorter this morning.

There is no crow in the yard, she said, were you dreaming?

I stood up and looked over her shoulder. The yard was empty and scary just like last night. Was I dreaming?

I'm going down, she said, tea is ready.

* * *

Ziynet put three spoonfuls of sugar in her tea. Then she stirred it for a long time as if she wanted to make that noise on purpose. She was half-asleep, half-awake.

How is she today, I said, still behaving strangely?

I haven't been to her, she said. She was looking at the glass as if it was the first time she had seen one.

Why not?

Don't know, I didn't want to. Maybe I was afraid. What if what you were saying is true. The creaks, I mean... What if the crows have told her everything...

You believe that?

Of course I do, she was so strange yesterday. And the crows shrieked all day as if there'd been a wedding or something...

You should have given her the medicine drops.

I will, after breakfast.

She poured some more tea. She put a thick layer of butter on her slice of bread and covered the top with jam. She took big bites and slurped her tea. I am sure she swallows without chewing.

When she was full she got up. Slowly she left the kitchen.

She was back in a second. There was fear and consternation in her face. My mother was not in her bed!

How is that possible! I exclaimed, springing from my seat. I ran to her room. The bed was empty. The crumpled bedclothes and the trace of her head on the pillow were still there. The blanket was opened carefully towards the wall side as if she would be back in a minute.

Did you open the window?

No, she said.

I went to the window and looked at the yard. There were hundreds of crows on the roofs and in the trees waiting quietly.

The crows, I said, look, none of them are shrieking.

And yesterday, said Ziynet, they just wouldn't stop, as if there'd been a wedding or something.

What happened to Mother? I asked.

Ziynet curled her lower lip. Then she sat on Mother's bed, covered her face with her hands and started to cry loudly.

The crows flew up shrieking. They circled the yard and came back to light on the trees and the roofs.

Translated by Ebru Diriker
"Kargalar Rotası," *Uzak Noktalara Doğru* (1995).
Istanbul: Can Yayınları, pp. 91-97.

CEMİL KAVUKÇU

Just Has to Be

You were standing in front of the shop, Mahir Abi, what a come-on you were. I could have pretended that I hadn't seen you if it hadn't been for your shrill whistle.

I'd just come up the street with shopping bags in both hands, breathing heavily and sweating. You're right—I could have taken the other road, or walked along the other side of the street looking down, without even glancing across to your store. As I was on my way to the marketplace, you were inside and there were no customers (naturally you don't have any—there aren't many goods on your shelves—times are bad); you were alone and were reading something with the help of your spectacles that had slipped down onto the tip of your nose. Apparently something interesting had caught your eye—politics, maybe—on those half-pages of newspaper you usually use to wrap the bottles in (on which you sometimes make difficult calculations, jotting down figures from top to bottom with your ball-point); maybe you were looking at the details of a provocative photo. I walked down the street and you didn't even see me.

When I was coming back from the marketplace, you were in front of the store. You were leaning lightly against the door-frame, your glasses in the upper pocket of your faded blue apron. When I tried to pretend not to see you and pass right by, you smiled, curling your lips in that strange manner—your face looks very funny, Mahir Abi, when you do that, but you don't realize it. I don't know what it was that made such a come-on—your 'know-it-all' smile or the way you were standing. Then, as if you too wanted to say "Enough of this game," your little finger at your lips and your eyes half-closed, you whistled: a sharp, shrill and penetrating whistle...

There was no way out, Mahir Abi; I changed my course, and putting my shopping bags down in front of the shop and sighing (there was no need for that, I know; could I ever fool you?), I wiped the sweat off my forehead with my arm. You, Mahir Abi, you old wolf, with that knowing smile on your face, went inside the store, shuffling your feet. From the shelf you took down a bottle of Çubuk Wine, and while I was counting the last change in my pocket trying to find enough money for it, you had already started wrapping the bottle in a piece of paper, maybe the same one you had been carefully reading or inspecting the details of a provocative photo on (oh no, you weren't born into the world too soon, Mahir Abi, you've just been a bit unlucky, that's all) just a while ago—that is, as I was on my way to the marketplace. While I was once again counting the change in my palm, you were thinking with an unseen smile (you're very good at that): *You'll find enough money, because you had this in mind when you were passing by the shop with empty bags, and you wandered all around the marketplace in order to save money for wine. You scrimped some from this and some from that. You looked for what was cheapest. You dug into the vegetable heaps and tried to collect the best eggplants, cucumbers, and peppers in your plastic basin. What for? Because the pick-and-choose heaps are the cheapest* (one eye narrowed, your forefinger on your temple). *Aren't I right?* In fact, Mahir Abi, you *are* right. You're right, but your posture at the door, your sharp, shrill and penetrating whistle...

Now Mahir Abi has a fatherly smile on his face: If you wish, you can hear a whistle or give a meaning to any posture!

We look into each other's eyes. On his face full of wrinkles you can see the sadness of having lived more than one life at once.

I want to say to him, "Whatever happens, Mahir Abi, this is the way it goes."

And he would say, "Just has to be!"

But what comes from his mouth is, "Enjoy it."

So my answer is inevitably: "Thank you!"

Translated by Evra Günhan and Jean Carpenter Efe
"İllaki," *Uzak Noktalara Doğru* (1995).
Istanbul: Can Yayınları, pp. 101-103.

MEHMET ÇETİN

Does What We Call a Human Resemble a Cloud?

a souvenir from Dersim in memory of Şeusen...

Actually, there never was anyone called Delican; this "Mad-John" was no more than a touched cloud.

Listen to me, he'd say; I was a deceived child in my previous life. You must listen, he meant. I have no place to call my own; don't prod me any longer with your bayonet. I have suffered too much grief... too long ago I killed and they killed my childhood and I have been left touched, *ahh lacêm ca perskena, houkı ma diya qı keş nediya,* by which he meant much more, though he held his tongue. Then, looking back to the days of life and death from which he'd been resurrected, stop, he'd say, startled. Fling up your hands, hide your eyes, and hold that position! May no one look upon this corpse of mine, Delican would continue. It was as if what he really wanted to say was: Don't let anyone look upon my dead body, don't look!

Havaar, havar...

It is a rare soul who knows of it.

My dear and respected friend, once Delican had said this, he'd define time with a terrible cry and would complete what he wanted to say; thus everyone would hear, but wherefore this cry, it's a rare soul who knows the reason behind it. I wouldn't find it at all strange if you say you haven't heard of it. You come from the Mediterranean; from that great distance you were taken in your childhood. You've grown up in exile in this foreign city. You've grown up at a distance keeping your silence. You've grown up concealing your native language, fearing "Kurdo... Kurdo" reproaches. You were always the one unable to find a friend to speak your own language with, the one suppressing your shame and hiding away inside. You've learned Turkish only later. When you first started school you were the one pulling at the teacher's skirt—was it because you couldn't figure out how to address her? You were the one who never tired of dreaming of the nights, the days, the countryside and the peers you grew up with in your own hometown. You were the one to follow up these images you'd collected in the heat of the Mediterranean and finally to return to your city after so many years.

My dear friend, yours is a different story, very, very distinct. You may attempt to tell your story, perhaps; it may be understood if you tell it. However, Delican can't tell his. There are few who can even understand his words. Everyone interprets his story the moment they set eyes on him. Anyway, how can the previous life of a touched cloud be told? There are few who even understand his "Listen to me; I was a deceived child in my previous life."

My friend, you can't imagine how Delican grumbles, "I wish I hadn't awakened this morning," and can't help wondering where he's come from. Likewise, you won't understand why there are so many touched ones in this city, why they're called "touched" instead of "mad." The touched ones of this city are never sent to a mental hospital. Why? Why does Musa Bey always wear a suit? Changing his clothes every day he puts on his clean, freshly ironed clothes of the 1950s and comes to the teahouse and drinks his tea. Without uttering a single word to anyone he gets up and leaves. You never know why no one's ever heard Musa Bey utter a single word. You wouldn't know that he was an aviation engineer, that he considered himself responsible for an accident resulting in the death of many and went out of his mind, that the spirits of the dead had paralyzed his tongue or he simply punished himself by not speaking at all. You don't know our Kartal who makes the crowd join in his laughter, do you, my dear friend?

You probably haven't heard the adventures of our eagle who takes very, very long steps swinging his very, very long arms. It was one of those days the city was under very strict martial law; picture a cool summer night with Kartal about to set out along the riverbank for a nearby village. The soldiers gave him a "halt" command, but Kartal, not accustomed either to being stopped or shouted at, became skittish and frightened, ran away, and found himself under fire. You probably haven't heard, have you, that the bullets couldn't reach Kartal, even that salvo, that he turned back from afar to say, "I've had your mothers—and how! I've wasted your ammunition—and how!" You wouldn't be able to picture what a child he was among the children, for whom he'd keep trying to pronounce "tortoise" at their insistence. "Turtuz" came out and then "tortiz... tortiz... tortiza... tortuaza..." Despite being such a child with the children, he was never on good terms with the government; even the touched in this city weren't at peace with the government.

My dear friend, you didn't know Fatin, either, did you? Fatin, whose sole anxiety was the fear of being enlisted? If you'd go and tell him they wanted to call him into the military, but you'd talked to the commander who promised to let him go for a five hundred thousand-note, he'd believe it. He'd rush off in a tizzy to find that money. However, he'd never be able to find it because he is one of the poorest in the city, one of the two street porters of the city... the other is İhsan, mentally retarded. Both are poor and both are touched and they're good friends. One has two sacks of flour on his back; the other, two sacks of sugar, and the two meet in one of the city streets that come quickly to an end. The moment they meet, no matter under what circumstances, they stop and talk. They never complain about the great load on their backs... they forget about it and talk on and on. What they have to say is only their business, as are their quarrels...

It is necessary to get to know the touched ones of this city, my friend, it is necessary to know and understand them. Then too, you should know Foterli, and then, the "Skeleton" and his touched assistant. He's a teeny tiny man who speaks a blue streak and spends the whole day running from one shopkeeper to another. He quickly stammers "Give me money, give me money," and because everyone knows what he's after, five-lira notes are handed to him. Once he has his five liras in hand, a long and hasty race begins, a rush from shopkeeper to shopkeeper asking each and everyone to "exchange... exchange" his five-lira-notes because he's in such a great hurry. Going around till he finds a new crisp one, he then puts it into his wallet and starts his second round from wherever he's left off. This is what he does all day long without tiring; but once evening falls, as if overwhelmed by his blood, he finds Skeleton or Skeleton finds him and takes from his hand the crisp, razor-edged five-lira-notes he's collected in his wallet.

I've told you, haven't I, how one needs to know the "touched" of this city, my friend, listen to me: Delican who wants to say "I was a deceived child in my previous life" is one of the touched in this city. It is a rare soul who knows his story.

It is a rare soul who knows why he went crazy...

Some supposed it was a summer night long ago. At Bükboyu, a pheasant in hand, he touched Gülcan's hair and kissed her on the spot. Even in the silence of the woods that summer night with the moonlight mingling in the river, the moonlight was enough to give Delican away. He was just leaving his childhood years behind; he was very ashamed of being seen. He was quite frightened that it might lead to a blood feud; they thought that was the reason he ran away from the village and went to the city. By the time he returned to the village, the heat of several summers had passed since he'd left; when Delican came back to the village as a young man having reached the proper age for marriage, the moment he came back having saved up enough money—if not to marry Gülcan in the name of God—at least for engagement, he learned that someone had died in the village and that the soil on the grave was still fresh and finally that it was Gülcan, who was heaped with reproach after he himself had run away from the village and humiliated because he himself, namely Delican, hadn't asked for permission to marry her. Then not being able to endure a forced marriage—as if a widow—to a man much older than herself, she'd poisoned herself. At the moment he learned of it, Delican went out of his mind as the soil upon her grave swelled and some thought his name was Delican from that day on, but they were wrong... Later on one summer night—some supposed it was again a summer night long ago—Delican pushed open the door of his home in Bükboyu with a pheasant in hand; he now had a home, children, and a wife who was lovely, attractive and somewhat flirtatious. He found his wife frolicking with someone just in front of the pantry; he looked and saw that it was his brother. In other words, he'd caught his wife frolicking with his own brother. Some supposed it was at that moment that he went out of his mind. He raised the axe in the air and immediately lowered it. As he was gazing down at the bloodied corpse of his own brother born of his own mother and his own father, they assumed his wife ran away and saved her skin... that he was imprisoned and released after counting long days, that he went to the sacred judges of the day, demanding that a higher court deal with the case and try his wife, but he was ignored even by these masters, which he found beyond endurance; they supposed he couldn't contain his wrath; the more he was ignored, the more frayed he became; the more frayed he became, the more he avoided people and began to resemble a cloud, speaking to himself at a distance so that people began to pity him, first consoling him with drink then offering him more and more so that he ended up as an alcoholic distant from human beings and thus he went crazy, they supposed, but they were wrong.

You know, my friend, there was a bloody defeat following the days of the revolt. On the days when the caves along the Laç Valley were bombarded and the odor of the scorched human flesh mingled with babies' cries, they supposed those shrieks have been left with Delican until today. The scarring from burns on his face was left from the gasoline poured down the cliff-side and lit to incinerate the people, and the scar on his breast left from a bayonet during that bloody silencing; they thought Delican was explaining this when he said *lacê me ca perskena houkı ma diya nâ dinade qı keş nediya.*

My friend, what does this thing we call a human resemble?

Delican couldn't explain.

He is old now. They thought he had always been old. He always appears in the restaurants, they put food before him; he sits and eats as if he is in a great hurry, and suddenly jumps up to leave as if he must immediately go somewhere. No, my friend, no one would refuse him a morsel. Nor cigarettes, nor tea, nor clothing... Whenever he wanted a smoke, he'd take a cigarette out of the hand of a person passing by and would smoke it; smoke it as if kissing it, as if kissing... Supposing that he wanted a drink and people are sitting around a table, drinking and chatting... He'd approach and pick up someone's glass, drain it and retreat at the same speed at which he'd come. People would look at his back with a smile or they'd tease him. Howsoever, he'd neither hear nor pay attention.

Delican was self-sufficient in his loneliness.

He couldn't explain. He'd always talk to himself, but they couldn't understand him. No, he wouldn't dress in white. He'd tie up his pants with a string, his zipper was always down. He'd make water wherever and whenever he pleased. He was privileged. He had paid his price. Could it be that he made water more often when there were women around? Or he'd occasionally feel an urge; it sometimes happened that he'd walk up and embrace a woman from behind without minding her laughter-like cries. Then he'd turn and spit over his shoulder.

Was it because this aroused a suspicion that he wasn't at peace with women or was it only after he'd embraced an officer's wife from behind and then spit that he was declared mad? That they wanted to take him off and shut him up in a mental hospital? Yet neither Delican nor the townspeople here would hear of it. Delican returned to his city. He returned and from that day on no one would ever have been able to put him in a vehicle that opened from behind like an ambulance or a police wagon. At such a moment he'd beat on the windows with strange cries, for example, and attack the people around. Whereas Delican hadn't ever previously been aggressive at all, not at all.

Since that time Delican kept living in his own way, kept walking on his own path. He'd generally even go without shoes. They bought him shoes, but he kept on walking barefoot even at the cost of a wounded and bruised pair of feet.

Delican is a Kırmanç you know, my friend; he wouldn't give up speaking his own language. Even though what he was talking about wouldn't be understood most of the time, he kept speaking as he pleased. He'd be understood only now and again when he said *çenî çenî çenamına rındekamı ahh dıle dıle ciğeramı dıle...* or *lacême çâ perskena huokı ma diya nâ dinade qı keş nediya*, but most often when he said: Listen to me, I was a deceived child in my previous life, you must listen, stop, don't, I have no place to call my own, stop don't prod me any longer with your bayonet. I have suffered too much grief... too long ago I was killed and today, I have been left touched today, ahh don't, don't let anyone look upon my dead body, don't look! Hold up your hands, cover your eyes. May no one look upon this corpse of mine. It was as if what he really wanted to say was: Don't let anyone look upon my dead body, don't look! He wanted to say, but they didn't ever understand, never...

Delican couldn't explain.

Actually, there's no longer anyone called Delican, my friend, he's a touched cloud; there is a rare soul who knows it.

He couldn't explain.

There's something strange on his forehead, they said, it must be a secret, they said, the kiss of an anafatma flower, they said, they were inclined to make a legend of it. That wasn't enough, either; they chose to feed him, to look after him. Whether it was because he was a joy to the small city or because they wanted to amuse themselves, they neglected neither his welfare nor his legends. You know, my friend, Delican would generally sleep under the overhang of the sole Turkish bath in the city. As he slept there on winter days, it would snow, of course, it would snow to the right and to the left of Delican but never upon him, never... he'd wake up just as he'd gone to sleep.

Contemporary Turkish Short Fiction: A Selection

Delican was a story in the legends of the city.

It was September, as far as is known, my friend; the chill of the early autumn days hadn't yet descended from the peaks of Delidağ. The riverbanks still preserved the warmth of the foregoing summer. On one night during those days, on the night that had brought on the day when I had to leave the city, Delican slept under the branches of a willow tree on the riverbank. In the early hours of the morning, he woke up and came into the city. With his sleepy eyes generally only slightly open, he started to climb the streets leading up to the main square of the city. In the silence of the streets he came, chattering to himself. He came with gestures of his arms that no one could understand, but that each interpreted differently. He came incessantly pulling one hand through his hair. He came murmuring one of the tunes he'd repeat without ever becoming tired of them. He came tête-à-tête with himself because he actually never looked to his right or left as he walked. He came without speaking to the people on his right and on his left because there was nobody around.

Speaking to himself on behalf of a city, Delican approached the square; coming up the slope, he raised his head to gaze at Delidağ. At that moment he became frightened again, *fındıre fındıre*, he said; stop, stop, he wanted to say after his sudden fright; don't, he said, I have no place to call my own, don't prod me any longer with your bayonet, I have suffered too much grief...

Suddenly he noticed that he was all alone, he looked around, and there was no one at all passing by to ignore or wonder at his words or to smile and tease him. He had never noticed whether there was loneliness or crowdedness at this hour of the morning in the streets he had just passed through; he found it strange. This time there weren't any of the sights he was accustomed to seeing at the intersection of the streets; he didn't understand. There was no one from whom he could take a cigarette without even a glance at his face, a cigarette to smoke as if he were kissing it. The restaurants where he could sit and eat, where he never found it necessary to ask for something, weren't open. The teahouses where he would go and drink tea weren't open. The stools left outside in the evening lay scattered, as if intensifying the desertion even more... Delican wasn't accustomed to this, he wasn't accustomed to stopping, to stopping, looking and asking why. He must have been desperate for a smoke followed by a tea, then a stroll through the square and finally a restaurant... where was everybody? His irritation soon turned to deep fright; he had no idea what to do with his hands. He raised them and put them on his head and stood like that for a while.

As he looked around, his eyes took on the color of the mountains left fading in the sunset.

Delican kept silent; in silence he raised his arms and shut his eyes tightly. It was as if he didn't want to see, he didn't want history to repeat itself here in front of his eyes. His tightly squinted eyes didn't suffice, however. With his hands he covered his face, the bitter lines of which were deepening minute by minute, and especially his eyes; he cringed. He doubled over. He cringed, doubled over with pain as if he'd been stabbed in the chest. He buried his face still tightly clasped in his hands on the ground. He wanted to spare his eyes the sights on the face of the earth. He waited. As he waited he began to tremble. His trembling increased more and more. Then...

Havaar, havar!

Then an infinite cry filled the time and space of the morning; fall, he said, bitch, he said, eyvaah... I wish I hadn't awakened this morning, just gone on sleeping. Is it thirty-eight again, what is going on? Havaar, havar...

My friend, few people know how much later it was that Delican raised his head, his face covered with a beard that had suddenly turned white, and looked at the crowd gathered on the square where the morning desolation of the streets ended. He watched with the lines on his face changing and deepening every moment. He watched with bloodshot eyes from the days at the river Laç.

He didn't just look.

Delican didn't just look. He arose from where he had fallen and with long strides entered the square. It was as if he were challenging everyone in the square. He saw the tanks, he saw the military trucks, he saw only men in uniform. In the hands of the men in uniform there were guns. On the tip of the guns there were bayonets. On the tips of the bayonets he could picture the frozen first smiles of babies. Raids of the villages. Gasoline poured over the people heaped one upon another and fire and cries and ash... people retreating to the mountains, people defending their rights at the cost of their lives. And a scorching and destructive defeat like death itself... he looked and couldn't endure looking any longer. Among the commands, cries and shouts Delican had no time to see the tips of the guns pointed at him.

He went on. He went on to seize one of the uniformed men by the collar. With his eyes blinded by blood, he could see no more. Among those who felt no surprise at Delican's behavior and those who didn't know Delican and were ready to shoot him, Delican called out to the man in the collar he had seized.

Commander, does what you call a human resemble a cloud, you, Commander... He meant: Where are the people... where have they been from dusk to dawn... where are my servants? Does what you call a human resemble a leaf fallen into the swift-moving current of a river... They're gone... Where are my servants?

Stop giving commands, Commander. What Delican wanted to say was, tell me, may this touched soul not smoke a cigarette, may he not have a bite to put into his stomach? Is every place closed that he can't have a tea? Have they been swallowed up by the earth, where have my servants gone? Were you gambling with them last night, where are they? Is it thirty-eight again, what is going on, what?

Payız, Delican wanted to say, that bitch of an autumn...

Stop shouting, Commander, he said, stop shouting commands. These mountains won't bow before you, this Delican won't bow... stop giving commands, Commander, my servants don't know how to bow at your feet, don't shout in vain... tell me where my servants are, where are my people? Is it again thirty-eight? Havaar, havar...

My friend, Delican was speaking with a howl that was drowning out his own voice. He was speaking as if swept into some eternal giddiness. Both his hands were on the collar of the man in uniform. It seemed to Delican that Delidağ was spinning around, and the ash trees on Delidağ—like leaves from the ash trees swept off by the wind— were swirling in the air; Delican had no more strength to withstand.

There was no one called Delican anymore, there was but a touched cloud.

His hands were torn from the collar of the man in uniform, he was knocked down by the sudden stroke of a rifle butt. With blood dribbling down his temple... before vanishing into a touched cloud, Delican rose from the ground like a bloody cry from the pages of history. Delican took a long look at the barrels pointed at him and said, alas, this *is* again the epoch of thirty-eight, time again has his hands handcuffed behind him.

Havaar havar...

At the moment he turned his face towards Delidağ, he described the September morning with a long wail and completed his days on earth.

It is a rare soul who knows it.

There was no one called Delican anymore, there was but a touched cloud.

My friend, do you remember, Delican would say, Listen to me, I was a deceived child in my previous life, you must listen, he meant; stop, don't, I have no place to call my own, stop don't prod me any longer with your bayonet. I have suffered too much grief... a long, long time ago I was killed and, I have been left touched today, ahh... don't, don't let anyone look upon my dead body, don't look! Hold up your hands, cover your eyes. May no one look upon this corpse of mine... It was that same morning when there was nobody to understand what he meant to say that I left the city.

Then, on the summits of the mountains towards which Delican turned his face, there were incessant night blazes, and fireflies incessantly lighting themselves to set the night afire.

The rest is a myth.

From that day onward, they say, a cloud has circled round the top of Delidağ as if touched... blood dripped over the city from this cloud prodded with the point of a bayonet.

From that day onward each person in the city looking at this touched cloud circling the summit of Delidağ began to ask one another.

What is this flower we call asmin, let's not forget it.
Does what we call a human resemble a cloud?

Translated by Esra Çarşıbaşı and Jean Carpenter Efe
"İnsan Dediğimiz Buluta Mı Benzer?" *Asmin* (1997).
Istanbul: Zed Yayın, pp. 28-38.

MURATHAN MUNGAN

Snow White Without the Seven Dwarfs

Once upon a time, in a far-off country there lived a princess called Snow White. But she did not have the Seven Dwarfs. Therefore, her only desire in life was to have the Seven Dwarfs. From morning till night, she would sit at the window praying to God to send her the Seven Dwarfs, and she never gave up expecting them to appear one day. Princes riding white steeds waited by the thousands at her door; a new one would arrive as the others were leaving, but what was the use? She did not have the Seven Dwarfs to begin with. The Knights and Princes all promised her riches and happiness; they all asked for her hand, and begged and beseeched her, but she would not accept any of them; she scorned all these early suitors.

"First I must have my Seven Dwarfs; I should be living with them in a small cottage. I should be cleaning their cottage, mopping the floor for them, washing their dishes and doing their laundry; then the witch should arrive and make me suffer; only after these things happen should you come and rescue me; it is pointless for you to come now!" she would say.

Knights and Princes were turned away from Snow White's door empty-handed. Her stepmother was extremely sad because of this; yet she could not do anything to change the situation. However hard she might try, she could not succeed in changing Snow White's mind. Of course Snow White had a stepmother, too. For in that country, everybody had a stepmother. All the young girls thought their stepmothers had "hearts of stone"; but like all the others, Snow White's stepmother was only a mother.

Snow White never got weary of waiting for the Seven Dwarfs. She just withered in front of that window. She would look into the basket of every peddler woman who walked past her house, saying, "I wonder if there's an apple in here?" But Snow White became tired of taking each elderly woman for an apple seller and checking each basket for a poisonous apple. In the meantime, she kept pleading with her stepmother's famous magic mirror:

"Oh, mirror, I beg you, I beseech you; go tell my stepmother to have me sent to the forest to be killed; get the hunter to have pity on me, to put rabbit's blood on my clothes... for the sake of my life, go tell all this to my stepmother."

Days went by and none of these things happened. Snow White was not able to get Seven Dwarfs for herself. Yet her expectations got stronger as they got older: They took root deeper and deeper in her being. Years went by pitilessly; she grew older; she turned into an old maid. Finally she completely despaired of ever finding the Seven Dwarfs; she gave up looking for them. Knights and Princes of the good old days did not stop by her door or at her window any more.

Thus, this particular Snow White could never enter any tale. She never had a tale of her own. And one day, she found herself quite old, an ugly spinster. She saw that her life had dried up as much as her body. She panicked so much that she became lost in fear and doubts. On the other hand, she would not give up neither her tale nor her dreams. Thus, she decided to acquire a new place for herself in the tale. She put her arm through an apple basket and began to go around to cottages in the neighborhood, not minding the rough countryside. She said to herself, "I can always find a Snow White at a window waiting for her destiny, anyway." She thought, "Maybe, in a far off cottage, at a dark window, a Snow White is waiting for me." She wanted, at least, to make her happy, to help make her wishes and dreams come true by giving her the poisonous apple.

She walked so many miles, she climbed so many hills, she went over so many hills and dales! But no Snow White ever called her to the window. She returned from each cottage, from each gate, empty-handed. Of their own poison all her apples rotted in the basket.

She lost all her teeth; her nose grew longer; she became a hunchback. Her legs became shaky; she developed chronic sciatica and she had rheumatic pains all over her body. Her eyesight grew weaker; she became hard of hearing; she had a stoop. All the same, with great perseverance and obstinacy, she went on traveling over hill and dale and through forests, to look for a Snow White that she could get to bite into one of her apples.

(Snow White was supposed to fall into a long dreamy sleep until the Knight on a white steed arrived... Whereas, all the tales had fallen into an endless winter sleep.)

In the end, she decided that time had changed everything, and she became unhappy and bitter towards the whole world. She withdrew into her own private corner. She spent heartbroken, disappointed days in poverty and suffering. Nobody had any respect for her ideals any more. Snow White had realized this at last.

She had sacrificed herself for her ideals. On her deathbed she thought of herself as a heroine—with some shortcomings. She had ventured to live a whole tale all by herself.

And Snow White died when she was ninety.

In her small cottage she died as a poor and lonely old woman.

When she died, the whole country was moved. National Mourning was declared and all the flags were lowered. A large, spectacular funeral was arranged. From seven-year-olds to seventy-year-olds everyone from all over the country came to attend the funeral. All the people shed tears for their Princess.

At the funeral, the coffin in which Snow White's body lay was carried by the Seven Dwarfs. Later, the Seven Dwarfs wept at length by her tomb, crying, "Oh, how can we ever live without you!"

The Knights and Princes on white steeds, who could not attend the funeral due to familial matters, simply sent telegrams extending their condolences.

Translated by Yurdanur Salman
"Yedi Cücesi Olmayan Bir Pamuk Prenses," *Kırk Oda* (1990).
Istanbul: Remzi Kitabevi, pp. 7-10.

MEHMET ZAMAN SAÇLIOĞLU

The Big Eye

A man asked a girl who was waiting at a crosswalk, "Would you have your picture taken with me?"

"I beg your pardon?" she said in amazement.

"I mean... I said, would you have your picture taken with me?"

"Are you nuts?" snapped the girl as she started out across the street.

The man stuck his hands into his pockets and glanced around to see how many people had witnessed the incident. Right then he noticed a pretty young girl approaching slowly from a distance, and he began walking decisively in her direction. Just as the girl looked up, realizing that the man was standing directly in her path, he said to her: "I'm sorry to disturb you, and it may sound strange to you, but would you have your picture taken with me?"

The girl started to look around her, then waved to a young man waiting at the far corner of the avenue and said, "Excuse me, but my fiancé is waiting for me," and slipped away from the man, walking quickly toward the young man awaiting her on the other side.

The man walked quickly in the opposite direction and entered a side street that crossed the avenue.

In order to disappear for a while, he had taken a bus three nights ago without letting anybody know and had come to this small town a few hundred kilometers from the city where he lived. He'd rented a room in one of the small second-class hotels under an assumed name and, with the help of a sleeping pill, slept for fourteen hours straight to free himself of the stress that he was under.

When he'd awakened, he had a headache. He got dressed, walked around a little and tried to assess the changes that had occurred in this small town since his visit several years before. Upon finding that the two restaurants and the small diner he'd frequented on his former visit were still there, he murmured happily to himself, "How nice, nothing's changed!"

The next day, however, extending his route a little further from the hotel and the restaurants, he said in surprise, "Gosh! How quickly this town has grown!"

After a couple of hours walking along the main avenue, he felt that someone was watching him from the other side of the street; his hand wandered across his jacket to the back of his pants where a gun was stuck in his belt. He hesitated and looked around carefully only to discover that what was watching him was the picture of an eye in a shop window. This big eye seemed alive. Although he walked about fifty meters further, the eye was still focused on him. There was a crosswalk not far in front of him, but instead of going to the corner, he jaywalked from where he was, and shook his fist at a driver who honked at him for going against the traffic. A few more steps and he was standing in front of the shop window with the eye. It was a photographer's studio. In this large window were many pictures, some side-by-side, some above and below one another, and others intentionally displayed at an angle, all arranged with the greatest care. At the center of the display was the picture of a giant eye. Upon closer look, the man became fascinated. This large eye had been created from many small eyes all cut out of a thousand, perhaps ten thousand snapshots and glued together to create one large eye; these thousands of eyes in a multitude of colors were set together so skillfully that you felt the giant eye staring right at you with every detail of the iris, the pupil, the white, the curving lid, and the eyelashes. The man examined the eye carefully and then noticed a sign in the corner of the window:

"Have your snapshot taken at our store and claim your spot in the big eye."

After hesitating a moment, the man pushed open the door and entered. The photographer, retouching a picture under the magnifying glass, glanced up at the man, smiled and said, "Welcome, Sir."

The man gave a cursory nod and asked, "Are you the one who made this picture?"

"Yes," said the photographer, "the eyes of nearly everyone in this town are in it. Ever since I got the idea of creating this eye, everybody in town has been coming to me to have their photographs taken. And as soon as I collect a certain number of pictures, I add them to the photograph and make the eye even bigger. I'm lucky it's not in a big city; otherwise the entire window would not suffice."

"I need pictures, too," the man said with a studied air of indifference.

"OK, let's take a pose," the photographer said. "Why don't you go behind that screen; there are some ties there. You can choose any color—unless, of course, you want a sporty look."

The man chose a black tie to go with the black jacket he was wearing. "That black tie doesn't go well," the photographer said. "Try that red striped one."

So the man switched to the red tie, knotted it, and sat down on the stool that the photographer pointed to. Irritated by the three bright lamps that were turned on one after the other, he squinted his eyes.

The photographer approached him, saying, "Just relax, turn your head a little to the left and bend it slightly forward," and positioned his head with his hands. The man posed as the photographer asked him to and held the position. The photographer then asked him to smile. The man tried to smile, but the photographer again said, "Smile a little bit."

"I am smiling! How much more can a person smile?" the man replied harshly.

"Soften your glance, think of things you like, look a bit tender," said the photographer, but there was not much of a change on the man's face.

The photographer muttered to himself, "Here's another one of these guys who don't know how to smile, God grant his family patience," and said to the man one last time, "I am taking the picture now, smile," and released the shutter.

As soon the picture had been taken, the man stood up, took off the tie, opened his top shirt button and tugged at his collar. When they'd returned to the front of the store, the photographer asked, "How many pictures do you want?"

The man asked what the price was for six and for twelve and decided on twelve.

"They'll be ready by tomorrow afternoon," the photographer said with a smile, expecting the man to pay.

"I'll pay when I pick them up," he said and headed for the door. Just as he was about to open the door, he turned and inquired, "Would you be willing to sell me this big eye?"

"No way. That's become the symbol of this shop," the photographer said.

"Then how about making another one for me?" the man insisted.

The photographer, as he wanted to get rid of this man as soon as possible, said, "I can't do that, I don't have that many pictures on hand right now," and sat back down at his retouching stand.

The man hesitated for a moment. "Well what if you made multiple copies of my pictures and put them together?"

"That won't work," said the photographer. "What makes this eye seem alive is the combination of many eyes at once. It's the shadow and the light that create the overall effect."

The man wasn't prepared to leave. He kept insisting. "I'm sure that you have at least a couple of snapshots on hand now. What if you just reproduce them along with mine? I'll pay you whatever it costs."

By now the photographer was getting irritated. "I can't just give the pictures of my clients to other people without them knowing about it. How would you like it if I gave your picture to just anybody who asked for it?"

The man retreated in face of this sudden attack and answered hurriedly, "Of course not, it wouldn't be right. Have a nice day, see you tomorrow." He opened the door and left, but before the photographer had even finished his work on the picture he was retouching, the door opened again. The same man, with an agitated expression on his face, entered again.

"How many photographs do you need?" he asked. "I mean, photographs of how many different people?"

The photographer was puzzled. He hesitated, and then said, "At least three." Looking the man in the eye, he went on: "Your eyes are brown. If we use your eyes as the darkest color, we also need a pair of hazel-colored eyes and another in blue or green, as the medium and light colors."

"So you can make me a big eye if I get you pictures of eyes in those colors?"

"No, I can't. I don't need pictures of eyes but people with eyes of those colors. I have to take their pictures so that I can control the expression in their eyes. The timing in the release of the shutter is very important. If I don't get the proper facial expression, the resulting picture won't be of any use."

"I could bring you as many photos as you like in a couple of days, and, if it would be of any help to you, I could cut the eyes out of the pictures and get them ready for you. Or look, I have an even better idea. I could cut the eyes, lips and noses out of a couple of thousand pictures and bring them to you. You can make a big nose out of the noses, a big lip out of the lips and a big eye out of the eyes. I can bring you so many pictures that you can also make a big nose and a big lip for yourself out of them. How about that?"

The photographer was irritated. He had never seen such a lack of consideration before. With a very serious expression on his face he replied, "Listen mister, you haven't got the idea. The photograph of a big nose made out of many noses wouldn't smell any better. The picture of a big lip, made out of thousands of lips, wouldn't speak or kiss better. This is something particular to the eye. A big eye, which is made up of many eyes put together, sees better than the thousands of eyes that create it. This is why the more different eyes there are within the big eye, the richer and sharper becomes its sight and, believe me or not, more mobile, too. In order to make you forget this idea, I have to tell you another secret. There couldn't possibly be anyone else as crazy as I am to cut out thousands of little eyes and paste them together. How many eyes do you think there are making up the big one in the window that's impressed you so much? I can tell you: There are thirteen thousand four hundred and sixty-five of them. I know the exact number because on the back of each snapshot there's a number."

"It might be on the front."

"But it's on the back. The number I've given your photograph today is thirteen thousand five hundred and thirty. How many does that leave?"

"I'm no good with figures."

"I'll tell you: only sixty-five. There are sixty-four—not counting yourself. The eyes of sixty-four people just did not fit in anywhere in the big eye. No matter what I did, I couldn't fit them in. I got fed up and just tried to squeeze them in, figuring that no one would notice the difference from a distance. Would you believe it, they each looked like a tear, or a piece of dust or sand stuck in the eye. I had to pick them off before the eye looked healthy again. I'll check yours tomorrow. Do not be angry with me if yours doesn't fit in either. Believe me, if I can find a place to paste you in, I will, and gladly; I'd be honored by your contribution to the big eye."

The man had finally begun to grasp what the photographer was explaining to him and appeared deep in thought. Then he said crossly, "But didn't you tell me that three eyes are enough?"

"Yes, that's the minimum for a healthy look. One eye is not enough, as it's only one single color. The second eye makes a contrast with the first, no matter how close the colors are. The third one both connects and separates them, and at the same time, adds a certain vividness to the eye. But this is only valid in regard to the nuances of color. It does not apply to eyes with a bad look like the 64 I mentioned. This is why the people who agree to contribute to your big eye should have different eye colors and a look that is similar to yours."

"I see," said the man. "I think I'll be able to find a couple of people who fit me."

That afternoon, he approached a group of high school students who were hanging around and joking among themselves and asked them to have their pictures taken with him. The kids were scared and ran off. Later, he asked a couple who were walking hand in hand and eye to eye, old people chatting with each other in the park, a middle-aged couple shopping with their children, a loafer sitting on the sidewalk watching the passers-by, insisting that they come with him, but all refused. In the evening, after all the stores had closed, he had dinner in one of his restaurants and, feeling down about having to spend three more days in this town where he had no friends, he wandered through the empty streets, before returning to his hotel late that night to fall asleep.

The next day, he definitely had to find someone, at least two people who would suit him.

But that morning also, the two girls whom he found worthy of asking had both refused to have their pictures taken with him.

Now he only hoped that the second girl's fiancé had not noticed him, as he would not be able to make anyone believe the innocence of his request. He wandered around aimlessly for a while. At another street corner, he saw a man sitting in front of a garden wall. This man, with his head raised towards the sky in thought, had extraordinarily beautiful blue eyes. As he approached, he froze at what the man was saying. "Alms for the blind..." He could not believe that these wonderful eyes could not see. He moved his hand quickly back and forth in front of the man's face. Yes, the man was really blind; yet he looked as if he could see. He shoved his hand in his pocket and pulled out a coin, then changed his mind and said to the man: "I will pay you well if you'll just have your photograph taken with me."

But the blind beggar was afraid. He took hold of the wall; he pulled himself up and started to walk with one hand against the wall.

"Stop!" the man said, and then whispered something in his ear. The blind man didn't seem to know what to do. Quite obviously he was frightened as the other man squeezed his arm tightly with his fingers. "All right," he agreed in a low voice.

The man took the blind beggar by the arm and they started to walk together. When they entered the photographer's, the man said, "Here, I've brought you someone. A friend who will have his picture taken with me."

But the photographer looked upset. He said to the beggar, "Welcome, 'Quiet One'"

The man was surprised and asked, "Do you know him?"

"Who wouldn't?" said the photographer. "He has the most beautiful blind eyes in the world. Do you know how many magazines have had his eyes on the cover? He talks very little, which is why everybody calls him 'Quiet One.'"

Then he turned to the blind man and said, "This gentleman wants to have his picture taken with you, to have me make a big eye out of the eyes of the two of you. Do you remember the one I told you about… the one on my window? Is it OK?"

The man thought that he had gotten himself into a bad situation and that the blind man wouldn't agree and would say that he'd been forced into the store. He became very tense.

The blind man said, "I don't care. Take it if he wants you to. It seems to mean a lot to him. But first I'd like to wash my face."

The man relaxed; he didn't say anything more. Now the photographer was in charge. He seated the blind man, straightened his clothes and said,

"Pose like you have before."

The blind man asked, "Like this?"

"Exactly. Smile."

The man watched without knowing what was going on. He didn't even try to understand. He didn't talk at all. He took the blind man to the door after the picture was taken and handed him some money. The blind man returned the money and said, "I don't take money in return for my services," and left.

The man put the money in his pocket.

The photographer said to the man, "I need to ask you something."

"Go ahead," said the man coldly.

"Do you really want that big eye to see you? I mean, to have it watching you?"

"Why do you ask?"

"Because if you don't want it to watch you, these two eyes will suffice. One of them will be your own, the other the eye of a blind man. The combination of these two cannot watch you. In fact, according to the proportion I use, it could be half blind, so that you will be able to see it but it will not be able to see you."

The man considered this for a while. "I'll hang the picture in my room, right across from where I usually sit. Actually, I shouldn't like being watched—especially when I am sitting at home. As a matter of fact, I liked the one in your window first, and then changed my mind. That one sees too much."

Then he asked, "But you told me that you needed three. Are two enough for you?"

The photographer felt he owed the man another explanation. "I'll try out a new technique with your big eye. In photography we call it the sandwich method. We superimpose one negative over the other and make a print of them. For example, when you print a negative of a fish and one of the sea, the fish gets put into the sea and creates a new image. This does not exactly look like a real photograph but expresses the relationship between a fish and the sea better than a real photograph. Have I made my point?"

"No."

"Another example. Now, if we take a photograph of your hand, opened like that, and put the negative of that hand over the negative of a gun taken somewhere else and print them together, what will we get? A gun in a palm. But the dark and light nuances of the films would penetrate so much into each other that the gun would not look like it was just in the hand but more as if it had melted into the hand, become a part of its cells. If you cut such a photograph with scissors, you cannot take the hand and the gun apart. It's not really a photograph of a hand holding a gun, but it expresses the strong relationship between the hand and the gun better than a real photo. Does that explain it?"

"Yes, I see. Is that how you are going to print these eyes?" asked the man.

"Yes, exactly," said the photographer. "I'll make the pictures of your eye and the eye of that blind man the same size, place one over the other and print them together. So, you will have a half-seeing eye. It won't disturb you at all when you sit around, but you can look at it as much as you like. You know, just like these windows that are mirrored on one side. But there may be one problem. Before I print the photographs of the two of you, I won't know which one is the seeing eye and which one the blind. As I said before, the instant of shooting the picture is so brief that you may catch a blind moment of a seeing person or the look of a blind one that looks right through you. We'll have a look together tomorrow."

The man said, "All right, I'll be back tomorrow," and left.

That night he slept very well and couldn't remember any of his dreams in the morning. After strolling about here and there until the afternoon, he made his way to the photographer's shop. The photographer must have finished his job because he was sitting and talking with a friend. On seeing the man enter, he went to the dark room at the rear and came back with a huge art board.

"It turned out quite well. I've glued it on a board for you so it won't tear. And here are your photos. I've written the price on the envelope," he said as he turned the big picture toward the man. For a few minutes the man gazed at this strange, empty-looking eye, nearly a meter high.

"All right, I like it. It looks as if it is looking at me and at the same time as if it isn't looking. It won't disturb me."

He counted out the money from what he had in his pocket and placed it on the counter, murmured something like goodbye, stuck the photo board under his arm and left the shop.

After he'd gone, the photographer's friend commented, "So that was the guy—he's exactly like you described him. But if he finds out that it's only his eye in the photograph, that the eye of 'Quiet One' is not included, he's liable to give you some trouble."

The photographer laughed as if there were no chance of this possibly happening. "I tried to print them together but they didn't fit with each other. The eye of 'Quiet One' looked as if it could see, while the eye of the man looked so empty. The only thing to do was to decrease the sharpness and print only his eye, which I did. I don't think he'll ever figure out that it's only his eye that's in the picture. He can't even see well enough to figure that out."

The friend of the photographer laughed, too. "That is if he ever realizes this is only his gaze—that'll be the day his eyes will be opened!"

"Exactly," said the photographer. "Anyway, we got rid of him. Come on, let's have some tea."

Translated by Carol Stevens Yürür
"Büyük Göz," *Beş Ada* (1997).
Istanbul: Can Yayınları, pp. 12-24.

HÜR YUMER

Just What I Had in Mind

What else would he do? He came and lay down flat on the linoleum again. Actually, nobody else knows that this is an obsession of his. He comes on Thursdays. In the afternoon, at four. He's never one second late. When the cuckoo clock strikes four, he rings the doorbell. He rings once. He's polite... I keep him waiting for a while. I don't open the door right away. He likes to be kept waiting. I always put on my flannel dress half an hour before; I get ready. If I have run out of cherry liqueur, I send the janitor to buy some. Not that he is going to have any, it's just for decoration! He likes a bit of dust on the linoleum. I don't clean on Thursdays, you know. I haven't had the doors oiled for a year now... to make sure they creak. He won't let me get rid of the old magazines. I throw them on the linoleum before he comes. He likes raving. There's this tape he brought. He gives it to me. I put it on for him. I close the door and sit down to knit. He's so quiet. He stays for two hours, sometimes two and a half. Wouldn't you accept such an arrangement? He even pays.

—I won't let strangers into my home. Home is sacred to me.

—At this age, there is nothing sacred about home. Used to be, when we were young. I am a lonely woman. Well, it looks like this poor soul is lonely too. A man who can pay so much to stretch out on dusty linoleum must be lonely.

—Couldn't he find dusty linoleum elsewhere? I mean he could go out and buy a roll of linoleum and spread it out in his own room.

—Is it the same thing? For heaven's sake, the man didn't even ask my name. He likes this. What do you care?

—He's a pervert, that's what he is.

—I don't think so.

—Just wait until he strangles you one day!

—God forbid! You should see him! He's just so nice! He never starts a sentence without "Madam."

—He must be rich.

—I don't know. But I can tell this is a big outlay for him. It looks as if he spends a good portion of his income on these visits. I don't know. I've never asked. But if you saw him on the street, you'd think, "Who is this dodo?" Shirts and jackets with worn-out sleeves, old-fashioned berets, you name it! A little shy... He's good with finery. Once he came with a white rose in his lapel, God knows where he got it. A white rose on a jacket with a worn-out collar... brings tears to your eyes. On one of his visits he brought sweet-williams for my vase with the girls jumping rope.

—You're making this up. There isn't any such person.

—Yes, there is. How do you think I could afford my color TV? He also brings books to read at my place.

—To read?

—Yes, to read. Why are you so surprised?

—You wouldn't be so tolerant if he didn't pay you. Let me take a look at those books...

—I can't show the personal belongings of my client to anyone, my dear.

—I'm just curious.

—You certainly are.

—Where did he ever find you?

—Nowhere... One day the doorbell rang. I went and looked through the hole: a decent-looking man. I opened the door...

—And that was it...

—Yes. "I like the way your house looks. May I come in and have a cup of coffee?" "Come in," I said. He came in and sat down. He started looking around. He had a strange smile on his face... Before I could even ask his name or where he lives or what he does, he said, "With a few changes, this could be just what I had in mind." Although I have been living here for forty years, at that moment I had the feeling that he might once have lived with me in this house. That day I had a chipped, pink, heart-shaped ashtray on the table next to the armchair you are sitting in—it's in his room, on the linoleum on the floor now; he picked it up and started examining it. Then he put it back on the table as if it were very precious.

—You mean he recognized the ashtray?

—I don't know... But the tenderness in the way he handled it implied it was a familiar object!

—If I'd been you I'd have asked if he'd lived here before...

—Don't be so silly. I've been living here for forty years. The man must be forty-five at the most. And there are no bastards in our family...

—So?

—I just couldn't ask him. And then... he popped the question.
—What question?
—He asked if he could come here on Thursdays and lie down on my linoleum for a couple of hours.
—Then...
—Then I tried to ask him why. He said, "Please don't ask! I'll pay whatever you want for those two hours."
—Such a professional!
—Yes. He's too old to be an amateur.
—God knows there must be other houses he visits. Maybe there are houses where he stands on one foot in the bathroom or in the closet! What did you say?
—I couldn't say "no."
—And you asked no questions. Weren't you curious?
—I was, in the beginning. Now I'm used to it. One gets used to it.
—If I were you, I'd look through the keyhole.
—I did.
—Are you going to tell me the whole story or not?
—I am! It was one of the first visits. I took his coat and hat. I showed him in. I told you he was shy. He always comes in like a guest arriving at a bad time. I saw a package in his hand. "I would like to open this if you allow me," he said. You should have seen the way he untied the knot! Looked just like a surgeon! All he needed was a pair of plastic gloves! It took him two minutes to undo the knot!
—And what was in the package?
—You know those plaid slippers with wool lining... A pair of those.
—He could have taken out a knife, you know.
—You are so suspicious. The guy just brought himself a pair of slippers. What's wrong with that?
—Nothing. Just go on...
—I said, "Good thinking. The linoleum gets so cold in the winter." He said, "I like it when it's cold. That's not why I brought these." I can be so stupid sometimes! The guy pays to lie down on ice-cold linoleum and I tell him that the linoleum gets cold in the winter.
—You should've told the janitor to buy some cotton balls. You could create a snow effect, you know.
—Oh, that's never occurred to me... Anyway, he said... What was it he said? Oh, right. He said, "A pleasant detail isn't it?"
—A pleasant detail...
—Yes.
—Detail of what?
—How should I know? I guess of a whole.

—So the guy knows what he's doing.

—You bet. Otherwise why should he give me so much money in a scented envelope after each visit? And the scent isn't like that of the scented envelopes you buy from the shop. It's oregano; it's the scent of good old oregano! He is so considerate. Just for variation, once a month he gives the money in a cinnamon-scented envelope. I guess it's what he calls a pleasant detail. Anyway... He put his slippers at the entrance to his room. Then he asked for my permission and went inside.

—He really acts as if he owns the room, doesn't he? What does he look like?

—Nothing special. Medium height. I think blue eyes. His eyebrows don't merge. You know I don't like merging eyebrows; people with merging eyebrows bring bad luck, they turn into birds and fly away. A nice mouth. Not too thin, not too thick. A long nose, very sensitive. No moustache, no beard. Nice haircut. His hands are the best part. You know I always look at a man's hands. He's quite charming. Sometimes I miss him. Sometimes I wish he came on Mondays too.

—Well, let him come then.

—I can't suggest it. He has to ask for it himself.

—What does he do on the linoleum for two hours?

—Nothing, really. He stretches out on the blue linoleum. He puts his cheek against the floor. He just lies there like that.

—Then?

—He reads. And plays with the veins in the linoleum.

—What do you mean?

—Just like that. He touches the veins with his finger.

—I wonder why. I mean, what's so interesting about the veins?

—How should I know? He caresses them. Or it's an excuse. He's thinking of something else. Anyway, are you crazy? The veins in the linoleum are nothing more than gray paint on blue.

—I don't know. It just makes me shiver. For a moment it felt as if the linoleum was alive!

—Perhaps it is alive to him, how do you know?

—A living corpse? All dusty, with veins... a perverted pleasure that costs so much per week!

—I don't mind. The guy is alive.

—You said he brings things. Things like what?

—Things he likes... A velvet needle-case—you've heard about the slippers—a chocolate candy wrapper straightened out with a pen; halva, purslane, toffee—I guess he makes it himself—marshmallows; bread with cheese, tomato and pitted olives; tin cans full of old-fashioned buttons; a jacket hanger—real mahogany, I don't know where he got it—then iodine, a bandage, yogurt in a glass bowl... Old tobacco cans. All kinds of spices, pocket watches with no hour or minute hand...

—He's into old stuff I guess! What about the bandage and the iodine?

—I don't know. They just sit there in the room.

—Just in case, huh? Purslane and marshmallows?

—He cooks them in a copper pot before he brings them. I put them on the stove. For the scent.

—Some strange incense! Doesn't he eat what he brings?

—No. He just wants the smell.

—Bread with cheese, tomato and olives. Don't you get flies around it?

—He is so thoughtful; he wraps it up in a piece of pale pink muslin. He uses muslin to wrap the pots. He never uses paper. Three days before he comes I spray the room with pesticide and then air it. That's the only thing he doesn't know I'm doing. He has four penchants. A needle, lace, eyeglasses and magnifying glasses. He has a huge collection of eyeglasses. He has all kinds, cheap ones, some in mother-of-pearl frames, gold, silver... There are glasses for everyone, the shortsighted, the far-sighted, the astigmatic... The other day I thought I'd try a pair to see better in my right eye; none of them suited me. Isn't it bizarre?

—Where does he put the glasses?

—On the floor. He arranges them on the linoleum. He makes a circle around himself. I don't know why, perhaps he likes to feel eyes on him. I'm so afraid I'll step on a pair and break it.

—Won't you show me?

—I can't. The room is locked.

—Where do you keep the key?

—He brought me a black velvet ribbon. "I would be very pleased if you wore the key around your neck on this ribbon," he said.

—Oh, that's awful!

—Why?

—I've seen this in a horror movie!

—That was a movie, what does it have to do with real life?

—Shall I tell you what I really think? You have become a part of the scenery. This man, he's... he's...

—You can't think of anything to say, can you? He is just a man, nothing else.

—A man with frightening obsessions.

—Fine. Aren't we all? What's wrong with that? I wish we all had such innocent obsessions...

—Yes, but not everybody gives out a room to a pervert like you do. Besides, you do it for money.

—You'd think I run a brothel... Anyway, I don't think I'll take his money any more. We've become friends.

—Don't fool yourself. You're used to the money now... What have you done with the money?

—I put it in a bank to get interest. Now every Friday evening I have an exquisite dinner in a restaurant by the sea. I've already been to every seaside restaurant in Istanbul.

—Now listen, I know you like to joke. You've made this whole thing up, haven't you? I refuse to believe it until I see it with my own eyes!

—Why should I try to convince you? But still, OK, I accept: You can come next Thursday. On one condition: You'll be quiet as a mouse. Promise?

—Promise.

—You can look through the keyhole and watch for as long as you want.

—Agreed!

A Friday evening. A long, narrow restaurant by the sea. The view out to the sea resembles an Ottoman miniature. A huge cargo ship and a white rowboat are gliding by in the distance. The rowboat looks like a white spot against the ship's body. The ship sails faster and is soon out of sight. The white rowboat now looks more like a miniature in the spring green of the sea. Through the clouds the rosy evening sun is reflected on the boat. A man with a raincoat and a beret takes one last puff on his cigarette, gets up from a bench a few meters from the restaurant and walks towards the edge of the pier. He looks around. He drops the cigarette stub into the water, slowly and discreetly. The stub disappears in the foamy green wake of the ship.

The man pulls his worn-out shirtsleeve back with his index finger to glance at his watch. Then he turns his head to the apartment blocks across the street, to their windows that bring back memories of bygone fires. He takes a bus ticket from his pocket. He walks away toward the bus stop.

Now on the pier there is no one but a squinting cat.

Two hours later, inside the restaurant... At one of the tables overlooking the shore, two women are sitting across from each other. One is sixty, the other forty. They are sipping their rakı. The cat walks into the restaurant.

—Why did you invite me here?

—Just to talk: He's gone.

—Sorry?

—He is gone. After you got tired of watching and lay down on the sofa, his time was up. "This is my last visit. I'm not coming back," he said. "I'll leave everything to you. Good-bye. I've spent some wonderful hours in this room. Thank you." So... That was it. I made a mistake. I shouldn't have told you about it. You got me all confused. On his last visit, I forgot to put the raving tape on...

—Did he record it himself do you think?

—Who else? I made a mistake.

—What was on the tape?

—Raving... A wonderful poem... if I were a honey cup/ children would dip their fingers into my eyes/ I would be blinded by those small hands/ I would tell a tale about today/ they would giggle/ I would laugh.
—Do you have the tape?
—He took it with him.
—You mean he didn't leave anything behind?
—No. Was he supposed to?
—...

The cat rubs itself against the waiter's leg. It starts nibbling a sea bream thrown on the ground as a reward. The woman in her sixties lifts her eyes from the fishplate in front of her and over her glasses gazes out at the still sea now turning gray. The sun has set. She places her fork and knife in a cross on the plate, narrows her eyes and enjoys another sip of her rakı. There is moonlight on the linoleum. The man props himself up on his hands eyeing the woman; after a brief moment on his knees he stumbles, but manages to get up. They exchange glances and laugh. The woman keeps her eyes shut tight not to lose that dream. She rubs her hand against her leg as if trying to enter the dream. Then she takes the hairpins out of her bun and shakes her hair loose. She takes a rubber band from her bag and pulls her hair into a ponytail. She puts her hands to her neck. She starts untying the knot in the black velvet ribbon carrying the key. When she is finished she takes off the key and throws it into the water.

Sleeping with eyes open, like all fish do, a gurnard watches the key sink slowly to the bottom of the sea.

Translated by Şehnaz Tahir Gürçağlar
"Tıpkı Hayal Ettiğim Gibi," *Ahdımvar* (1995).
Istanbul: Metis Yayınları, pp. 180-188.

HÜR YUMER

The Best Sunday

"I tremble too much," he thought while staring at the grass and the creepy-crawlers. He was sitting on an armchair of red velvet, worn at the arms. On his feet were brown leather house-shoes with holes at the toes. The armchair had been loaded onto the back of the truck. Everybody else was sitting on cloth- or plastic-webbed lawn chairs. He, on the other hand, because of his illness, was regally posed in this armchair just beyond those fast youngsters immersed in a ball game.

İpek approached Gülten at a skip, dragging her plastic picnic chair over the grass behind her.

"Şeref Efendi certainly looks healthy."

"Yes," agreed Gülten. "I noticed myself a little while ago. Among all these youngsters playing ball and so many husbands dozing behind their newspapers, only he has a lively glance..."

"He was quite a rake when young," said İpek. "Look at his cigarette, how it teeters up and down at the corner of his mouth."

"Yees!" cried Gülten, shaking her torso as if there were a bug in her blouse. "The weariness of years seems to be showing up!"

"Do you think so? Perhaps it is distress or anger..." suggested İpek, half-examining over her bare shoulder a familiar itch on the wrinkled skin of her elbow. She'd squinted one eye and contorted her mouth.

Gülten, not overly convinced, silently tucked her bra strap back under the shoulder of a dress covered with cherries, oranges, toy monkeys, teddy bears and a teasing snake with arrow-like eye-lashes and a tongue darting in and out among dried flowers.

A bee, undecided as to whether to alight on the remains of the salad or the leftover meatballs on one of the tables, was tracing small circles and quadrangles in the air. Şeref was looking at the calendar-girl on the center-page spread of the Sunday edition that his son-in-law, lying on a cot nearby, had left open, perhaps as a shield against the sun or perhaps for no particular reason at all. Frilly black satin panties hardly as big as a baby's head covering the woman's indecent parts caught his eye. The fingers of this Sunday-girl seemed to be glued to her waist.

Her hands with their dark red nails resembled the webbed feet of a goose. The nail of one forefinger was near her navel as up to something malicious; it was obviously different from the other fingers, a privileged and cruel creature. Her one leg was thrown aside: the familiar sexual posture with the hip tensed... Perhaps she was both distracting his son-in-law with her eyes dulled by lenses, with her richly powdered nose resenting the tampering of aesthetic surgery and with her crooked breast bone just striking the fold of the middle page and enjoying his approval as he gazed at her so long. The legs of the Sunday-girl had been cropped from the knee down to fit the dimensions of the page. When the bee alighted between the legs of the girl where there was hardly any hair and frightened the son-in-law, Şeref laughed, turning his head to another side perforce.

While İpek, with the end of her ring-finger, was prying up the tantalizing and persistent young skin of a hangnail on one of her big toes, at the same time searching in vain for those little nail scissors which she always left in the dresser drawer and never put in her bag before she went out, she bent down, spying on the ground some unknown object she couldn't care less about.

"Look how he's laughing; he must be thinking of the women he ran after when he was young," suggested Gülten.

As Gülten said, "Don't say that," İpek suddenly felt the urge to say something ridiculous: "Why 'Don't say that!' One doesn't grin without a reason. His eyes are tightly closed!" She spoke and then burst into laughter.

"Not closed but narrowed... Don't say things like that. What a pity!" opposed Gülten again.

My mother always used to say, "Poor Şeyda, she was never happy, this fellow was the reason for her death!" Look, his head is trembling again! I wonder if he could even get his meatballs down! Old age is something horrible! I'd commit suicide before I got that old."

Şeref had been a maker of frames. He placed the coffee cup on the grass slowly with the care of those fortunate enough to spend all their lives working at a shop counter. From a distance he waved to İpek and Gülten. They were probably gossiping. He shouted, "What are you gabbing about, girls?"

"We're talking about you, Uncle Şeref," answered Gülten. "You look very spritely!"

"Well, carry on!"

"Why are you lying, Gülten?"

"I'm not lying. You're the one who's lying."

"What have I ever said? My mother was in love with Uncle Şeref. He never gave mother any hope at all! He'd always enter the house, saying 'Is Hüsnü home?' Think back! He never loved poor mother! Did he ever once come to the house to see her?"

"He came, and many times. Uncle Şeref never left mother alone after father's death."

"Couldn't he have come while father was still alive?"

"How could he come to flirt with the wife of his best friend?"

The boys' ball grazed a swaddled baby with her face covered as well and sped as far as the tea-house, ricocheting off the trunk of a sycamore. Thanks to a long kick by the keeper of the tea-house, the ball this time missed the baby's cart by some three spans. Once it had reached the playing field safe and sound, Şeref—taking a deep breath—raised his hand to warn them not to play so roughly; though he shouted to one of the boys "Son," they didn't seem to hear. Fortunately, the baby—as if she'd seen the danger in her dreams—had suddenly awakened. As soon as her mother had run up and rescued her from the cart, she began to kiss her avidly and squeeze her by the arms and legs. Although the baby cried even more, everyone was satisfied that she was now out of harm's way.

Şeref Efendi bowed his head over a neat right angle at the corner of an old frame he had very much enjoyed making in the shop he'd had to liquidate. The very day when his hands and head started to tremble...

His son-in-law had fallen asleep with the newspaper supplement folded over his face. The wind was beating the reversed kneecap of the Sunday girl against the earlobe of his son-in-law...

The painting with the swans was just a picture of a lake, but it seemed to him that it would look dazzling in the dentist's waiting room in this fine old frame he'd carefully sanded down. He'd finished the small frames rather quickly. These were pictures that he didn't find at all suitable for a dentist's office; not pictures actually—caricatures; he hadn't liked them: a poor fellow with his teeth and skeleton being pulled out through his mouth, his legs thrown up. The dentist with forceps in one hand and his other hand pressing against the patient's chin. Twisting the tooth... A chubby boy with his cheeks ruddied by drops of blood, about six years old, and grasping the dentist's arm. A series of caricatures all like this, the product of an "if you see the pain, you don't feel it," know-it-all attitude. Dentist Nevzat had told him the client would feel relieved by looking at these, forgetting his own tooth being drilled. He'd commented, dropping his jaw, "Really? How nice!" and gone back to his work, waiting for the dentist to go away. When Dentist Nevzat had returned a week later to pick up the pictures, he couldn't help asking where the doctor had been educated.

"In Europe, master." Nevzat had answered. His machines were brand new and they were all from abroad. But it was that very day, while stuffing his caricatures proudly under his armpit, that he'd left the painting with the swans behind; Şeref had hidden this swan lake away for himself. Actually he'd simply neglected to remind the dentist of the picture—he couldn't bring himself to it.

While he was—as if for the first time—reflecting on this single theft in his life, one of the screechy-voiced boys shouted: "Off-side! I saw it." He concluded that this game had no referees; everyone was saying something different. At that very moment Şeref saw the flag hung on the branch of a walnut tree; as the wind blew, there it was ruminating as if grinding something between its jaws: a skull in the middle of two crossbones... A fun-loving kid had put a wreath of creepy-crawlers on the skull. Which one was he? Most likely the boy sweating on the sidelines!

From that day onward the swan lake had become a familiar sight to his tired eyes. Then, a long while afterwards, one day as he was watching *Swan Lake* on television, this swan lake so familiar to him flashed before his eyes. Turning off the television, he set off bravely for the shop in that cold weather "to watch" his own swan lake under the fluorescent lights with as great an exhilaration as it had been on the very first day he saw it. It was an exquisite painting lacking in primary colors, with pastel purple water lilies and many shades of deep green—a dark clouded dawn when black and white swans were preening themselves, their beaks under their wings. Couldn't he see one group fighting and one swan swimming gracefully alone far away? It'd been ages; was something different?

The painting remained for a long time near the counter in the shop. Then he had given it to that İpek, the daughter of his best friend Hüsnü—may he rest in peace—as a marriage present.

Gülten had never married; Hüsnü, however, had been much fonder of Gülten than of İpek. Şeref looked around for his own daughter. While these two had been sitting and gabbing all day, Sedef had arranged the meatballs on the brazier, fed the kids and looked after the crowd as always. İpek, Gülten and Sedef had all grown up together. When Saturday came around, he and Hüsnü had taken the girls to the cinema for the 4:30 matinee. If only for once poor Hüsnü—with his little money—had been able to say no to them! Cake? Cake... Ice cream? Ice cream... Clack... clack! Cluck... cluck!

"Parkinsons," the doctor had said. "Parkinsons! What work do you do?"

"I make frames." The doctor had said he couldn't expect to work as he always had. On his way out—perhaps he hadn't recognized it earlier because the lights were off—he saw his Swan Lake in the corridor, near the door to the toilet. On his next visit he inquired, "Where did you get this painting? Magnificent. However, I suspect it doesn't like where it's been hung!" The doctor shrugged this off with a wave of his hand, implying that it was something trivial; he said it'd been a gift from a girlfriend.

He looked at İpek. Gülten had risen to her feet and was helping Sedef stack the dirty plates in a bag. İpek's husband had put his head on his wife's knees and was going on about something, posed like a rascal film star with a sprig between his teeth. İpek was nodding and picking things out of the poor fellow's hair. Şeref had never mentioned the fate of his Swan Lake to Sedef in order to prevent any rumors. He'd been visiting the doctor with his son-in-law—İpek's husband, a pharmacist—who also brought him his medicine... He burst into laughter. While the two players who had little by little practically turned his armchair into a touchline—or a strange shelter to catch their breath—were running towards him, he felt the furious glance of the boy who already realized he'd lost the ball this time.

Şeref had a close call. To pacify the furious boy and to do something really naughty for once in his life, he said, "Shouldn't this be a corner?" Making out from the discussion that even the players didn't know what was going on, he became upset and sulky. He didn't really want to be a referee at this age. Not a referee, quite obviously a judge... No, that wouldn't be enough, what they needed was a lawyer.

"Uncle, say something! Didn't this cross the sidelines?" There wasn't any sign or line aside from himself! He was ready to comment, "The goals are clear but the side lines are rather vague," but then he gave up.

"If I'm on the sideline, then it's a corner, son; I saw it." He couldn't keep himself from pacifying the furious kid, or from doing something naughty. He grasped the boy by the arm to ask who'd stung the creepy-crawlers like hair on the skull's head. "My brother," said the boy. "He's short of breath! He is always sweating and goes off to drink water. They scored two points against us because of him. He's spoiled our team." Şeref wanted to twist the boy's arm hard, but he knew he wouldn't be able to. Pulling the boy towards himself, he whispered in his ear: "It's not a corner; it's a throw-in; you should be ashamed of yourself!" The boy was amazed. Şeref shouted in a voice the others could hear. "Think for a while why I say a corner. How can you draw such random lines and play a game? You head towards me because I can't move. What a sport you are!" Now the whole team was ready to attack the boy. "No lines," he continued. "No sidelines! You can't play a game from a grandpa in an armchair to a walnut tree with a terminator."

He called out to his daughter, "Sedef, wake up your husband, gather everybody up. Let's go as soon as possible. I'm tired." He bent over and picked up a creepy-crawler. Opening his palms he looped the creepy-crawler in a line over his two little fingers. He then teased the creepy-crawler as far as his wrist by moving his hands back and forth; the rest would be more difficult; his hands began to shake more and more. Slipping between his wrists, the crawler fell to the ground, glancing off the sunlight reflected on one side of the chair. He used to make it crawl as far as his elbows. His head fell back as they were seating him in the back of the truck. Through the darkness a pair of golden earrings glittered past, dancing up and down—the same as his wife's, but it was as if he were seeing them for the first time.

Translated by Hande Öztürk and Jean Carpenter Efe
"En Güzel Pazar Günü," *Ahdım Var* (1995).
Istanbul: Metis Yayınları, pp. 189-195.

SİBEL BİLGİN

The Blue Dress

"Look," he said, "I don't know what you're looking for, but I am sure you won't find it in this city. This is a city where people can't find what they're looking for. This square—comprised of a few gothic buildings that lost their grandeur long ago, a dry fountain, and a café that welcomes those who've lost their way—is always deserted. The streets, which at first glance you think meander like the tributaries of a river and wander to mysterious parts of the city, in fact lead to nowhere. The entire city is what you see from where you are. Behind those houses, penetrated by a dispiritedness that reminds one of inexplicable miseries, lie barren fields. As if a still, flat russet were fading steadily away into the horizon. You feel as if you've reached the point where Earth ends and space begins. There's nothing behind this façade, which recalls a stage set. It's also impossible to find your way. You keep wandering around in the same desolation."

"I'm sorry, but the road you came by is the only road you can take to return. I know it is never an enjoyable journey to return by the same way you came. Especially if the only thing there is to pass by is an old graveyard. Well, of course you have one other option. You can follow the path that winds between the rocks and walk down the cliff to reach the river. It is weird, but in this city that offers nothing, you will find a pier, a boat that is tied to it, and an old boatman."

He pushed his chair back slightly into the shade. He pricked up his ears to the bells. From his pocket he took out a watch on a chain and studied it closely as if he wanted to engrave in his memory a picture he was seeing for the first time; then he placed it back in his pocket. Sunlight filtering through the vine leaves sprang from the lenses of his glasses to the frames, and from the frames to the lenses, forming a small triangle on his forehead. His silhouette falling in the partial shade gave away his age. Apparently he wasn't as young as his voice. He was relaxed, sitting on a familiar chair like always. "Forget about your return for a moment," he said, moving his slender hand from right to left as if he wanted to push aside something that only he could see. "The nights come late during the summer months anyway. Maybe I can beguile you with a story, and prevent you from setting out at an awkward hour. I will start with myself. Then I'll tell you an old story of which your blue dress has reminded me. Now don't jump to conclusions. This is not a love story or lovers' ballad as you might think. I am too old to tell about love I'm now experiencing, yet too young to play around with love stories. For now, let's call the story 'a city, a museum, a museum's security guard, and the blue dress.' Later you can use your own imagination and think of another name. The city is this city, as you may have guessed. As for the museum, that you can't guess: It's a gloomy building, a single-storied museum next to the old graveyard you pass by; it looks more like an orphanage.

"I don't know why, but I could never understand the secret of museums, I could never truly acknowledge these strange places that separate the living from the dead. It was always an affliction to think that pictures, sculptures, temples, and pirate ships—in other words things that should take their part in life—are buried in the dark behind the doors of these inaccessible buildings. When I see these thousand-year-old pieces of life rent asunder from the time and place they belong to, exhibited in showcases somewhere in the world, a feeling of betrayal pervades me. I have always believed it could be no more than an illusion, this walking from the memories of one century to another in a single step, piecing together in my imagination a statue that has been dispersed to the four corners of the world, whose helpless hands rest there as if they've been angrily wrenched from the head, the body and the wrists.

"I walk about in museums for hours examining the facial expressions of the visitors. I feel pleased when I see someone who feels this same illusion and shares the feeling of being lost, a pair of eyes shaded with suspicion, and I tell myself, 'He knows.' He's gazing at the laugh of the Inca women on the golden cups in the treasury of Saint Mark's. He knows that every museum writes its own history. 'You're right, my friend. If there are four different names for Christopher Columbus in four different languages, and he has tombs in four different places throughout the world, each celebrating that they have his tomb, then in fact his real name is written in a fifth language which we don't know, and his real tomb hidden in a fifth place we don't know of. You're right.'

"I had so little knowledge of art or history when I decided to write a book of travel notes on museums. Perhaps I still have too little. Was I supposed to start out with art and move towards history, or the other way around? I was especially desperate about the puzzle called art history, which combines these two. Perhaps for this reason as well, I took the easy way out and decided to start with the human being as an individual. This was a safe and enjoyable way. I'd be able to travel through art and history without involving the artists and historians. I'd be able to rewrite the story of the very same seas in my own way, just as a captain writes his logbook.

"So the adventure I set out on some twenty-five years ago is still continuing. By the time I had completed my journeys to the major museums in the world, the sixth volume of my travel notes was also complete. It was complete, but it felt to me as if I had just begun to write. This time, unknown stories from unknown museums were awaiting me. Like the story of the museum next to the old graveyard...

"Have you ever asked yourself just what the distinction between city and town is? Don't bother to look it up in the encyclopedias. For one, the basis of the distinction is a train station, for another a cathedral; it's a seaport for still another. Yet at this point in our world, it's the museums that make the distinction between the cities and the towns. So the first thing an ambitious administrator who settled here years ago did was to turn the ruin next to the old graveyard into a museum. Thereby he proclaimed the town a city, and himself the governor. Well, the museum was built but there was nothing to exhibit except for an altar from an old church, one icon and a few candlesticks. Yet the young governor was determined. One by one, he visited all the houses in the city, and took all the items he thought worth exhibiting to the museum. Things that had been left forgotten in some corner of the house for years and that nobody cared about would be exhibited in the museum. The people, who were proud to have their names carved on plaques and thus immortalized, gave the governor their full support. The governor is also said to have used his own fortune to collect pieces from all over the world. In this museum, you will see paintings and sculptures that you won't see even in the greatest museums, even Egyptian tablets. The young governor, who devoted his whole life to creating a museum, had these words written over the museum portal: 'Where life ends, a museum begins, and where there is a museum, life begins.'

"If there's a locked door, there is certainly someone guarding it. So there was a guard for the museum, too: a sorrowful young man with a pale face. Or better, a silent man whom others took to be sorrowful. When, nights, the museum's door was closed and the museum buried in silence, he was lost in the inner world of this ever so mysterious place. He would look at the yellowed pages of the registers and try to figure out the stories of the sculptures and the pictures. What interested him was not where and when they had come into existence, but the adventures they had been through. For instance, he would spend hours imagining what a woman sculpted in bronze might have seen and experienced, having been dragged to the Dominican Islands through Seville, then to Havana, and finally consigned to loneliness in an isolated corner of this museum. From love stories in hanging gardens to sailors' ribald songs, from slave markets to the lace veils of noble ladies in mourning...

"It was one of the dream-like evenings when he was walking about in the museum—one of the evenings when the moonlight filtered in through the high windows and played with colors and shadows, the Egyptian tablets were reflected with lake scenery in the water, and the silhouette of a bronze woman was wandering among the candlesticks from the old church. The young guard was inspecting the paintings, watching the colors transform. 'After midnight,' he said, enjoying the fact that he knows what is happening, 'all the browns will turn to blue, and all the blues to purple. And the limpid faces of the Renaissance women will slowly pass into shadow.' He paused to light a cigarette in front of 'A Venetian Woman,' a portrait from the sixteenth century. That was one of his favorite paintings. This Venetian figure was a woman in a blue dress, silently wading among columns rising high out of the water that rose to her waist. Although half submerged, she had a peaceful expression on her face as if she were wandering in summer gardens. She held a mask in her hand. A big gray mask. He sensed something strange as he came nearer the painting and perused it. In the moonlight the colors were fading instead of becoming brighter, with the blue of the dress becoming ever deeper. Flurried, he struck a match and approached the painting. For a while he thought he was losing his mind at what he saw before him. Instead of a Venetian woman, a real woman in a blue dress was gazing out from the frame. And with a peaceful expression just like the Venetian's. Who are you and what are you doing here? he wanted to cry out, but not a single sound could be heard. Frozen where he was, our guard stood without turning his glance from the woman, as if under a spell. The woman's lips did not move, yet a woman's soft voice was telling a story. As if telling for the thousandth time a story she knew well.

"The woman went on: 'The first time I met her was in a gallery years ago. She stood alone, distinct among many other paintings. Silently, I slipped out of the crowd; I recognized her when we came eye to eye. She was telling my story; she was me. The one who drifted through the vestibules was me, and so was the one who wandered with the traveler's dream of buried cities. Only I could know what she was looking for. Maybe she would reach my destination before me and I would start over again on the path she left behind. I had to figure out which one of us was the past, and which the future. Every day I would go to the gallery and stare at her for hours without getting bored. But there was a slight difference between us. She was carrying her mask in her hand, and I, mine on my face. She was one of those who had real faces behind their masks, while I was one with no face other than a mask. I was living behind a mask, but she behind her own face, so to speak.

"'Unfortunately my happiness in finding her didn't last long. One morning they said she had left for a faraway country, an unknown city. I decided to go after her—after my own story, in other words. When I finally came to this city in my travels from one country to another, from one museum to another, I was really afraid that I might have lost all track of her. It was beyond my imagination that there would be a museum in this city that offers nothing. Just when I had lost all hope and decided to go back, I saw her by the river one night. She was wading in the water in her blue dress. You know, the figures in the paintings leave their frames when night comes, and disperse to all corners of the city. When they come back and take their places as day breaks, they have left another adventure behind. If you examine them carefully, you will notice that their faces have changed. Since I met her by the river, our adventure has changed, too. Our stories have merged into one another. During the daytime I live her story, and at night she lives mine. One might say we have a single story. As for the question of who is the past and who is the future, I really don't care anymore. Because I know I'll never be able to figure it out. It's only that I feel there is one actress too many on the stage.'

"The guard, holding his pulsating head between his hands, stood motionless for a while; then plucking up his courage, he lightly touched the woman's cheek. The last thing he could remember was the warmth of her limpid skin burning his fingers.

"When he came to, he was still lying on the stone pavement just as he had fallen. Pulling his aching body onto his feet, he slowly gazed around as if searching for some clue from the night. By then, however, day had already broken; the ghost-like shadows were long gone. No longer were the Egyptian tablets reflected with lake scenery in the water, nor was the bronze woman's silhouette wandering among the candlesticks. He turned a suspicious glance on the Venetian woman's portrait once more. It was in its proper position just like the other paintings. It was there, yet there was something strange, something different about the painting; what it was he didn't know.

"'I must get out of this place,' he thought, 'before I go insane.' He rushed out of the museum and following the railway, he stumbled along until he reached the city. He could neither forget the night's adventure nor pull his thoughts together. 'There is something different about the painting,' he kept saying. 'Something different, but what?'

"One cannot get lost in this city even if he wants to. It is always this old square where you will end up. Our museum guard, having wandered about the streets for a while as if sleepwalking, found himself in this square. There was a crowd. One of the traveling theaters that pass from city to city in the long days of summer was setting up for a show. The clamor of youngsters cheering and clapping their hands reverberated in his head while he made his way to the front row, his eyes glazed. He felt he was becoming lost in the crowd that was weaving to the left and the right, weary of waiting under the hot midday sun. Now he felt all alone amid a mass of healthy skin and bones—not a single soul had any idea about his story and anxiety.

"The curtain opened. Silence enveloped the square. The actors and actresses took their places on stage. As one player began to sway her body back and forth like a dancer behind the large mask she held in her hand, our guard lost his balance. It was as if the ground was slipping from under his feet as he was being rapidly spun up into the air by a wind funnel. He was trying to escape from the square, staggering and supporting himself on the arms of those around him; a woman's soft voice was ringing in his ears: 'Our play is a mask, and the mask is a play. One crying, one laughing, one living, one dying, one crying, one laughing, one living...'

"He was exhausted by the time he reached the museum. He could barely drag his body to the portrait of the Venetian woman. Now when he dropped to his knees in front of the painting, he knew he wasn't mistaken. Indeed there was something different about the painting. The Venetian woman quietly walking through the water in her blue dress did not have a mask in her hand. She was no longer carrying that big gray mask; the Renaissance face was no longer shaded with suspicion.

"Those who heard it did not believe the guard's story. Young people don't know how to embellish a story to make it more credible, and our young guard was no exception. People are strange. They are not surprised to hear that Christopher Columbus has four different graves at four different sites in the world, but somehow they just cannot believe that the mask the Venetian woman had carried in her hand for centuries could disappear with the magic of one night. They dismissed it as the imagination of a melancholic youth. Just as no one cared when an old boatman found a woman's body in a blue dress in the river shortly after the event. Just as nobody noticed the big gray mask that slid from her pale stiffened fingers to drift with the current into the reeds near the shore. No one except the young museum guard...

"Since then a more lucid guard, sensible enough not to be carried away by stories called to mind by every blue dress he sees, has been watching over the museum. As for the young guard, they say he left the city after a while. Who knows, perhaps he is still traveling around the world in search of the mask carried off by the waters of the river.

"As for me, soon I too will leave this city. I don't have much to do here. For some reason this city reminds me of those children's books with standout pictures. When you open the cover to ninety degrees, like opening the cover of a box, some of the details in the pictures come to the fore, creating a three dimensional world. But your joy doesn't last long, because in fact everything is only half there. The trees, people and houses don't have any depth. There is only emptiness behind them. And just as when you close the book that three-dimensional world is buried in emptiness and all you have in your hand is a book, it seems to me that this city will return to emptiness in the barren fields. Maybe that day masks and faces will merge, and the last volume of my travel notes will be complete. All that is left behind will be a museum.

"I don't know if you still want to go back. If you do, don't hurry to take the riverside route. Rivers are not like seas. They definitely take you to a shore. Besides, on your way is a museum, the story of which you know. Don't forget, where life ends, a museum begins, and where a museum is, life begins. And do you know what? I would have told you the same story even if your dress hadn't been blue. Well, museum guards here don't have any other stories to tell."

Translated by İlke Deniz and Jean Carpenter Efe
"Mavi Elbise," *Bana Bir Harf Söyle* (1993).
Can Yayınları, pp. 37-48.

ÜMİT KIVANÇ

A Crossing of Paths

"I've killed her," said the man rather unusual in dress and appearance. "I've killed her; her body's now married to a yuppie in Izmir."

I was drunk. "I know the story," I said.

"There's no way you could know this story," he said. "At best you might know the cliché. But you don't know the story."

"Uh, that's what I meant to say," I spoke only with effort. The words bloated in my mouth; they seemed to swell with some substance, whether gas or liquid I wasn't sure. "Don't make it too long," I said. "If you're going to tell it, get on with it. Don't expect any comment from me, though. It's all I can do to speak straight."

"A pity," said the man in the double-breasted jacket. "At least you're not the type that refuses to admit being drunk. In fact, one could have told you things..."

Surely he'll get up now and leave, I thought.

He didn't. He was still seated there.

"Eh?" I uttered. I don't know why.

He took one bite of his white cheese. And a sip of *rakı*. Each of us had two wedges of cheese. It looked as if he would leave one behind when he got up.

"They haven't come," I said.

"Were they supposed to?" he asked.

"Uh, yes."

"Did you want them to come?"

"I don't know..."

"After this hour I don't suppose they'll come," he said, "will they?"

"No, of course not. In fact, for the last hour now there hasn't been much hope."

"Would it make any difference if it were earlier?"

"I don't know."

"... since you said 'they'..."

He hesitated.

He didn't go on.

His cigarette had gone out in the ashtray. After removing the stiffened filth at the tip, he lit it again. I too lit a cigarette. I could smell it burning. I felt I was about to get sick. I didn't have a watch. He didn't either; that is unless he had one on a chain or something like that. He just might have a pocket watch, though.

"Have you ever carried a pocket watch?"

"I always wanted to. How about you?"

"Nope. I like them too, but I never thought I could use one. I kind of feel that it would seem somehow like putting on airs."

No reply. What was it that seemed so strange to me about him? Were the lapels of his jacket wider than the ones I see all around? I could confirm this by having a look. To do so, I'd have to turn from left to right. And to leave, I'd have to stand up. Wasn't this man rather old to be having a turbulent love affair and to be left in a melancholic mood when his girlfriend had been snatched up by a yuppie? Weren't the lapels of his double-breasted jacket too wide for this?

"Is she aware that you've killed her, Sir?"

No reply. A question followed.

"Shall I tell you something about yourself?"

"This will be the second time."

"If you don't want me to, I won't."

"Ahh, please go on, Sir, go on."

"You're beginning to sober up. If you don't want to, go and hit the hay at once."

"Am I coming around?"

"At first you simply called me 'you'; where has this 'sir' come from? It's because you've diagnosed and put a label on me, isn't it?"

"From time to time I'm rude or distant to avoid being pestered."

"If you can make a diagnosis, this means you're using your head."

He took a sip of *rakı*. He takes such small sips! Never releasing the glass on the table, he once more grasps it firmly and takes another sip, and then another, and another... As long as he's been sitting down across from me.

Of course not! He only ordered a small one and three quarters of it is still in the glass. Ha, now I understaaand! I'm composing a montage. I've outdone even the Hollywood movie-makers. I'm condensing ten meters of life onto scarcely fifty centimeters of film.

"If only there were cinemas with very late matinees..."

"Video?"

"That too means going back home."

"Well, I wouldn't know about that, nor do I have any comment there." He leaned slightly forward as he said this. He wasn't old at all.

"Moreover, everybody's brain works well when drunk. It works like a whiz!"

"That's different. Then it works by itself, that's different. Different from using your head..."

"What's the difference?"

"Isn't there a difference?"

"There is."

The waiter came. He removed one or two empty plates. We didn't have much ice left.

I pondered the next morning. Surely I'd wake up with a terrible headache. In that case, I'd never be able to time my boiled eggs right. That's for sure. Dirty dishes were also piled up.

"Eggs," I said.

"Are you thinking about women, too?" he asked.

"What?"

"Don't they show a great similarity to eggs?"

"How?"

"You never know what to expect before they're peeled. You can sort of predict but can't tell for sure."

"Every time you undress another woman, Sir, do you put a notch in the butt of your gun?"

"Do the eggs at your place peel themselves?"

"No, but women..." I'm about to smash the pit of a green olive between my teeth. I suspect that my anger here might be unfair. This is a castrating feeling. That's why I'm becoming more and more rabid. It won't do. The olive pit, I mean. In fact, both. Not only has my fury been repressed but I've had to take the pit out of my mouth and drop it into the ashtray. The metal ashtray makes it clear that it doesn't want to cooperate by leaving steamy, dirty flecks on the parts of my cigarette that touch it. Now, at this hour, I'm sure she's peeled. They didn't come, anyway..."

"Look," he said. "The subject of women is delicate. It's not one to be spoken of lightly." But whether he's just now said this, I'm not sure.

I suppose it was the way the man's coat was draped over his shoulders, or perhaps his carefully ironed pants—dark with pale pinstripes—or his shiny polished shoes, how should I know! Maybe all of it. Why should I find this man awkwardly dressed, anyway...

"The subject of love is not one to be discussed just anywhere," he added.

"I see that you've begun to speak philosophically."

"There's been murder committed," he said. "Hasn't that sunk in yet? I say I've killed her."

"Well, I can't even bring myself to kill. That's even worse!"

"Then commit suicide and let her live."

"Oh dear, is there any need for one of us to die?"

"Who said there was a need?"

It had become very difficult to breathe because of the smoke. In defense and resistance I lit still another cigarette. What time is it, anyway? Late enough that I'll have to pay a fortune for the taxi...

The same old man who always sold lottery tickets here came in. The man opposite gestured to him in such a discreet and artful manner that I felt a twinge of insufficiency.

"Shall I ask you something?" I said.

"You already have," he said.

I went to the men's room. I didn't have any difficulty walking. I had some difficulty in getting up, though. I was relieved once I'd pissed. The need must have been more pressing than I'd realized.

While walking back to our long table crowded with men who either knew or didn't know one another, I caught a glimpse of him from behind. He looked quite strong and well built.

"You must buy lottery tickets regularly, Sir," I said. "Every week, every fifteen days or what-not, maybe only once a month, but certainly on a regular basis..."

"Do you want an answer?"

"Not necessarily," I said and leaned back. "Look, like this, it was just like this. I just wanted to say it. It certainly looks that way."

Finally my *rakı* was finished. To keep from drinking any more, I needed something sweet.

Out of the blue he asked, "So, peeling them doesn't mean loving them in your opinion, huh?" he asked.

"In love," I replied, "I am unfamiliar with various processes ranging from peeling to killing. I wasn't raised in those lands where they grow."

He spoke as if surprised. "If what you're referring to by land is really a land, then only such things would grow there!"

"Then it means that love's lifetime doesn't correspond to ours," I muttered in retort. "Our lifetime is too long."

"It's not that way," he said. However, he spoke as if behind a veil of indecision.

I'd changed my mind about the dessert. I'd buy a chocolate bar or something when I went out. I requested the bill. He had at least two glasses of *rakı* to go. I didn't want to go out and head home. I didn't want the moment to come when I'd enter my room and turn on the lights. But I'm going, right now, for sure!

"If I didn't tell anybody that I was a murderer, it might pass for suicide."

"I... Why should I lie..." I stammered. "Honestly, I found it difficult to believe."

"Me, too," he admitted.

I had very little watered-down *rakı* left in my glass. I grasped it and raised it. We toasted. Emptying my glass I couldn't see his; I suppose again he barely touched the surface of the *rakı* with his lips.

As I closed the door of the pub behind me, a cold wind struck my face. I stuffed my hands into my pockets and walked down the dim side-street towards the avenue.

Translated by Bilge Kıral and Jean Carpenter Efe
"Kesişme," *Erkek Hikâyeleri* (1990).
Istanbul: İletişim Yayınları, pp. 312

HALİL İBRAHİM ÖZCAN

While Rain Was Falling on the Hazar

The month was April; the destination, a long, long history consumed within the lethal, scorching flames.

With a greeting matching the cloak of dampness in which the lonesome boat on the shore of the Hazar had enveloped itself, the huge rings inside the military transport encircled our wrists and ankles. On the planks of the benches remained only short gaps in time. A man approaching the boat asked where it was going. Without raising his head, the other shouted out, "To remote distances within ourselves. To remote distances within ourselves." His sincerity touched me. I intimated to him that he could share any advice of his with me. "You know, you young people have a desire to relieve the troubles that pester the elderly. So let me know if there's any change, okay? My address is clear."

"I would like you to know that I will take into account all your warnings, but I do request that you not assume to hold any authority over me."

"Don't worry too much about such things. We all know that when what one intends to say becomes blurred, we people should all know how to speak less to one another. As well as you can, you must face tooth-and-nail the difficulties life brings against you."

The waves. The waves were like the gait of a drunken man. The belated spattering of the raindrops newly falling on the shore forced my muddied tongue back into my mouth. The water lay glimmering, observing the absurdities of her new lover. As the drops became a shower, together with my intuitions I was shrouded by them. As if this weren't enough, I leaned on the raindrops. I thumbed my nose at the place where those drops were shedding their evil. In a rage of confusion bribed to "silence," upon hearing a forbidden sweetheart crying out, in a remote square set up for a celebration I tempted her toward "sin." Now, in their lack of daylight, let the enlightening scribes of blindness write this as well.

I was trying to catch my breath in tomorrow's yesterday. The drops formed rivulets in my hair, streaming steadily down my chest and arms. Each and every longed to pool together, merging into one—just as people do. Over a lunch break—during a lapse from the irreversible struggle—the irresistible passions of shores yet to be explored were calling. With my constant mention of her name, a chaos of impressions was left behind. If there were a price to pay for washing one's dirty laundry in the sunlight, I might have to pay that price.

The shore was just disappearing from sight, smiling at the back of the rain clouds.

* * *

As I sat at my seat on the bench comparing the irregularities falling from the awry lips of the houses yawning up and down the street, I discovered the reason behind it all. Or did I? Everything is blurry and smelly. You should be glad I think this way. You should be thankful you know the less-than-nothingness of those hiding their wounds. You should leave aside your dirty tricks, without taking shelter in the daylight-clear lies that have rotted certain documents from the inside out. As children we used to have such great fun. Indeed how impatiently I now track down those small souls with hearts so black. I should have been summoned earlier. I had no chance to speak out. We all speak with such intermingled voices that one cannot tell whose words are whose. We are self-created monsters. Not even to mention the curious just out for fun. Everything's written here. Even details concerning possible confusion with the guideposts heading us towards our destination lie within the palms we rub together. The journey might take a very long time. It might end soon, however, if there's nothing more for us to learn.

Starting out with others, we get caught in bottlenecks and progress no further. If congratulations ever reach me, I will settle and clear in the stream where I flow. My child, your desire for immortality has pulsated long enough. In the idiocy to which you've been led, you can scatter ash into the eyes of anyone who's asking for it. Who's speaking here? I'll tear these senile lips to shreds if I can grasp ahold of them where the objectionable words escaped. Simple, very simple. Speak with simplicity's voice. You too will see. Bring simple things before your eyes and think. Try to make sure that the branch you grasp ahold of bears no flowers but is green rather than dry.

* * *

Nothing remains of either the raindrops or the irregularities falling from the awry lips of the houses yawning up and down the street. All of a sudden they have disappeared. Let it be. Take me away from here, into the embrace of a heartbroken, forgiving mother. Again you're not being fair. You must decide what it is you're up against. This morning too will reach an end within time's borderlines. Only as much as the songs we've sung under our windows compare with all songs, so great is the separation between you and me.

"Good morning. Daylight unto you."

Good morning, unnecessary. Good morning, separation—as light and bright as splashing water. Good morning.

Write your names down here and then pass on. You will not take me anywhere unless you want to be consoled. Let us leave and let the others talk, starting where they left off.

Translated by Ayşegül Eryılmaz and Jean Carpenter Efe
"Hazar'a Yağmur Yağarken," *Randevu Hazırlığı* (1993).
İstanbul: Metis Yayınları, pp. 37-40.

HALİL İBRAHİM ÖZCAN

Preparation for a Rendezvous

In that watchtower of mine where I was spreading my heartbeats with an unguent black flux over the whiteness of the snow, there was a woman walking with a mechanical gait. I wouldn't have minded her dragging me after her from where I was but I could hardly have ignored the bicycle with broken pedals I was pushing along at my side. For some reason the snow wasn't falling on her. I was like a shadow under the ruins of the minarets, following her without destroying the vision. There where she was walking towards openness, freeing herself of the ciphered burdens of life, she still was letting me hear the sound of her mechanical steps. She wasn't delivering her message in her own way, either. If I'd tried hard enough, a projection of possible quarrels between us might have emerged.

The images I expected fell from my periscope at last. I was confused which to deal with. All were hiding from the others' fuming jealousies and almost savored of showering exotic tales. There were moments when the woman let herself be heard in academic lectures lingering in her painful joints. Whose business was it if she behaved this way... The references lingered with me as the sum of everything needing to be done in the fictitious loneliness of heaped up neglects; what was even more interesting was that my steps seemed to become mechanical as well; I began to strut for no reason at all.

With sweeping glances as obstinate as those of a ruthless dictator, the woman with a newly-found expression appeared to be saying that I must not follow her. I couldn't have remained silent in the face of this unnecessary obscurity. I increased the rhythmic pounding of my steps. Following a beautiful woman wafting of sandalwood was like hearing the breath of shy lovers on a bench. It reminded me of some hidden danger in the faded reflection of a stain I found superfluous. At the crossroads of my choice, I thought I'd be able to give her a name. To be able to bring it to an end, moving into further bedrooms, creating intimate lovemaking scenes, lying together as if committing a dangerous crime—hers was a very short past within a grandiose history. Although she was carried away by her dreams, I couldn't say "never mind," unable to resist the softening effect of her warmth. My body was mine, but I neither wanted to fear the heights nor to reach them. I'd already let my whims disappear behind Kaf Mountain. Well, if I were a desert lord this would be fine; I'd take her out and present her with a new gem while searching for the misplaced key of the hotel room I'd taken her to. I could speak of pine needles, dead fish, and the smell of wheat were she to listen to me.

Passing by a source of inspiration from the days I've been living through has made me lose the fright of falling off the path and tumbling down. Strolling the streets aimlessly now also means sharing fancies. It's clear that I wouldn't succeed in this game either. What aimless man has ever succeeded in playing games with the square roots of his own destiny? Why should I do the same? The woman must have guessed the color of my thoughts because she paused before she turned the corner and looked back at me. First she pretended to be tightening the strap on her shoes. Realizing that I wouldn't fall for such a cheap trick, she began to look directly at me. I was indifferent, trying to reach a feather's lightness as I followed her, smiling at the ground I'd covered between my childhood and my puberty. As she climbed up the steps in front of me at the entrance to the side street, I could feel the burning heat of my first ejaculation. It was there when I first noticed her slightly aquiline nose, there where she again hastened her gait. I thought I'd be lucky if I found enough time to write down all that was happening. Because I knew that it was impossible for me to note down each and every detail in its own right. Once the face of the word appeared, the word whose sense of touch I'd felt, I wished my path were leading to the outlying districts of a city in the woods. Yet she just walked along the route she knew. As I wasn't the one who'd created her guiding compass, I had no other choice except to follow her.

As I—accompanying my curves drawn on the sand—followed the woman, she pursued the path she'd taken as if irreversible. Her situation seemed close to mine. Though I was hoping to catch up with her in front of the door to the corner supermarket, I couldn't reach her there either. In the monastery—just as with the coinciding of my candle clock and hourglass, I would retreat into seclusion on schedule twice a day and would have had time to think about how to reach her—instead, behind her, I was still trying to divide time into smaller units. The division of deceased seasons would be seemingly hard with the ruler lines I'd keep redrawing within my calculations. According to the lines, one third of the mistakes were snoozing beneath the remnants of my imagery. In the time allotted, scarcely enough to motivate the entrepreneur in me, I'd arrived at the disciplinary door of greedy haste. She hadn't been able to see me there either. My legs were moving so slowly. They were likely to bring about unwanted situations in the want of tick-tocking of accurate clocks. On my very way I had the impression that some were coming forward to ask if I were rushing after an advanced cure for loneliness. No, no, the woman was reality and she was walking right in front of me. My strength wasn't enough to make proper use of time; it seemed I wouldn't be able to catch up with her. Progress, regress, both felt like acrobatics assessing the depth of the sea. The rest disappeared in two giant universes of escape.

    I was wasting my minutes, my seconds, following her as if she were a noble creature whom I'd never be able to find again. Centuries of mine mingled with my steps. Because doing anything else would appear to be imitating her, the drawbacks of following her faded one by one. One side of mine having aged only modestly was running its natural course in harmony with my interior organs. I was looking through the equally deceived child-like eyes of many fine dervishes, but as I tried to reach her, surprisingly, she didn't turn a hair. Besides the aspect of savage bravery that I couldn't then put a label on, it was also that I didn't want anyone else approaching her. If I hadn't believed in her, I'd have been smearing every pure experience on earth with evil. I was also aware that I could insert into the pages of my lost years that leaf wrapped in lost words brought by the wind. What if I should become more attached to her than I have ever dreamed? What would my end be? Screaming, I was grasping the guile of my lips in my palms. I wasn't wondering where the odd rattling of my timid strokes was coming from but the glitter of the little words crippling my feet... I was making the mistake of waiting for them to fade out. They glitter infinitely, never ending. As I cannot do without following her—no matter what—I should amplify my indictably criminal preparation for the rendezvous. Indeed, where has she gone?

Translated by Ayşegül Eryılmaz and Jean Carpenter Efe
"Randevu Hazırlığı," *Randevu Hazırlığı* (1993).
Istanbul: Metis Yayınları, pp. 21-25.

CEZMİ ERSÖZ

The Writer Unable to Write

I hadn't been able to write for days. And this time it was different. It was not like any of my previous impediments at all. It was as if an emigration had begun in my soul. As if I had absent-mindedly offended and hurt the existences inside that kept me going. While they were making their way towards a new valley, giving up their hope of me, the places they left immediately turned to desert... I had always had large mirrors of my own and I used to host faces, dreams and stories from life in these mirrors inside me. Then I would see them off into life again... I was certain which people's souls they would visit...

But now, in the place where the mirrors used to be, was only a cavity, whose depth even I couldn't fathom. Faces, dreams and stories would disappear in this bottomless pit, creating neither reflection nor light. I could no longer reach the things inside me. I couldn't write; nor could I do any other work. I was madly jealous of working people. The grocer's apprentice, the neighborhood tailor, the street hawker, the plumber, the baker... I stood guard over this deep void inside myself all day long. This waiting, this uncertainty of destiny that had lost its way was far more frightening even than death... It had been quite a long while, and my first fright had diminished. My void had made peace with itself. Both my ambition and my touted ability to reflect everything I saw or experienced—and bring them back to life—had surrendered to silence and simplicity...

I felt a sympathy for myself that I had never felt before. I would treat myself as if I were a very dear and close relative who had just escaped a terrible misfortune by a hair's breath. I felt as if I had come back to the inside of me from far away—from an exile full of trials—after long years... Now, towards evening, when I went out to stroll through the book exhibitions with tranquil steps, I would see my books, once published one after the other by the leading publishing houses, thrown into heaps and sold under a sign reading "Everything for 100,000 TL," and then this sympathy I felt for myself would there and then turn to joyous pain; and in order to give even more significance to this pain I would bend over quietly, wipe the dust from my books and line them up properly. As if they had been children of mine who'd died when young. While I was dusting them, putting them in order and smoothing their pages, I would envision the bookseller as the cemetery watchman and look at him as if I were saying, "Take care of my children, don't let anyone crush them in passing or disturb them in their final sleep." I had become one with the void inside me; however, my loneliness—the throb of which was gradually increasing in my soul—didn't seem to acquiesce with this secret agreement.

None of my readers had either phoned or written even a short letter to ask how I was. None of the associations or societies had invited me to make a speech; the newspapers and the magazines were not asking my opinion on current events... The next generation of writers were not sending me their files anymore.

I didn't know how they'd treat me any longer, but I didn't want to feel their existence. If they didn't call me, I'd call them. If they didn't come to my place, I'd go to them. My pride never revolted against these decisions of mine. Who knows, maybe just like the faces, voices and stories, it too was lost in the void inside me.

Taking out my address book, I started to call them one by one. Except for a few, nearly all of them told me that they were following other authors and wanted to spend time with those writers; moreover, that I had betrayed them somehow by leaving off—and then they just hung up on me...

I received similar answers to the letters I wrote. They'd say that I had suddenly deserted them in the middle of difficulties; I had left them in the lurch and they could never forgive this abandonment... Actually, I could see their point of view. However, I too was still unable to grasp the meaning of my sudden abandonment and my being unfair to both them and myself... How great was my blame in this offense, who knows...

Nevertheless, some of my old readers agreed to have me as their guests. They were also offended, but the pity and the sympathy they felt for me concealed their offense. They would treat me like an old patient who has lost both his energy to live and his memory during a fatal illness. There was no sign of their former artificial and exaggerated respect. Without hesitating at all, they'd read passages from the books of writers who were once my rivals and speak of their growing admiration for these writers—increasing day-by-day—right in front of me...

In fact, I was at first upset about this situation, but later I began to overlook it, even to take a strange pleasure in it. This pleasure gave me a sense of freedom. I could observe myself like the hero of a novel or movie, from far away and carefully. I was that hero and at the same time I was not. I could observe with great curiosity whatever might happen to me. Furthermore, I could clearly see many details I'd missed in that half absent-mindedness and comfortable inebriation of conceit in my old environment, plaited with a circle of love and admiration.

Sometimes curious friends would come along to the houses of the old readers I was visiting, and to them I was introduced as "our guest writer unable to write..." At these moments I felt like an exotic creature on the verge of extinction.

Sometimes the little kids in the neighborhood looked through the window into my room and made fun of me: "The writer who can't write! The writer who can't write!" And then they'd run away...

Some nights my old readers would show me their poems and stories and ask me for a critique. These readers, who in the past had listened to my critiques with great attention and respect, now immediately took offence and ranted at my criticisms; they found them ill-timed and went so far as to accuse me of being jealous because they could write—and went away slamming the door in my face... Nevertheless I was still not tired of criticizing, of condemning lecturers with harsh words at panel discussions and seminars... Moreover, I would do this more courageously than ever before, being forthright stubborn until the very end because in the past I too used to write—and since I had never had enough confidence in what I wrote, I'd always shown others a more moderate and self-possessed respect... But I no longer had anything to lose. I even started to take a strange secret pleasure in the wounding, despising objections of the writers or lecturers whom I sometimes criticized, such as "Start to write again first, do what you say first and criticize us afterwards!"

Because I'd suffered such great pains at not being able to write, these words no longer affected me at all. For a short while they numbed even the pain of my loneliness, which couldn't be removed by my old readers—by whom it had been, on the contrary, intensified...

After a while, I began to seek out people like myself. Now we had a small group formed by poets and novelists unable to write, painters unable to paint, composers unable to compose and actors unable to act. Nearly every evening, we'd gather in the same pub and share our sorrows, our loneliness. Although no one took us seriously, we participated in press conferences, demonstrations and political activities. We even went to support the "Saturday Mothers" a few times... I no longer had any doubt that the people demanding a social revolution could be led by those like us.

Everyone misunderstood us... We did not feel any hostility for those who wrote and produced. Moreover, we never showed any hint of the jealousy and the filthy ambition which they felt for each other. Our anger was as naked as our souls and was vented only against the system itself... Now that we no longer encountered any respect or attention from anyone, we could see the oppressive power of the system, see how ruthlessly injustice suppressed the people, how painful it was to live like the ordinary person without any protective attribute to shield him... We had nothing to lose... And so, unbending we remained till the end... And we had to defend each other in the quarrels we initiated, because an assault similar to that which would be made tomorrow against a poet friend of mine who couldn't write, might be aimed at me the following day... We were despised, never esteemed, never asked for our opinions, and always ill treated;

however we didn't worry about all this too much because we could be ourselves everywhere, every moment. I was no longer imitating what I had written. I didn't fall into artificiality as I had done for so long when I was trying to persuade my readers that I was as frank, consistent and compassionate as what I had written...

I was not throwing my soul into the fire for the sake of defending my writings. I was not a symbol or a theme in the eyes of others; I was now an ordinary person. Nobody was searching for a secret meaning in my words or suffocating me with a hypocritical and compulsory respect that bound my hands and restricted my freedom. Thus no one else was being suffocated, either.

No longer was making love a single-handed journey for me. While making love, it was as if I were free from my body and from that diseased observer in my soul who was always splitting hairs—and whose curiosity sometimes turned into cruelty. I could now lose myself within the body next to me the moment I wished...

I experienced a deep pleasure in watching the faces I constantly encountered in the street, each of which was more interesting than the next; the reflection of moonlight in a broken bottle, the passions, the hearts that made themselves believe in the meaning of life; the pains that were hidden inside the greed and shadows—and were about to fade away, with all my self-respect and without any anxiety to write.

So much for this; now I want to confess something to you. Yes, maybe all this was real. However, there is still another truth, which is that I had deceived myself. However free, happy, and "myself" I thought I was being, I could never staunch the pain of my loneliness and its bleeding like a cry...

Even though I was exiled within myself, I must still have regained my mirrors that reflected faces, stories and dreams. Perhaps I should have never started out in the beginning. Had I never decided to dedicate my life to writing, I would have been happy forever, perhaps. But I had started out. Once I had traveled into those dreams and stories and those souls I knew so well... Halfway through, I was not able to put an end to this journey by making peace with the growing void inside me. I had to go on together with that diseased observer inside me always splitting hairs—whose curiosity sometimes turned into cruelty—till the bitter end, although it made me suffer...

Because I was now sure that what made me suffer was not that observer in my soul, but what he could never see... What had exiled me within myself was not that I had lived in a montage, but that I still did not know where my real homeland was...

I understood...

What had set my soul on fire was not writing, but those things I had never been able to write...

Translated by Esra Çakıruylası and Jean Carpenter Efe
"Yazamayan Yazar," *İçime Gir Ama Sigaramı Söndürme* (1999).
Istanbul: Gendaş Kültür, pp. 5-10.

PERİHAN MAĞDEN

The Secret Meanings of Unappreciated Words

Back then I was working at the paper factory. The workers shunned me for having been to such places as Singapore, for wearing black all the time, and for eating my mother's completely tasteless roast beef between thin slices of bread instead of the factory rations. Yet I was so lonely, so distressed. I passionately yearned for them to come up to me so that I could smash them from floor to floor, astonish them by wrapping them around my tongue, and drive them to frenzy when they finally grasped the meaning of what I had said after a week or two.

But they kept their distance with an animal-like instinct, and they would establish no relationship beyond giggling over the aphorisms I would mumble every now and then. As I was undergoing a distressing period, I was too lazy to get into their kind of clothing and ran around like an unfortunate, lonely wolf among little red riding hoods.

This sense of desertion was the reason why I had written the dictionary *The Real Meanings of Some Unappreciated Words*. I, who had succeeded in penetrating the heart of the most secretive societies all over the world by impersonating a variety of characters, would never have lived through the night's experience I'm about to narrate if I had not been pushed to write my dictionary by the obstinacy of the workers at the paper factory. That's why I'm grateful to my sisters who work at that factory.

That day, like every other day, everyone hurried to the gates upon hearing the bells ring. I was walking slowly because I had no one to meet and nothing to do—other than to go back to my dictionary—and I had no idea on how to triple this sentence. It was as if the five-o'clock-bell had been invented to remind me of how busy they were, and of how idle and free of appointments I was.

Upon reaching the front of the factory, I stopped and looked up at the two statues which the wrought-iron gates separated. Icarus and Pegasus. The two statues rising on top of white pillars and the iron gates which separated the winged figures were perhaps the only reason why I wanted to work at the paper factory. The monotony of work, the matchlessness of feeling like an extension of the machines, the bells, the rules, and the insidious pleasure of watching the workers were in fact responsible for my spending more time here than I would have ever imagined, but the gate of the factory was the seal, the signature of the time I spent there.

As soon as I'd left the gate behind, quickening my strides I started walking as though I was late for something. No, tonight I could not endure the annoying dishes prepared by my mother nor the painful hours spent over the table extracting the meaning of an unappreciated word and making up its sentence. I turned into one street, and then into another. The restaurant, frequented mainly by single male workers, was right across from me with its steamed shop-window. I pushed open the door and entered.

The next day, on the road, I remembered in bits and pieces, in the company of a bad headache which was the souvenir of the red wine, the hours I had spent at the restaurant. This happens to me every time I drink a lot and fast. The incidents I will narrate might be more or less than the whole. Who could ever resist the fact that the whole is not equal to the sum of its parts; I beg you not to expect this from me here with this headache of mine.

I settled at a table for four in a corner. Contrary to my habit of ordering kidneys or pork chops at restaurants, I remember ordering a meat dish with carrots and peas, and after having eaten the meat, playing some sort of chess game by myself with the peas and the carrots aligned and facing each other. However, I was drinking the dry red wine that was placed in front of me so fast that I won't be able to go into the details of the game. I vaguely remember that the peas were pure spiritual states whereas the carrots were spiritual states which were polluted.

I don't belong to the tribe of human beings who can keep themselves busy for a long time. As the wine in the glass bowl was emptied, I lifted my head and shouted at the owner of the restaurant: "Sabartés! Sabartés, another bowl of red wine please."

The restaurant owner was a man of experience; he was not one of those immature souls who would question you for addressing him by this particular name. Also, distressed, dissipated, evil-hearted people like me, who are stricken with an affliction to behave as they feel, immediately sense how long they can dance on others' territories. Even in my half-drunken state, I had felt what a decent man the restaurant owner was—this world is full of restaurant owners who would feel threatened upon being called by a Catalan name.

Sabartés had just left the wine bowl on my table when the door opened and a broad-shouldered, tall dwarf entered. Since my childhood I have never been able to keep my eyes off a dwarf whenever I see one. Years ago a dwarf I had run into on a road in

Peshawar, upon catching my eyes crawling like snakes all over him, had devilishly punished this habit of mine by turning somersaults and wrinkling his face as he madly swung his arms: There, isn't that what you expect of dwarfs!

Whenever I recall this incident, my hair stands on end. However, I was not able to keep my eyes off him; I was staring at him as if I were watching a skyscraper on fire. On top of everything he was a tall dwarf. It would almost be appropriate, if he were to portray himself as tall and broad-shouldered in the "Lonely Dwarf-Hearts" column of a newspaper for dwarfs. He was received with enthusiasm by the two dignified gentlemen sitting at the table right across from me. It was evident that he was a well-liked dwarf. But he was a dwarf nonetheless, was a dwarf, a dwarf, a dwarf.

I was so deeply immersed in thought that I didn't notice that the chair right by my side had been pulled out and that someone was sitting on it until the man turned his head and fixed his eyes on me. I guess it was not a common habit at this restaurant to ask for permission to sit at someone's table. The man talked with the deep voice of a heavy smoker: "Aren't you the author of the dictionary *The Secret Meanings of Unappreciated Words?*"

He had skipped "Some" and had replaced "Real" with "Secret." Wasn't his perhaps a more correct, a more attractive title? I was stupefied.

"Could you please move to the chair across from me?" I asked. "I can't see your face easily."

He moved to the chair across from me and sat down. He was a beautiful dark man. He had dirty, combed back hair and glaring eyes. His upper lip was conspicuously thinner than his lower lip. This gave him a covetous expression. He spoke in a fast and broken manner that would not be expected from a heavy smoker. Moreover, I remember he had long and slender fingers. I always try to be cautious with people who have slender fingers, perhaps because my fingers are so thick.

I pulled the wine bowl closer and reached for his glass. "I hope you won't say 'No' to a glass of wine."

Bending his head forward he smiled as if to say "Please." It can't be said that he really smiled, for he was one of those people who do not have smiling souls. I placed his glass in front of him after filling it up. At that moment, coming over to our table, Sabartés handed him and myself a pair of woolen socks.

"One of the customs of this restaurant," he said. "At a certain hour of the night, customers whose feet feel cold get a pair of woolen socks as a present."

"I only have tonight to get used to the customs of this restaurant," I said. "Tomorrow I am setting out on a long journey."

"Then, you will be quitting your job at the paper factory," said the man.

"That job has never been important to me."

Narrowing his eyes, he again affected something which resembled a smile. He knew that neither this nor any other job was ever important to me.

"How do you know all this?" I said.

"I paid the price to find out," he said.

"The price," I said. No one can top me in meaningless conversations. I can talk for hours jumping from the ant to the clove. But I get tongue-tied whenever someone utters a meaningful word.

"You are someone who goes on journeys," said the man. "You always go on long journeys."

"But then, you are not capable of smiling," I said. "I wonder if this is the price?"

This is my quick-to-reply affliction with no remedy! I will drop dead one of these days because of the shame this affliction brings on me. I turned bright red; lowering my face, I fixed my gaze on the floor.

I was so ashamed that I could not sit at the same table with him for another second. I jumped up from my chair and within a second I was at the table where the dwarf and the two dignified gentlemen were sitting.

"Gentlemen, may I sit at your table?" I asked. "I am in need of a shelter at this moment."

"Our pleasure," said one of the dignified gentlemen, the one with the blue eyes. He had blond hair turning gray and a thick neck. He resembled a lion.

"Geishas speak of music, politics and poetry," I said. "What would you like me to talk about?"

"Our conversation was going just fine," said the dwarf.

This was more than I could take. I had gotten tired of this world where dwarfs gave me lectures on life. Calling Sabartés I ordered a crème caramel.

"Please excuse my brother," said the man resembling a lion. "No one can surpass him in outspokenness."

"Your brother, eh?" I said. "The dwarf and the lion!"

"You said it so beautifully!" the dwarf burst out laughing. "Who are you? Scheherazade?"

I hardly restrained myself from saying: You are the one who belongs to the story books, my dear dwarf. "Whatever you wish, Sir," I said. "I would like to eat my dessert now, if you don't mind."

But my sadness wasn't likely to be appeased with crème caramel alone. Calling Sabartés, I ordered a potato salad. I like eating something sweet when I am distressed. And something salty after I eat something sweet. The dwarf and the other two plunged into deep conversation. They were talking about Burma, the price of lapis, giraffes and such things. I was watching the dark man, doing all I could not to be too obvious. He ate a plate of pork chops.

Sabartés, picking his plate up from in front of him, said: "How strange! Weren't you the one who always ordered a dish with peas and carrots and played some sort of chess game with them?"

"Tonight is different, Sabartés," said the beautiful man.

Sabartés? Wasn't I the one who gave this name to the restaurant owner? Paying the bill, he got up from the table. He walked out. There went half of my heart with him. And he left me with the desire to plunge the other evil half into a river to cleanse it. Or, I felt that way for five minutes.

Five minutes or so had passed when the second gentleman, who was the friend of the brother of the tall dwarf, or of the lion of a man, said: "Don't be saddened please, he was trying to change you. They would give you a little bit of love, not at all uncalculated or unlimited love, mind you, a little bit of love with their miniscule scales, a little bit of intuition; and in return they would want to mold you from scratch. Not that you would be better or worse, but simply that you would be molded by their own hands."

"You're right, Sir. I am glad to have met you," I said. "After all, it only lasted five minutes."

"There are some instances when it lasts for five weeks, five years, five thousand hours," said the man. "Unfortunately mine lasted a little bit longer. Do you see my eye? This right eye of mine?"

"Yes, Sir, I see that your right eye is artificial," I said. It was hard not to notice it. His left eye was brown, whereas his artificial right eye was blue and gleaming like a glass bead. He had light auburn hair and a thin, flat nose. Honestly speaking he was a fine man and he was very well-dressed. If you met him on the street, you would definitely say Harvard Anthropology major. Or at worst, Columbia Social Anthropology.

"I lost it during the war," he said. "I was eating soup at a table with a white tablecloth—with my two children and my beautiful wife. Suddenly I felt as if I was swimming in the soup bowl. It was stupefying. I was swimming but it wasn't possible for me to get out of the bowl. I still continue to live at home with my wife and my two children. I just don't go home for dinner, that's all."

I tried to say things such as, "I understand, Sir." But I was so shaken that my heart was full of a desire to run away from their table. Furthermore, my head was spinning violently. Asking their permission I returned to my table.

"Yes, it is better if you return to your table," said the married, artificial-eyed gentleman from Harvard. "And also, you have a new guest, a hard to find guest. Mister Elya will become a rabbi in two weeks. Furthermore, he is a convert himself—he wasn't born as one of the chosen few. He became a Jew with his own sweat and blood. Quitting the Music Academy in order to walk through the labyrinths of religion! Tonight the stars are shining for you."

"Thank you, gentlemen," I stuttered. "And please, good night."

As soon as I reached the table, I said: "I heard that you have been walking through the labyrinths of religion. What's more, you have quit the Music Academy which you enrolled in with great difficulty; you have quit everything I'm afraid. But your yamuka looks good on you, I must admit. Do you take it off when you go to bed?"

"There is nothing in life that can't be quit," said Mister Elya. "Everything is worth quitting. We exist in this world in proportion to the value we attach to this truth: to quitting, and our existence in this world is our conduct in a prison yard. Don't misunderstand me—by quitting we should not only widen the yard; we should define our status at the time of our quitting this world, in other words the yard."

"Don't be afraid of my misunderstanding you, Mister Elya," I said. "Because I do not understand you at all."

"Principally, your vulgarity is a threat to the guardians," he said. "And please, how about leaving the "Mister" aside. My name is Elya, only Elya."

"I understand, Sir," I said. To tell the truth, this word was my lifesaver tonight. The moment I grasped the little bits, I would jump on it.

I filled his glass which was emptied of wine, and while he was taking his first sips I examined him carefully. He had curly, fluffy hair and green eyes with long lashes. His complexion was whiter than white, almost transparent. For some reason the complexion of those who stroll through the labyrinths of religion is either transparent or has become transparent. This must be a small compensation for moving away from the works of the world. He wore a dark green shirt with the first three buttons undone. A black T-shirt with the word "first" in white letters was visible under the green shirt.

"I can guess what is written on your T-shirt," I said. "It must be on sale at the synagogue. Is yours a special print for the rabbis? 'First There Was the Word' is written on it."

He smiled. His smile was a very soft, very forgiving and a very luminous smile. Our table and the neighboring tables were illuminated by it. The gentleman from Harvard blinked his eyes. Elya slowly unbuttoned his shirt. On it were the words,

> First
> There
> Were
> The
> Rolling
> Stones

"Nobody would believe me if I told what happened here tonight," I said.

"You are individualizing everything," said Elya.

My mind had gone to the dark man again. What's more, I had no strength left to deliver ripostes to Elya. "How beautifully you put it," I said. "How beautifully you put it."

Right at that moment the dwarf sprang up right by our table. His eyes, looking at Elya, were gleaming with love. Apparently he wasn't only a loved dwarf, but a loving one as well. It was obvious from their manner that they had many topics to discuss.

I got up slowly, went over to Sabartés and asked for my bill. "Your bill has been taken care of," Sabartés said. Reaching into the first drawer of the counter behind him, he pulled out a red rose with a long stem. "And he also left this for you."

"Good evening Sabartés," I said. "Thank you for the socks."

"It is a custom here," he said. "Have a nice trip."

He was a man of dignity indeed. There was no need to stretch the word. Picking up the rose, I left the restaurant.

It was late in the evening; there was no one on the streets. As I walked I smashed the rose petals between my fingers. Breaking the stem again and again, passing through winding streets, I reached my mother's house. All the lights were out; my mother had probably gone to bed much earlier.

I entered the room which was allocated to me and turned on the dresser lamp. A shaky light illuminated the surroundings. My rough leather suitcase was in its usual place—lying under my bed like a loyal dog. My heart full of delicate affection for it, I pulled it out and placed it on my bed. I packed my notebook with the blue cover, my three books, my soap dish, my little pillow and a few pieces of clothing. I like living off what I get from the places I go. Traveling heavily is for people who don't know how to travel.

Sitting on one of the chairs at the round mahogany table that is right in the middle of the room, I wrote my letter of resignation. I started emptying the pockets of my jacket, as is my habit every night before I go to bed.

From the right pocket, which usually stays empty, came a ticket, a rose stem, and a handkerchief. My keys and the coins would be in my left pocket—I put them all on the table. A gleaming, blue glass bead, detaching itself from among the coins, came rolling out. I picked it up and looked at it; this was more than I could take! I threw it back onto the table. Picking up my pen, I wrote on a sheet of parchment paper which was lying right there:

Very Deserving Sabartés,
I think that the artificial eye which came out of my left pocket belongs to the gentleman from Harvard who is the friend of the lion-like brother of Mr. Dwarf. No knowledge in my mind, nor in my hand is enough to explain how it ended up there. But of course, we can always say: Let an artificial eye be among the many occurrences tonight beyond explanation. I say so whether I like it or not, and I beg you to return the eye to its owner as soon as possible.
Thanking you in advance for all your assistance,

Signing the letter, I placed it in an envelope along with the glass eye. Sealing the envelope, I felt as if some great weight had been taken off my shoulders. Believe me, it isn't an easy task to get rid of an artificial eye that has entered one's pocket.

I immediately called one of the private messenger centers which are open all night.

Five minutes or so had passed when a messenger boy rang the bell. Like all the messenger boys of this city, he had curly blond hair, clear blue eyes, and dimples. Like all the messenger boys of this city, he wore lilac and yellow striped pants buttoned at the knee, white stockings with pompoms, patent leather shoes with bow-ties, and on top, a short jacket of the same lilac velvet with starched white lace at the collar and the cuffs.

"You can deliver this letter to the paper factory in the morning," I said. "And you will take this envelope to a restaurant with a steamed shop-window. The name of the restaurant owner is either Sabartés, or that's what I believe it is."

"I understand," he said.

"Good evening, Messenger Boy," I said.

"Good evening," he said.

He went out. He disappeared with fast and silent steps.

Transl*ated by **Cem** Yegül*
"Kadri Bilinmemiş Kelimelerin Gizli Anlamları," *Haberci Çocuk Cinayetleri* (1991). Istanbul: Afa Yayınları, pp. 20-30.

PERİHAN MAĞDEN

Courage Does Not Reign

I was kicked out of the Conservatory. When called to the office of the elderly director where I was handed my dismissal papers, I said: "Sir, believe me Sir, I am not concerned for my sake regarding this decision of yours. What concerns me is how the St. Petersburg Conservatory will shoulder the heavy burden of having kicked out the best student it has ever had—just for one or two disciplinary offenses: That is what concerns me."

"I do not know what to say to you," said the director. "Therefore I shall say nothing."

Undoubtedly by my use of the words "one or two disciplinary offenses" he thought I was making light of having gotten drunk in the dining hall and making scenes, of having sent the music history professor to the hospital with a diagnosis of neurosis, and lastly, of having burned down the dormitory using gasoline. Therefore, he did not know what to say. I was tired of people who didn't know what to say, and even more of those who didn't know what they had already said. I always know what I have said.

Naturally, a conservatory student has the right to make scenes at school, to act this or that way with professors, even to burn down the dormitory. The things I did were not insignificant. Besides, I do not wish to do insignificant things. Then again it would have been to no avail for me to discuss with the old, white-haired director where my rights started and where they stopped. In a way I also liked him. And I knew that no matter how hard he tried to hide it, he felt a fine thread of love for me; yet because I was beyond his limits of endurance he would never admit it.

Politely I bade him farewell. My dismissal papers in one hand, my purple velvet cape and rough leather suitcase in the other, I made my way to the train station. I was going back home after seven years.

As my father had died years ago and as my mother was a rather "different" person, my home was not one of those real family homes which are like a distress balloon, filled with a sort of sticky, stale, castrating gas: thank God! But home is home after all, and I felt stifled with nausea, having to go back.

When I reached the station my train was about to depart; I followed the numbers until I found my compartment. Breathless, I plunged in and to my great surprise I saw that I was sharing the same compartment with a dwarf and his monkey.

The monkey had on an astrakhan coat fitting tightly around the waist; on its head was a kalpak of the same astrakhan. The dwarf wore a gray-striped black gabardine suit with a purple satin waistcoat inside and a purple-gray striped silk tie around his neck. His tiepin was a diamond the size of my thumb nails. His thick red hair was meticulously combed back, emphasizing his disturbingly blue, sparkling eyes.

I put up my suitcase and cape and took my place by the window. On such a miserable day for me as this I must admit I was rather annoyed to be obliged to travel with such a dolled-up dwarf and his dolled-up monkey.

People with certain flaws comfort me. They entertain me with their flaws and absurdities; they show me that I'm not alone, that I'm not the only one with handicaps and misdemeanors; they almost bind me to life. But honestly, I cannot make such generous comments about physical disabilities. Facing such people here and there distresses me, obliges me to wonder why they don't sit at home rather than poison my day. This dwarf was a festival in and of himself: Let alone not hiding his faulty body in his nest, he was parading it on inter-city rail with pride, underlining it with his nerve-wrackingly chic outfit. With a look of almost anger, my eyes became anchored to his cuff links. One of them was an emerald-eyed grinning cat's head made of diamonds. The other a porcelain-faced head of a little girl with blond bangs. This was Alice. Alice in Wonderland.

"Yes," said the dwarf. "Alice, Alice in Wonderland."

His tone of voice was astonishingly beautiful: soft, hoarse and deep. I couldn't fail to be impressed. I hold one's tone of voice to be of importance. I am a fine conversationalist as conversationalists go, but I have a high-pitched, horrible voice. Such a lovely tone coming from this dwarf... Now fancy that!

"Oh," I said so as to say the least possible, and also so that my voice was heard as little as possible. At any rate, I do not enjoy traveling companions: Intimacy suddenly established beyond any logic with a person you've not met before is not my style, definitely not.

"Let me introduce you," said the dwarf. "Isabelle!"

The monkey, I mean Isabelle, politely held out her hand. Reluctantly I held out my own and shook her small warm little monkeyhand. I do not like shaking hands at all, especially with a monkey—especially on such a miserable day for me with an astrakhan-coated monkey of a dwarf I've met for the first time! But there was something about that dwarf's voice: an imperiousness wrapped in unmatched politeness, a magical air which made one take pleasure in obeying.

"Isabelle is ill," said the dwarf. "Indeed, very ill."

While the gentleman spoke with his astonishingly beautiful voice, Isabelle was shaking her head with melancholy. When the gentleman, I should say the dwarf, finished his sentence she rolled her eyes and inclined her head to rest on her shoulder.

"In your hometown there lives a very famous physician; he is the reason for our journey. Otherwise, I agree with you absolutely: I wouldn't like to exhibit this faulty body here and there, distressing people with my appearance."

The train had just started; it was moving very slowly. Otherwise I would have opened the window and thrown myself out in order to smash that spoilt head of mine with its burning cheeks.

"Isabelle liked you rather much," said the dwarf. "When she saw you coming towards us with your purple cape and rough leather suitcase in your hand, she prayed that you would be traveling in the same compartment with us."

"She must know a very short prayer," I said, for I was running in fear of missing the train."

The dwarf, I mean the gentleman, laughed. It was the nicest laugh I'd ever heard. Isabelle smiled politely. What a sweet monkey she was!

"I've been kicked out of the St. Petersburg Conservatory," I said. "You must have known it anyway; I'm going back home."

"That was quite obvious," said the dwarf. "If you would like, let us pour cognac on your dismissal papers, and then throw them out the window. That way you can clear your mind of the conservatory, the music, and St. Petersburg. One should never carry around the places one has been kicked out of."

I don't know why, but all of a sudden my eyes were filled with tears, my voice trembled: "I wouldn't compose emotional arias starting with minor and ending in major keys," I said. "I also relentlessly cursed certain classics which are regarded as sacred. Frankly, I have also committed one or two disciplinary offenses; but no one should be kicked out of any place."

"It's such a coincidence; I have a wonderful bottle of cognac with me," said the dwarf. "Let us drink together and talk of other things."

We poured cognac on my dismissal papers, threw them out of the window, and talked of other things. I fell asleep drunk. When I opened my eyes we were halting in front of a large station. Isabelle was sleeping under a mink coverlet, sighing deeply. The gentleman sat erect, with his sparkling eyes fixed on me.

"You have slept for hours," he said. "Isabelle, too. She is so happy that she met you; she hasn't had even one single nightmare about death tonight. Isabelle is very afraid of dying." He stopped and lowered his eyes: "She's about to die," he said. "My sweetheart is about to die and is surrounded by fears. All I want is to rid her of her fears. Death is nothing to be afraid of. But it is not only she who will be lonely; I will be too..."

He couldn't bring himself to complete his sentence. He fixed those madly sparkling, big blue eyes of his on the train windows. I also stared out of the window, whether I liked it or not, and started watching the people at the station. Ahhh, but what was that?

Six people in strange outfits had surrounded an unbelievably beautiful dark young man, whose long black hair reached his shoulders. The young man was wearing a white robe which touched the ground and on his feet were roman sandals. His eyes, which heralded the existence of other worlds, were dreamy, dazzling. In his hand he gently waved a peacock feather. I looked more carefully; it wasn't a peacock feather after all, I had only assumed it was. In his hand was an old book with a black cover. I felt I couldn't breathe, and my heart pounded wildly.

"The Prince of Manchuria," said the gentleman dwarf. "The Prince of Manchuria—according to some—the New Messiah."

"The Prince of Manchuria!" I exclaimed.

The Prince and his entourage entered the compartment just next to ours.

"Manchuria is a very poor country," said the gentleman dwarf. "He's a prince, but when the British discovered him he was covered with dirt playing marbles in a muddy street with his friends. The moment the British saw him they said: 'Here is what we have been looking for; here is the Messiah.' It's obvious that they were impressed by his beauty, his extraordinary beauty. In haste they kidnapped the child from Manchuria. It's presumed that the Prince's mother was an alcoholic Irishwoman. She was an anthropologist, living in Manchuria for many years. She died while giving birth to the Prince. Also, she had six toes on her right foot. Unfathomable details! I report them to you as they were told to me. The British held him in absolute isolation so that no worldly events could sully his spiritual world. As you can tell from his expression, the New Messiah or the Prince of Manchuria doesn't like people; indeed, he is incapable of love. If one can recall how hard it was 2000 years ago for Jesus Christ to love mankind, one has to admit that he's right. Moreover, the British fastidiously protect his person, which becomes thoroughly exhausted from his spiritual journeys. That's all I know. I presume that no one knows any more than this."

While the gentleman dwarf was relating the story to me, Isabelle woke up. She started drawing circles in the air with her index finger. As she had taken off her kalpak while sleeping, I was able to see her head easily now. On Isabelle's forehead were deep scars, and in one of her ears there was a butterfly-shaped earring made of diamonds.

The dwarf burst into one of his beautiful laughs. "Dear Isabelle," he said, his eyes shining with love, "you forget nothing, absolutely nothing."

Isabelle was smiling as she went on drawing circles in the air with her index finger.

"Isabelle is reminding me of another detail I forgot to mention to you," said the gentleman dwarf. "The British desired that the Prince of Manchuria or, according to some, the new Messiah, be given a classical education. He was tutored privately for three years by the most esteemed teachers in order to take the Oxford Proficiency Examination. The result was a complete fiasco. All through the examination he did nothing but draw pictures of snails on the papers. They weren't even good drawings; they barely exhibited the talent of a terrified five-year-old. When they told us this story Isabelle laughed so hard that she almost fell off her armchair."

Isabelle smiled sweetly. It was obvious that she was ill, very ill, and far removed from the days when she fell off armchairs from laughter.

"Isabelle's earring is eye-catching," I said. "So are your cuff-links and tie-pin. Believe me, to this day I have never seen such precious jewelry."

I had barely finished my sentence when I blushed from head to toe. The more I tried to avoid being tactless, the more tactless I became. All right, but isn't this the summary of life? Don't we always get caught by what we are running away from?

Isabelle and the gentleman shook with laughter. While wiping his wet, mirth-filled eyes with his purple silk handkerchief, the gentleman dwarf observed, "Oh, you are tactless! That's what makes you so charming, so entertaining. Some things slip from your tongue before they even cross your mind. You are charming, believe me, very charming."

The sound coming from Isabelle wasn't quite laughter, her laughter was more of a gasp. "Her lungs are rotten, too," I thought. But believe me, I held my tongue.

"All this precious jewelry is a must in my profession," said the dwarf. "The more precious jewels you have, the more others feel 'obliged' to give you precious gifts. Or shall we say feel 'compelled' rather than 'obliged.' They encourage, stimulate, and force one into competition. As money begets money, our dear traveling companion, jewelry invites jewelry. Besides, it's a good investment, takes up little space, is easy to carry, and can be cashed anywhere."

"Ah," I said again. This time my voice was rather hoarse. With all these precious gifts, what could this dwarf's, this gentleman dwarf's profession possibly be?

Right at that moment there was a polite knock on our compartment door.

"Come in," said the gentleman dwarf. "Please come in."

It was one of the weirdly attired Englishmen from the Prince of Manchuria's company who entered. He was a tall, beak-nosed, sandy-haired man. He smiled like frozen fat: that most renowned British smile—obligatory, inevitable, only arousing the feeling of "uff... why is he doing this?" In his hand was a basket of luscious figs. With his long arms he placed the basket next to me.

"From His Majesty the Messiah to your mother," he said in his Oxbridge accent, Oxbridge voice. "His Majesty the Messiah, hoping not to disturb you, expressed his desire to relate his wish: Your mother..."

Interrupting his sentence with all my nastiness; "Yes," I said, "my mother really likes figs. You may extend my deepest gratitude to His Majesty of Manchuria... uhhhh, the Messiah. On behalf of my mother of course."

The Briton, in order to steer the conversation to warmer waters, fixing his frozen eyes on Isabelle said: "Oh, what a cute monkey this is." He tried to reach out to pet Isabelle.

"Don't ever try to touch her please!" I screamed. "Don't touch Isabelle, Sir. Besides, let us not detain you any longer. Thank you for the figs and may you have a good day."

My voice sounded so sharp, so crazy that the Briton was utterly shocked. Making sounds like "aaaah, uuuh, oooh" and saluting each of us with his head, he departed.

The gentleman dwarf and Isabelle, barely glancing at each other, burst into laughter.

"You are terrific," said the gentleman dwarf. "You are one of those whose species has become extinct... Because courage doesn't reign anymore."

I inclined my head slightly. I liked Isabelle and the gentleman dwarf, and I liked being liked by them.

"It has been months since Isabelle has laughed this much," said the gentleman dwarf. I am so thankful to you."

He took Isabelle's hand. Isabelle shook her head sweetly, as if to say: Yes, darling, you are so right.

Isabelle and the dwarf loved each other. There was no doubt about it: They loved directly and grandly! How cute, how cute, I thought. It had been months, years, since I had seen two persons or two things or one person and one thing—whatever—in love.

"Your mother must be an important person," said the gentleman dwarf. "It is no small thing to attract the attention of the Prince of Manchuria, the New Messiah according to some. The poor kid is engulfed in such immense loneliness, his life is so miserable that he views the world from behind a heavy curtain of selfishness. In the lines of a favorite poem of mine, 'If the universe burst into pieces one afternoon,' that young man would not even be aware of it."

"You never know from under which stone my mother will pop up," I said. "I wouldn't know whether she is important or not. We don't see each other that often. She lives in a house she inherited from my grandfather, with her servant Wang Yu. You might consider me a stranger in my hometown; all my life has been spent in boarding schools and on journeys."

"I see," the gentleman dwarf said. And believe me, when he said this phrase, which is usually used when people understand nothing, it was as if he really saw everything.

Isabelle felt warm. She took her astrakhan coat off. Around her neck she had on an exquisite necklace wrought in the shape of butterflies adorned with rubies, sapphires, diamonds and emeralds.

The gentleman of course noticed my saucepan eyes.

"Isabelle has a passion for butterflies. A lady admirer of mine who knows my passion for Isabelle had this made for her in Burma. The stones are quite good, the craftsmanship excellent. Isabelle likes to wear it from time to time—what more can I say?"

"You mean your lady admirers buy all this jewelry?" I said. At that moment I could have swapped voices even with a peacock.

"I work for money because of my profession," said the gentleman dwarf. "I live in a mansion with Isabelle, and though we rarely go out, our expenses are rather high. In short, my income only just suffices to cover our expenses. As I said before, I have to accept such presents, moreover, encourage them. We have a very poor background; you could also call this passion for jewelry the fear of going back to the past. The moment I cease to excel in my profession, I must be able to quit. When that moment comes I will be in need of this jewelry to live in comfort with Isabelle."

"Excuse me, but if you don't mind... I mean, if I don't ask I will burst. What's your profession?" I exploded.

"Ah, I thought you already knew," he said sending me one of his beautiful laughs. "I am a gigolo."

"But you... how come?" I screamed. Yes, I also performed this insolence.

"You mean because I'm a dwarf?" he said. "That's the key point."

While I was screaming, "Key point, your being a dwarf?" Isabelle was laughing uncontainably, looking at my surprise-smothered face.

"Yes," said the gentleman dwarf. "Forget about the psychological theories that claim women always seek their fathers. Women always seek their children to fall in love with, their unborn children. My being a dwarf is functional here. I am not their equal nor am I above them. Plus, I am not trapped in the ignorance of being spiritually inferior and being unaware of it like so many men are. I am full of flaws: from head to toe, very obviously and clearly! They can feel as much pity as they want towards me, they can shower me with all the passion that they suppress, they can make me the object of their desire. I am only myself, not like those men who drive them crazy with stupidity and heartlessness in their flawless bodies: I am certainly not like that. They know I do this for money, that I'll never love, wouldn't love, any of them. I wouldn't pretend to make a place in my heart for them: I wouldn't cheat them because I wouldn't cheat myself. They know that I only, and only I, love Isabelle; but I do my job perfectly. They accept me as I am. This is a great relief for them. Women either poison their lives by trying to change their lives for a man who does not accept them as they are, or by trying to change a man whom they can't accept as he is. As they feel the greatest love for those who cannot reciprocate—their children—they fall in love with me. When they are making love to me they feel the highest of all pleasures, the most inhibited and inevitable pleasure: the pleasure of incest. Very complicated and very simple. I have never tried to explain it before; I hope I've made myself clear."

Like a child who is bent from his waist over a well in which he has seen hundreds of unknown stars, I was shaking my head in wonder when a loud voice was heard outside the compartment.

A young man was screaming: "I want to talk, leave me alone, I want to meet them and talk to them."

Two or three other people were whispering things to calm him down, begging him to go back to his compartment. I recognized one of the voices. It was the Oxbridge voice of the tedious Briton who had brought the figs a while ago. Suddenly the conversation was cut short. The door of the neighboring compartment was aggressively slammed.

Indicating the neighboring compartment with his eyes, the gentleman dwarf said, "The Prince of Manchuria. He tried to meet and talk with us." He sighed deeply. "Ahh, poor young man! They don't even allow him to breathe and then they expect from him philosophies which will salvage the world... Believe me, nothing will come out of sterile circumstances: comfort, peace and isolation. If something were going to come out of these, our world's greatest thinker would probably have been Rudolf Hess."

"You're so right!" I shouted. "Either he or Howard Hughes."

"The New Messiah wrote an incredibly good book when he was twelve years old. However, seven years have now passed without his writing a single line. What could one feel with men who are like funeral attendants? What could one feel, what could one write? Whatever I learned about life, I learned in the circus in which I was born. Everything beyond that, I've learned from Isabelle's love."

He turned and looked lovingly at Isabelle. Isabelle shyly nodded her head.

"Were you born in a circus?" I asked.

"Yes," he said. "I am the son of a dwarf clown and the world's most beautiful woman acrobat. I have something in common with the Prince of Manchuria: My mother also died giving birth to me. Imagine how insufferable it would have been for such a beautiful woman to be the mother of a dwarf like me. When I was a child I tried to be glad about my mother's death by thinking of this. My father was so in love with my mother that he couldn't even bear to see my face. Abandoning me to the circus in which I was born, he joined another. After three or four years he died by falling from a trapeze: one of those deaths which is a mixture of accident and suicide. It could be said that the circus cook brought me up. She was a very fat and lonely lady. She loved me madly. Isabelle was the baby of the most renowned monkey in the circus. She was very feeble, and guess what happened?"

"Her mother died giving birth to her," I said mischievously.

"Yes, that's exactly what happened," said the gentleman dwarf. "Monkeys are like human beings; they need a mother's care. The other monkeys didn't look after Isabelle. She was a teeny-weeny thing. She was so sweet, so pretty... I looked after her. I gave her her name, I taught her everything she knows, and Isabelle has made me happy."

He turned and gazed at Isabelle for a long time. Isabelle was again under her mink coverlet, sleeping and sighing deeply.

"I have tired you," he said, with heart-winning politeness. "Look, you've become sleepy."

"Oh no," I said. "Never! It is such a pleasure to listen to you."

Our compartment was warm. Beyond our window was the night and trees. I fell asleep.

When I woke up the train was about to enter my hometown station. The gentleman dwarf and Isabelle were gone. Feeling almost melancholic—without even saying goodbye, I was thinking—I noticed the envelope on the basket of figs. On the envelope, in incredibly beautiful handwriting, my name was written. I opened and started reading the letter which was inscribed on exceedingly fine, beige-colored parchment.

"Our Dear Dear Traveling Companion,
You made me and Isabelle so happy... When Isabelle woke up she was a different person; your liveliness, your youth and your courage towards life have made her a totally new person. She does not want to see the doctor in your hometown anymore, or any other doctor for that matter. Her desire is to pass her last days in peace and happiness in our home. We are glad to have met a person like you. I hope you will accept a small remembrance. Perhaps we shall inspire you to sell it and set off on journeys. What do you think?"

His signature was eye-catching, displayed a special character and was absolutely illegible. In the envelope was his diamond tie-pin the size of my thumbnail. I placed it in the palm of my hand and looked. In it I could see India, Nepal, Sri Lanka, and Burma. Nothing else happened on the journey.

Translated by Alin İnce
"Cesaret Kol Gezmiyor," *Haberci Çocuk Cinayetleri* (1991).
Istanbul: Afa Yayınları, pp. 7-19.

NALAN BARBAROSOĞLU

The Daisies of My Spring Morning

The coolness of dew covers my body... The scent of the countryside wafts from somewhere... When I open my eyes, nestled in my sleep-warmed right hand on the pillow beside me, I find a bunch of daisies. I wonder whether I'm dreaming. I move my fingers; it's not a dream, I can feel the freshness of the daisy stems. I sit up in bed with the bouquet in my hand. It's my own bed, the bedroom is my own... On the bedside table is the ashtray with the stub of my half-smoked bed-time cigarette from the night before and the book titled *Midnight Crime* that will finish in one or two pages; there's the wardrobe, the chair with the clothes I took off... Nothing's out of place; everything is familiar, even the morning voices coming in with the daylight from the street through the open window. I stare at the daisies again and try to recall whether I could have drunk enough to fall asleep with a bunch of daisies in my hand. No, I couldn't have. After coming back from my grandmother's, I'd only had one or two glasses of cherry juice laced with vodka while watching the film on TV, but still I can't quite remember everything I did before I went to bed. As I get up now, I feel even more confused. The entire floor is covered with daisies; they look so sad on the polished wood... Trying not to step on them, I make my way out of the bedroom, but it is the same story in the hallway... This is a bit agitating; I glance into the other room and the living room; there are daisies sprinkled all over the place, even in the bathroom and the kitchen... With my fingers I check the balcony door... It's locked. Thank God there is nothing on the balcony floor. "The balcony must have been forgotten," I think. The apartment door doesn't look as if it has been forced open. I just can't say for sure whether I fastened the chain last night, but it isn't fastened now. The door opens quite normally... Daisies—as if they had always been there—lie sprinkled on every step of the staircase. I don't even dare guess what my neighbors coming downstairs will think about the daisies leading away from my door. Because *I* don't have a clue... I rush in; grabbing the broom from the balcony, I worriedly start sweeping the stairs before the janitor, Tahsin Efendi, starts his morning rounds. The two flights of stairs leading to the front door of the building are full of daisies... They form a huge heap in front of the doormat. Beyond the mat they descend the five steps in a single line and continue to the garden gate, again, in a single line... I wonder again whether or not I'm in a dream. The anxiety of the situation is too much even for a dream. When I can't sweep up the daisies, I realize that they are stuck to the marble and the concrete with thin strips of tape; like it or not, I fear that there is someone or perhaps several people trying to blow my mind... And pulling the tape off piece by piece, I throw the daisies I've pulled off onto the heap. Prodded by the devil, I open the garden gate and glance into the street. I freeze... Taking a sharp left, the line of daisies continues to the main street... Remembering Tahsin Efendi, I rush up to fetch a trash bag; using my hands like a ladle, I stuff the pile of daisies into the bag. I throw the bag into the trash. I know that I am being unfair to the lovely daisies but I have no other choice. I'll bet the ones in the house are a good four or five times this many. Brooding, I climb the stairs; I have finished with the building, I won't bother with the apartment, but how about the street? I can't believe I'm experiencing such a morning. I go to the kitchen and prepare myself a cup of strong black coffee. The daisies underfoot get crushed. Who *is it* that has done this or who *are they*? Who will take the responsibility for turning my morning into a daisy-mare? Wishing to forget about this morning, I lean against the kitchen counter and take a huge swig of coffee. I close my eyes as I swallow. This is my last chance. When I open my eyes, the daisies will either disappear—nothing more than a figment of my imagination—or take their place in my life with their beauty as a nightmare—a reality. At the warmth of the steam rising from my cup and warming my face, I shiver. I realize that I haven't put anything on over my nightgown since I got out of bed. I open my eyes. The daisies are still in front of me. I am playing a game without rules. There is no other explanation. Whoever has done this obviously entered the house without force, just walked in. In fact, one of the keys to my house is with my mother, one with Mrs. Nurten and one with the boyfriend I broke up with seven months ago... And we broke up with such a ruckus that about the only thing we didn't do was to tear each other's hair out. There is no doubt that when he found my keys in his pocket he threw them into the toilet and flushed them down. Since neither my mother nor the neighbor Mrs. Nurten, who comes in to water the flowers and take care of the canaries when I am away, is the Queen of Daisies... The bell rings. I place the empty cup on the table and walk to the door. "Thanks, Tahsin Efendi... but I don't need anything this morning," I call out without opening the door. I hear his footsteps proceeding up the stairs. The question whether he will recognize the daisies when he walks out to the street passes through my mind, which I cannot seem to organize... I have no choice but to follow the line of daisies in the street. Taking in stride the risk of being late to work, I quickly put on my clothes and fly out into the street. I start walking alongside the daisies. There is no time to pick them up from the ground, and furthermore, I hardly want to make a weird impression on the people hurrying to school or work. I follow the daisies, some of which have been crushed, not knowing where I am going or what I am going to find there. I feel like Hansel and Gretel. As they tried to find their way home, they first followed breadcrumbs and then shining pebbles. In contrast, however, I could be at the beginning of a journey with an uncertain end. I've started to talk nonsense. I should stop pitying myself. The street has come to an end. I turn left, following the daisies. I walk along the avenue against the increasing stream of people. I look at the faces of the pedestrians and drivers passing by. Do they realize in what a funny situation I am, I wonder… What about the person who has done this to me? What was the point in scattering the daisies through every corner of the house—except the balcony—arranging them down the stairs of the building and out to the gate, even sticking them onto the road? Did it occur to him how passive—how helpless—I would feel? What conclusion should I draw from this many daisies? Or is it just a sadist that I am dealing with, one with rich fantasies who has chosen to sacrifice me to one of them? Did I say a sadist? Thank God, the avenue is at an end. I now enter the park, and advance along a path. No sooner do I wind past a huge round pine—whatever its name is—the kind I've only come across in such parks, than I stop stock still as if I've run smack into a wall. There's someone sitting on a bench; the daisies lead right up to his feet. His newspaper is wide-open in front of him; I can't tell who it is. I am ready to burst with impatience. I take a deep breath, walk over very calmly and sit next to him. He turns and looks. "Good morning," I say. "Good morning," he says without paying much attention… Behind a pair of thick glasses, his eyes are a deep bright blue… His hair is graying. He seems to have an honest face. (Whatever that means…) I place my elbows on the back of the bench and lean my head way back. The sun is dazzling… In fact, if this were a normal morning, I would enjoy bathing in this morning sun which has just begun to warm up… I must find a way to communicate with this middle-aged gentleman. But how? Unable to think of anything original, "It looks like the weather will be nice today," I comment. He raises his eyes from the newspaper, first looks at me and then at the sky. "It will rain before evening," he says. "I wouldn't know, I haven't heard a weather report," I say. "Me neither," he says, starting to read again. "Then why did you say it would rain?" I insist. "Look," he says motioning toward the sky with a movement of his head… I look in that direction and see clouds stretching out like a net curtain. "I learned this from a fisherman when I was still a child. Those clouds are called 'storks' wings.' No matter how sunny it is, if stork clouds spread thin wings like this, it'll rain that day, or that night at the latest…" The attention in his glances toward the sky diverts me away from my own reality… "I've never heard any such thing," I say. The doubt that vibrates in my voice, if only for a moment, scares me. I wouldn't want to offend this man getting on in age. "You are right," he says, folding his paper, "today's been really nice to me so far. I come here every morning, unless it's cold and rainy, of course... There is not a single bench in this park that I haven't sat on to read my newspaper. When I arrived here this morning, I found a bouquet of daisies and an envelope on this bench..." "And what did you do?" I ask rather excitedly. "What should I do, I was surprised," he says. "Yes, I meant with the envelope," I say, advising myself to calm down. "Nothing, this is it," he says and takes the daisy bouquet and the envelope out of the bag next to him. "Is there anything in it, did you have a look?" I ask. He smiles. "Yes, I couldn't resist my curiosity and I looked. Wouldn't you? It's good that I did. It's been ages since I've seen such a thing." "What was in it?" I ask curiously. "A note," he says. "May I see it?" I say. "Of course," he says, "it doesn't have any name on it, so I take it it's anonymous." He carefully slips a sheet of notepaper from the envelope, and hands it to me. "To make up for the daisies I haven't been able to give you for the last three years..." it says. I know the handwriting well. The squarish lettering reflects his self-confident personality. The handwriting that I used to say came from hands with the delicacy of a calligrapher, confronts me once again... How many years has it been? I don't even want to think about it. The handwriting of a man who had kept me evenings by the window and days by the telephone... Every time I cleared the untouched food—cold by then—from the table and threw the salads into the trash, "I'll never again set the table before he arrives!" I'd promise myself... The handwriting of a companion who might arrive at any time during the sleepless nights I spent getting infuriated at myself and who would then fall asleep unbelievably fast, without even seeing me... "Excuse me, I didn't catch that," I say, "did you say something?" "I was saying that I think there aren't many thoughtful people anymore. What a nice gesture, isn't it? But whoever this person gave it to, has left it here." "Yes," I say, "a very nice gesture... Well, I must get to work." I hand the note back to the gentleman I've just met and rise to my feet, "Have a nice day." "You too, young lady, have a nice day... I'm going to keep this note—and the daisies, too," he says. I'm sure he will. For a moment I wonder if I shouldn't tell him everything. But I'm very late for work. Besides, right now, I don't really know what the note and the daisies mean to me. I'm on my way to work.

Translated by Seda Tahan and Jean Carpenter Efe
"İlkyaz Sabahımın Papatyaları," *Ne Kadar da Güzeldir Gitmek* (1996).
Istanbul: Oğlak Yayınları, pp. 63-69.

NALAN BARBAROSOĞLU

Teller of Tales

—No, I was not there.

—*They say they saw you.*

—They told me about it, and I felt as if I'd been there. Those who were there are no longer here.

—*Always the same story.*

—They're gone. One of them was a man. Gray skies always would bother his eyes; at night he used to create daylight indoors. "I cannot stand the grimness anymore," he exclaimed one day and emigrated to a sunny climate.

—*Goodness, she's starting again.*

—They'd told him the days were sunny and always longer than the nights there; that's what he said. He was off without a backward glance.

—*Who was off? Who did you say?*

—His name was Ali. His departure and absence begot a new existence inside his mother. It was as if he'd been born again.

—*So?*

—The other was a woman; she used to construct very long sentences; adjectives and particles would dance between the subjects and the verbs; by the time she'd start to say, "I really don't want to talk any longer," she had indeed already swallowed up the borders of communication.

—*Shall I open the window?*

—She went flying off by balloon to a community with people whose language she didn't speak and would never be able to learn.

—*I say, we really ought to get some okra from the market; they say there's a good price now. Are you listening to me?*

—She chose the loneliness of unread books over a crowd of magazines. And we've never heard from her again.
—*Have you called the bottled-gas man?*
—Her name was Selin. Those who went to her place told me she hadn't taken a single thing with her.
—*Hello-oo! I'd like a bottle of gas delivered to Violet Street, Number 7...*
—Still another was neither a man nor a woman; it had been many years since he'd freed himself of sex; he told his story one night steeped in alcohol—stretching into the morning... With his mind overflowing, where he went no one knows.
—*She's started again... She'll probably go on and on now...*
—His name was Cemil. After he left, we realized that we hadn't even known where he lived. He became a past dream never to be forgotten; as misty and pastel as a pastoral film.
—*Have you tried the new carpet shampoo that's out? Once you try it—just try it—listen to me, try it... That red stain will be out in a whiz, believe me.*
—I'm the only one left here as the witness of witnesses. I can't escape from myself.
—*So, I'd better get up and go now. What else can I do? I'll go then.*
—That's the way it is... I'm left all by myself.
—*No, no. I'd better go then; I can't stand her today. She stares straight ahead as if there's someone opposite her. You'd sometimes think there's really someone here. I swear!*

That evening, the evening of a sunny day, the first one to come to my house had been Selin, with her nails filed straight and in a long skirt. With a silk scarf made of the same material, she looked chic and glamorous. Her long, slender face was pale and her glance was distant. (Selin, Ali, Cemil and I used to meet at my place every Friday except when we weren't off traveling; to the accompaniment of chat, tidbits and tea we'd listen to the music that we'd brought back from our trips but had never had time to listen to during the day and on weekends. Then we wouldn't sleep and sat up till dawn in our own houses with fresh melodies in our ears.) Ali and Cemil had come together. They entered the room with faces at least as pale as Selin's. On that stagnant evening when nobody felt like talking I'd gotten out the tumblers and fixed hors-d'oevres as nobody wanted to drink tea. After a while, as the water one could see from the window gradually darkened, it was Cemil who started to speak:
—Actually there's not much to tell.
—All three of us were there. It was just one of those hospital rooms, you know. Seated on the long couch we were telling Hande what had happened that day. It was not clear to what extent she was listening to us or whether or not she was interested in what we were saying. Murat came in. There was a bouquet of wildflowers in his hand. As soon as Hande caught sight of him, she leaped from her bed, grasped his hair and began pulling at it; meanwhile she was shouting at the top of her lungs, but whatever

she was saying was incomprehensible. Even today I can't possibly imagine where she'd found so much strength. The broken mouth of the serum bottle was dangling from her arm; the bandages on her wrists were soon soaked in blood. We were in a state of shock. While I was trying to separate them someone—I think Selin—was constantly ringing the nurse's bell. Murat stood there passive, not even trying to protect himself. His face was covered with pollen. Hande's face, which kept changing hue, had gone yellowish green by the time she was forced to lie on her bed. I think one of the nurses must have given her a tranquilizer at that point. Ali had taken Murat, who looked an absolute wreck, out of the room. The doctor later pronounced it "toxin poisoning"; they'd been too late in giving her a blood transfusion. "We were too late to save a life..."

Cemil paused. He took a huge gulp of his drink. His face flushed red. He looked at Ali as if to say, "You tell us."

Ali, doubled over on the couch with his elbows on his knees, was rolling his rakı glass between his palms and staring down at his socks. The eyelashes shading his eyes behind his glasses formed a stark black line. As Cemil was silent for too long, Ali raised his head and looked at Cemil. When their eyes met, he swallowed hard. "I was thinking that suicide is the worst punishment there is," he said. "It's punishing everyone who knows you. It punishes a whole lifetime. It sentences us to lifelong pangs of conscience without giving us any right of defense. In this context it is sadism par excellence."

Selin intervened, "Don't be silly! Hande had no strength—neither to judge nor to punish nor to do anything else. Which one of us has ever heard of criticism coming from her mouth? She lived in her own world; she was so introverted that even when she saw two strangers quarrelling, she'd blame herself. She'd feel responsible for whatever circumstances had caused the quarrel. Should a war break out even in the farthest corner of the world, donning mourning—offended with both the world and herself— Hande would be cringing, feeling guilty that she could not be there to help those suffering. Neither the circumstances that kept her here nor matters of common sense could help the guilty feeling within her. If she did commit suicide and if suicide is a kind of punishment, she must have done it only to punish herself. Certainly she had no dispute with anyone else."

—What about the things that happened between Murat and her?

It was Cemil who asked that.

—I suspect she thought Murat didn't understand her, replied Selin.

—She didn't think I ever understood her, either. She used to get angry with me for being a peacemaker. She used to claim that I had no principles—that I was inconsistent... That I'd change with each situation. She was always ashamed of having a sister like me.

I was the one who said that.

—Don't exaggerate, Selin continued. If you ask me, she'd solved the problem with you on her own; she was just trying to get used to you; she'd been looking for ways of accepting you as you are. But you know she had no time."

—Yes, I said and went on.

—She always lived a busy life... Time for me seemed to be endless... When Murat chose Hande instead of me, my days and nights came to a standstill; for a long time they were endless as far as that's concerned, but...

—Oh come on, said Cemil,

—You're doing an injustice both to Hande and yourself. I know you're angry and it is not easy to put up with this or to get used to it, but... I think you should be a bit calmer."

—She left me. When I saw her stretched out in the middle of the carpet, a pool of blood flowing from her wrists, I understood that she wanted to leave me once and for all, I said.

—Hande didn't desert just you; she left everything, everyone, Ali said.

He seemed sad. It was as if he were in a sweat. He pushed his glasses back into position on his nose. He seemed distressed, wretched. Perhaps he'd fallen in love with Hande as well. But he hadn't run after her as Murat had. He did not say this but I could understand it from his posture. But Hande might not have understood it. She's so far from the others, distant from those outside herself. I mean she used to be.

—You all loved her so much, or am I wrong? I asked.

Selin looked at me, squinting her eyes, bloodshot from the wine.

—Didn't you love her? she asked me.

—She disregarded it, but I loved her very much. And she always pushed me aside; she didn't love me; she looked down on me. She never used to love anyone. She thought she liked others, but she never did.

—I think she only liked their child-like faces. She tried to console each of them like a love-lorn child. But she couldn't.

These were Cemil's words.

—What could any of us be consoled by! exclaimed Ali.

—This is our life. Whether we're consoled or not, Selin said.

—Hande took everything I wanted and then left. She's left me all alone in these rooms. Nobody hears my voice. Nobody sees my face. Most of the time I don't even see my face in the mirror, I said.

Everybody sipped their drinks; I refilled the glasses. In broken, incomplete sentences we tried to speak. It didn't work; we couldn't. After a while we stopped talking and drinking as well. That was the last evening we spent together. We wrapped up all our memories, opinions, heart-aches, loves and hopes in a bundle and put them away. I don't know about the others, but I can't help sometimes taking that bundle out of the trunk and rummaging through it to examine what's inside. Each time the contents look different but they're all still there. This is my story. A short story told in the blink of an eye. I've told you now, as well.

—Hasn't she shut up yet?
—I used to have a sister. Her name was Hande. She stopped speaking to me. She didn't want to see me, even. We stopped seeing one another.
—I spent hours looking for okra but it was all sold. Hard to believe it!
—And she left. The way she went she took my past as well.
—Please pardon her. She always goes on this way... Never mind. Hande also says, "Don't do that, Dear Sis, shame on you." But she doesn't listen to her... She won't listen to anybody. Shall we change her medication again, what do you say?

Translated by Fatma İdin and Jean Carpenter Efe
"Anlatıcı," *Her Ses Bir Ezgi* (2001).
Istanbul: Can Yayınları, pp. 18-25.

HAKAN ŞENOCAK

Ci Ci

His father never asked Ci Ci whether he wanted to go to school. There wasn't any need. Theirs was a family destined to poverty, and since they had no other option, they had to choose silence. While silence may often create emotional images, for Ci Ci and family it meant a ramshackle shanty, endless illnesses with moans and groans and periods of unemployment with tears and tattered hopes. There wasn't any need; his father never asked Ci Ci if he wanted to go to school.

It was a spring day. Time was ebbing towards evening. Returning from work, the man would want to see his wife and son at home. It never failed; they were always home.

He went in, exhausted. Mother was prepared for the ritual. "Welcome home," she said. Ci Ci was in his place beside his mother. "Welcome home, Daddy," he said in a voice slightly ridiculous and rather novice. "Daddy, dear," he should have said; he knew that. Father would never reply. He glanced out of the corner of his eye to make sure that everything was exactly as he'd left it. He put one foot forward. Mother knelt down, untied the laces, took off the shoe and put a house-shoe onto her husband's foot. She repeated the same procedure with the other foot.

Father's imposing stature filled the house. Taking a few slow steps, he slouched onto the couch and revealed the fatigue of the day with a deep sigh. The atmosphere in the room became heavy. Mother's shoulders drooped slightly.

They had their meal and Mother cleared the table. Father sat on the couch and lit a cigarette. Mother stood waiting. Soon Father would say, "Sit down." Ci Ci was tumbling with Boncuk on the carpet. Father was watching, lost in thought. He took a long puff on his cigarette and commanded his wife "Sit down."

Everything unfolded as usual. Ci Ci continued the game he'd started with his cat, but all of a sudden he felt uneasy, lifted his head and looked up. Father and Mother were both looking at him. Under these two pairs of eyes, Ci Ci felt embarrassed and stood up, not sure what to do. With questioning eyes, he looked at his mother and father. Then frightened by his father's glance, he collapsed next to the docile Boncuk who always followed him about. He'd tried this before. This way his fear would subside. He pulled angrily on the cat's tail. Boncuk shrieked in pain, and Ci Ci laughed in joy. Soon, however, he could no longer bear his father's glances on his back, and let go of Boncuk's tail. He stood up, looked at his father and again fell to the floor to pull the animal's tail.

Nothing was ever discussed in this house because Ci Ci's father was a very clever father, and he would make all the decisions. Therefore, a peaceful and trustful atmosphere always prevailed in the home. Although sometimes this atmosphere of peace and trust was interrupted, this was only temporary. For example, a few days ago Mother had dared to create a problem by suggesting that Ci Ci himself should be asked about his schooling. However, Father, who as the real intelligence would have axed right there on the spot anyone who tried to axe the future he had in mind for his dear little lamb, his dear son, didn't do anything to his wife because there was really no need to.

Father took out his prayer beads and started passing them between his fingers, click-click-click. He made a small sign to his wife. The woman ran into the kitchen. Her husband wanted hot water for his feet. She knew every one of his signs. Actually, all these signs meant, "Do what you're supposed to do. It's time." Everything was repeated every day, and everything had a sequence that had gradually become set. The water was already boiling on the stove. The woman took it off, poured it into a bowl and brought it in. From where he was sitting, the man raised one foot. The woman first took off the slipper and then the sock. She did the same for the other foot. The man put his feet in the hot water. The water was hotter than usual, and it burned his feet. He hit his wife on the head with the prayer beads.

"The water's hot! Hot!" he grumbled.

The woman immediately rushed inside, brought some cold water and poured it in. She glanced up at her husband with questioning eyes. The man nodded. He was now pleased with the water. Again he went on with his beads. The woman washed and washed her husband's dirty feet. The warm water relaxed the man. A little later when his wife asked, "Shall I bring some more hot water?" he awoke from a daze.

"That's enough," he said briefly.

With the towel she'd brought along, the woman dried the man's feet well, slipped his house-shoes back on over clean socks, and took the bowl away. When she returned, she collapsed in fatigue onto one of the chairs.

"I've thought it over," said the man in a calm voice.

The woman and Ci Ci looked at him. The man never looked at his wife or son while speaking. This showed his superiority. Tormented, his wife and son were forced to gaze at him while he spoke.

"The boy is going to become an apprentice!" he said in short.

Neither his flesh nor his bones were yet his. Father held a dominion over the household that was like a heavy bloody ax. After all, he was the one who worked from morning till evening to look after the family. Father's general attitude towards Ci Ci might be summarized as follows:

"Your flesh is mine. Your bones are, too, because I am your father!"

One chirruping spring morning Ci Ci woke up early. He was filled with joy. He jumped hopping and skipping out of his bed, wanting to clamber into the grand trees all in blossom. In excitement he threw on his clothes and rushed down to breakfast at his mother's call. Boncuk ran at his heels.

A smell of toast filled the kitchen. Mother was sitting on a stool, waiting.

"Good morning, Son," said Mother.

Ci Ci laughed with the joy of a pupil just released from class.

"Good morning, Mummy dear," he said, jumping into her lap.

They were suddenly quiet.

Then Mother asked, "Are you starting work today, Son?"

Ci Ci giggled.

"Yes..."

"Well, do you know what an apprentice is?"

Ci Ci laughed just like Father.

"I'm going to become an apprentice. I'll be hanging lambs on hooks."

The woman swallowed with difficulty, but didn't say a word.

Ci Ci, however, wanted to play.

"Didn't Father go to work today?"

"No, he didn't."

"Won't they fire him?"

"No, they won't."

"Why not? Won't the master get angry?"

"Your father doesn't have a master."

"He doesn't have a master?"

"No."

"Why doesn't he? Everyone does."

"Your father doesn't."

Ci Ci chirruped cunningly.

"Because my father is his own master!" he gloated.

Mother replied, laughing, "Yes, Son."

"What's my father's job?"

"What is it?"

"Papers and raaaaaags!" imitated Ci Ci.

Mother looked surprised. "Good for you! How perfectly you imitate him!"

"Papers and raaaaaags!"

They were silent.

The man awoke with a wide yawn. He cleared his throat. He walked to the open window and spat outside.

"Your father's up," said Mother.

Ci Ci anxiously waited to hear those well-familiar footsteps.

"Yes, he's up!" he screamed.

"Son," said the woman and didn't speak again.

Father came down and ate breakfast. Mother knelt in front of Ci Ci and first put on his socks and then his shoes. Ci Ci looked up at Mother with pride.

"Okay, now let's go," said Father to Ci Ci.

Ci Ci hugged Boncuk tightly and yanked at his cat's tail. He laughed. Mother knelt, kissed Ci Ci, inhaled deeply, and kissed him again.

They went out. The woman watched from the window. She slowly closed her eyes.

While walking up the road, Ci Ci enjoyed himself, trying to pace himself at two steps to each of Father's one. Then they'd arrived. Father took him into the butcher's shop. The Master was there. Father and the Master shook hands. They greeted one another politely. Then the Master looked at Ci Ci.

"So this is our new apprentice, huh?" he said.

Father nodded, bobbing his head up and down, up and down. He laughed, and the Master laughed as well. Ci Ci laughed, too. Father and the Master laughed once more. Father shook the Master's hand up and down, up and down, "His flesh is yours." The Master took his cue and promised, "All right, and his bones are yours." Ci Ci laughed again.

"This is your Master," Father warned Ci Ci. "You'd better do what he tells you."

Ci Ci looked at the Master. "Yes, Daddy," he said, "I will do as I'm told, I promise."

"Good boy!" said Father delightedly and stroked Ci Ci's slender young neck.

After a while, once Father had gone, the Master took Ci Ci's little hand in his palm and led him into the cold room. There he showed him the sharp hooks ready for the little white lambs.

"This is where you hang the animals," he said.

"Little white lambs," Ci Ci corrected him.

The Master laughed.

"You're right. Little white lambs."

Then he took Ci Ci, raised him into the air with one hand and suspended him by his slender young neck on one hook ready for a little white lamb.

Translated by Eda Taşkınarda and Jean Carpenter Efe
"Ci Ci," *Karanfilsiz* (2001).
Istanbul: Can Yayınları, pp. 11-19.

SUZAN SAMANCI

Click-Click

The end of the month. I can't take a taxi. Walking in this viscous darkness, I feel the coldness of death on the nape of my neck. Turning, I glance behind me—and at those passing by. There's someone following me, I'm sure. A hand will touch my shoulder. A small chapped hand will cock the trigger: click-click.

Taking the minibus is no good either. Yesterday, from a back seat they squeezed the trigger right in the back of the doctor's neck.

They're waiting at a corner, maybe in the side-streets. Couldn't that man in dark glasses and trainers in front of the tobacconist's be one of them? How he defies his surroundings! He's hiding a dirty face behind those dark glasses, that's for sure. Quickening my steps, I cross the street. Again I've splashed mud on my trousers. There's not a spot to be seen on the man walking in front of me! He's walking at a good pace too, glancing left and right. Should I take a different route? My heart skips a beat at each corner; my face flushes. The chestnut seller there keeps fanning his coals, calm as a cucumber. As for the women sashaying by, wafting of perfume—without any fear…

Born into martial law… to die under it, I envy those who live in other cities. The horses pissing in the street make the damp air heavier. Water falls in droplets from the rustling trees. I quiver in fear. Maybe there's somebody hidden behind that tree. Or somebody about to step out of that black automobile pulling up and open fire. I spy the young poet. On foot he's exchanging a few words. He greets me in passing, a crooked smile masking his fear. People no longer care for either books or poetry. The day he was promoting his second volume one simpleton actually asked, "Do you make good money?"

Military vehicles: long-barreled guns protruding from civilian autos.

I hear short panting breaths. Then: click-click. If only I could whirl about and attack, wresting the gun from his hands and pressing it against his temple. My legs are numb. To overcome my fear, I light a cigarette. There! I'm not hearing things. "Click-click." Suddenly I turn; I'm face-to-face with an old man and his cane. He stretches out one wrinkled hand. "Alms for the poor, Sonny," he murmurs. Quite automatically, I press some change into his palm. With a hiss, my cigarette falls into a small lake at the edge of the curb.

In the pulsing bustle of the evening rush people jostle against one another non-stop. Beyond the Dörtayaklı Minaret begin the narrow shadowy streets. If I could just find someone to walk with… Deep inside I shudder at the rasp of the gratings descending this early to close up the shops. I wander into the courtyard of the mosque. Poor folk are murmuring, accompanied by the trickling streams of water they use for their ablutions. Under the dim lights white skullcaps come and go. Glancing at me, a bull-necked agha pulls his jacket onto his knees. He's obviously been relieved more than once of the change in his pockets. Without wasting any time I begin ablutions. From the corner of my eye I watch the man beside me. I try my best to do what he's doing. Not a single acquaintance in sight! I leave the mosque. A strong wind blows up; I'm shivering to the marrow. The narrow streets are nearly deserted. Ahead of me there's someone waiting. I pause. I pretend to tie the laces on one of my shoes. The tip of the man's cigarette glows in the dark. "Click-click" sounds multiply inside me. I cough and cough. Burying my hands in my pockets and my head in my coat, I walk on. Seeing me, the man waiting takes two or three steps backward. Just then a box of matches falls from above. I relax. A happy relief floods over me. Looking back, I see the man pick up the box, wave to a shadow that flashes in a window, and walk on.

From aged houses waft the smells of impoverished dishes. Threadbare laundry flutters in a courtyard. With *"Cenderme hat!"* mothers try to hush their crying children… Now wouldn't there be someone hiding behind the post at the corner! I wasn't seeing things; there's a shadow there. A cat leaps out in front of me. My stomach lurches into my throat. The power goes out. I want to mutter a curse, but my throat's too parched. As I spy a light in Hacı Yakup's shop, I breathe a sigh of relief. There sat Hacı Yakup, bent over his notebook, settling accounts for the day. The shop was helter-skelter as always, tainted with the aroma of sundry wares. He glanced overtop his spectacles at my arrival and rubbed his chin. "So it's you," he announced with a smile. The sputtering candle scattered wax upon his scales. I asked for a lollipop and gum.

"I come out short—it doesn't balance," he bemoaned.

"You'll settle it in the morning light," I assured him.

Accompanied by the racket of planes and helicopters, I reached home. I grabbed at the knocker and rapped a firm click-click. My heart was pounding. The iron door creaked open slowly on its iron hinges. In the candlelight my wife smiled a sweet welcome. I ducked quickly inside and locked the door behind me.

The room was in twilight. It was warm. Behind the smoldering embers of the stove my daughter slumbered. I placed the gum and the lollipop just beside her. "You're late," my wife commented.

"I walked; didn't do too badly considering that," I replied. I straightened the curtains and slumped down. My wife calmly came in and out of the room. I pulled the linoleum roll out from under the divan and spread it on the floor in front of the stove. Steam from the potatoes now fills the room; it seems that the only taste in my mouth is that of metal cartridges.

"Too salty?" asks my wife.

"I have a toothache," I say.

Pursing her lips without much expression, "Take an aspirin," she murmurs, and then goes on eating with appetite. Taking a seat in the candlelight and picking up her knitting, she continues, "They shot Nergis' son today on his way to school." Her voice echoes in my ears and spreads out over my temples. Everywhere I hear "click-click" and shiver.

When my wife roused me, I stumbled into the bedroom. She helped me undress and then curled up herself in bed with her back to me. I cannot sleep. Someone's wandering about in the paved court below. Mirza's dogs aren't barking for nothing! They'll force the door now! My breath comes irregularly, out of control. I gaze at my wife; under the glow of the night-lamp above, her cheeks are as rosy as a pomegranate seed. Her black hair spills over her glowing face, and within the flannel night gown her neck shines like satin. The vein down the side of her neck pulses evenly. I envy her this peaceful face, this deep sleep. I pull the blankets up over me. I cuddle up next to her, prodding her into a corner. Murmuring unintelligibly, she nestles into a fetal position, tucking her hands between her thighs. I look at the clock—it's a little past three. In the old days we'd be hearing the laughter and shouts of the drunkards. They've retreated into their chimney corners. I hear only the rumble of planes and helicopters deep inside...

On tiptoe I move to the window. I pull the curtains aside just enough to see out. A breeze wafts between the joints in the window-frames. In the silence of the night I gaze at the houses that have lined this narrow street since the Middle Ages, their every stone a treasure trove. Then I'm sure I want to trod upon the "click-clicks" building up inside me.

Translated by Aysel Yıldırım and Jean Carpenter Efe
"Tık Tık," *Kıraç Dağlar Kar Tuttu* (1996).
Istanbul: Can Yayınları, pp. 37-41.

SUZAN SAMANCI

Two Mothers

This river Tigris, how she rises and overflows! She's gone berserk again. A soft breeze is carrying the scent of newly ploughed soil and of narcissi. How nice to feel the warmth of the sun on my back! Well, it's almost time for the third *cemre*... How many *cemres*, how many springs have passed, and yet the pain in my heart has not eased; it keeps growing and gnawing away at my bowels. It's not easy to endure such pain: He disappeared right in front of my eyes... If it had been death, I would have mourned over his grave. Son, how difficult it was to bring you up in all this poverty! Did you take no pity on us? We've been crying night and day, our eyes riveted on the TV screen, on the pages of the newspapers, our hearts in our mouths...

It was a beautiful day just like today. He had come back from school; without talking to me or looking at my face, he kept staring beyond the Tigris. He didn't like what I cooked any more; after eating just one stuffed chard he pushed the plate away, went out into the courtyard, and kept gazing at the mist beyond the river. Then, without ever glancing my way, he asked for his green coat, the one he'd recently bought. When he leaned over to lace up his sports shoes, his face turned rosy. Son, how handsome you looked with your light beard, your henna-colored moustache! As he went down the stairs he searched through his pockets and looked inside the wallet his uncle had sent from prison. I ran to the window when the bell of the garden gate tinkled; he was putting on his coat. He turned his collar up, put his hands into his pockets, and started to walk away. When he saw Şirvan, our neighbor's little girl sitting at her doorstep, he stopped, stroked her hair and gave her something—later they said it was a five thousand lira bill. Before rounding the corner he stopped for a moment, as if he was about to turn back and take a look. I couldn't take my eyes off his long legs, his broad shoulders. Did I know it then? My heart was filled with fear. I went to visit my neighbors, from one house to the next to get rid of the anxiety I felt; and when the night fell, I didn't want to go back home. Later, Filit's son took me home. My heart was fluttering like a bird, I was sweating. I saw the girls sitting on the divan embroidering their trousseaux and I yelled at them about the courtyard being muddy. I wished to smother my husband who was snoring in bed. I looked at the clock on the wall. It was early yet.

Spring heat strikes fiercely and makes everyone lethargic. These linnets, they pierce my ears. I feel as if I'm swaying in the blue void of the sky. One moment my ears start ringing, the next, darkness sinks into my soul. Memories seem to spring from every corner. They slowly surround me. I don't have anybody any more. I'll be alone forever. I'll sit in front of the window and count the neat Mondays, the slovenly drunken Sundays. Here comes the postman, waddling again. If he would only bring letters as he used to, grinning and lisping! If only I could melt away in the letters starting "Mom," if only I could caress his slanted handwriting, desolate photos falling from among the stained sheets of paper: I was a mother, a widowed mother, oh God, how can one endure such pain!

On weekends, when I was exhausted by constant sewing, I would rush to his school. With long leaps he would come to me and hug me. He always felt embarrassed when handing me his dirty clothes. "I'm making work for you again," he used to say with a warm and shy look. We would walk past shop windows and booksellers, then sit in the park under the acacias and drink something. His friends, with their youthful laughter, would sometimes join us. I felt younger when I was with them. On winter nights I would sit by the window, my hands busy with my work, my eyes expectant. He would never ring the bell; creasing his nose, he would gently tap on the window-pane. He would clean his shoes on the doormat with extreme care. After taking his bath, he would sit on the pillow next to the stove and start taking the basting out of the sewing, as if that was his duty. He had learned to play the bağlama from Sadi, the son of our next-door neighbor. While the tea steeped on the stove, he would start playing his bağlama softly; sometimes he would even hum the tune. My hands would become stiff; I would stop to watch him. My heart would fill with strength, my body would shake with vibrations of happiness. Noticing my glance and as if he was irritated by my doting, he would stand up, hang his bağlama on the wall, pour tea into the cups which I kept behind the stove, smell the aroma, and say, "Hmm, bergamot..."

I walked up and down in the room. The clock seemed to stand still. When it finally struck two, I went out onto the exedra. Everyone was asleep. The breeze from the river brought the smell of clay and rotten plants. It felt as if in my heart a rabid puppy was turning round and round. I was restless. I lay down on the paved stones. Now and then my daughters came and took a furtive look from the window. I wanted to cry but I couldn't. I scratched the cement I laid on. I felt as if I was burning on charcoal. I went to the cistern; when I drenched myself with ice-cold water, a hawser broke in my heart and I wept. My voice expanded in the dark; in the end I was afraid of my own voice.

Even the dogs echoed it. With my wet clothes I lay down on the wooden divan in the courtyard. I heard the hushed sobs of my daughters. Then I started to count the cars leaving the city: one, two, three...

I used to lie to him; when I gave him the secretly-bought almond kernels and walnuts I would tell him they had been brought by some neighbor. He never learned that I had bought them for him. In the summer we used to have a wonderful time. Early in the morning we would water the plants in the backyard; when the grass and the flowers were still gleaming, we would go under the trellis covered with ivy and bindweed to avoid the sunlight penetrating through the black cherry and plum trees. When I was busy with my sewing, he would read, playing with an ivy rose in his hand or munching on the fruit he had picked from the trees. Sometimes he would fall asleep with the book on his chest. Waking up to the noise of the neighbors who came for a visit, he would say, "I'll just go and take a walk," and then leave. When he came back in the evening, he would bring some Maraş ice cream. He would laugh and say, "I must marry a girl from Maraş so that her father will supply us with this..."

My hands shake; I cannot sew any more. I'm scared of the furniture in the house. Loneliness, desolation is overwhelming me. It is daytime; I'm scared of the light outside. Oh, God, should I go out into the garden? The gate opening into the backyard has gotten rusty, it creaks so loudly. I feel nauseated; weeds have overtaken the garden. It smells like a graveyard and chills me. My eyes become blurred: I see soldiers running... The fog rising over the mountains... My son is running through the fog... He falls, blood gushes from his forehead... Did I hit my head against the door? Was it the doorbell? A telegraph... Telegraph... Your son, stop, died for his fatherland, stop, in the line of duty, stop...

Was it a place called Şırnak? My son, where is he? I want my son back... I want him back...

Just before dawn I woke to my husband's tobacco-smelling breath. "Piroz, wake up. Come inside," he said indifferently. I was stiff all over, my voice had become hoarse. For days on end I had waited. I chatted with the clock on the wall; I kept looking at his white labcoat. Every night I took the artificial bones out of the cupboard, the ones he'd put on his lap to study; I caressed them. The wound in my stomach keeps troubling me; he was going to have me operated on... This irresponsible bum, he should repair the roof this year. I must go downstairs; tomorrow we'll have the *henna night* for our second daughter... The sun has gone down beyond the mountains. If only I could reach those mountains! The birds keep singing. Son, how I miss your face! The Tigris, she knows my sorrow. I pour out my grief into her, I pray, I send you my greetings sometimes, do you hear me, I wonder...

Translated by Şebnem Susam
"İki Anne," *Reçine Kokuyordu Helin* (1993).
Istanbul: Can Yayınları, pp. 17-21.

GAYE BORALIOĞLU

Subtle Calculation

He said it at such a moment that I couldn't utter anything but "all right." I simply said "All right." No sooner had I said it than he opened the door and went out. He dashed off. I couldn't say, "Let me come, too." In a terry robe with my hair wrapped up in a towel and water dripping off my body, how could I suggest going with him? He'd bolted. He didn't even ask me, "Want to come?" He must have been waiting for this moment. He'd been on the lookout for a moment when I could only say "All right."

How despicable is this behavior of his! He must have calculated it carefully. He may have been scheming ever since our arrival. He's been waiting for my bath. If that's the case, I really have to laugh at him. That means he's been waiting for three days. Because I haven't had a bath for that long. Because it gets chilly in the evenings and I dread catching a cold. Then, too, I like wandering around with saltwater all over my body. The salt and the sweat intermingle; it's like pickle juice. It could be too that I'm a bit of a sloth. Why have I taken a bath now? I've run headfirst into trouble. I could easily have gotten along a couple more days. He'd have had to wait another two days then. That would've been perfect!

What would've happened if he'd waited longer? Would it have changed anything? Two days more or less, what's the difference? Once he makes up his mind to phone someone, he'll phone.

If I slip into my clothes and rush out, can I catch him? I should run and catch him in the phone booth and slam down the receiver. "Get out!" I'd say. "Out! Don't burn me up! Here am I in love with you. Don't spoil it all!" If I go out before my hair dries, I'll catch a cold. I suffer from sinusitis. It's quite risky to go out with wet hair. My coming down with something now would be the end of the world; it would ruin everything.

Then I'd be in bed the whole day and he'd go out to the phone every day. Nobody can take this, actually. For my own part, I can't. I'll die first, not of sinusitis but...

I wish I'd brought my pocketknife with me. Then I could commit suicide, slashing my wrists. Yes, I'd have filled the bath, slashed my wrists and held them in the water.

Would slashing them hurt? I've never even cut myself before. I have no experience at all. Once as children one of my friends and I became blood-brothers. I pricked my finger with a needle; that hurt a lot. That's all I know. If pricking your finger hurts that much I'd hate to think how awful slashing your wrists would be. How people dare do it in one stroke! My blood-sister proved to be a real goof-off. I haven't seen her for ages. She wasn't worth pricking my finger for.

How surprised he'd be to return and find I'd committed suicide. I'd like at least to make the attempt. He'd appreciate my value and my love for him. Yes, that would be good. I don't want him to pity me but come to terms with reality. He shouldn't squander his time on these matters. For his own sake. For his own sake and mine. At some point there must be an end. An ex- is an ex-. They must all remain in the past. If you don't let them go, all your ex-es will pile up. You have many ex-es in your life. If you hold onto all of them, you'll always be on the phone—furthermore, in the most underhanded of manners. All ex-es must then take baths at the same time so that the original ex- might be phoned. Obviously, it's not possible! Then, consider, everybody has an ex-. If everybody were phoning his ex-, no work would ever get done. Do I call my ex-boyfriends? They don't call me, either. I wonder why not, really. Maybe it's because we never split up on good terms. Actually, one likes to be asked after. It's a warm feeling. A lover is always a dear. Even with an ex-lover there's that nearness between two people.

If I were his ex-, would he call me too? But no! I don't want to be any worse for wear. In any case it's undesirable to be an ex-. Your being an ex- means there's someone new. Can you imagine? Instead of you, she's the one who's now sniffing his hair and kissing his lips. I wonder whether or not he treated his ex- like he does me. Did he, for example, close his eyes while making love to her, too? Maybe he's still after her. Why not? At least he's obviously still interested in her. If he weren't, would he desert me here with wet hair? He feels sympathy for her. Maybe he's still in love with her even. He's so preoccupied with her that he can't help phoning her. Actually in love with someone else, he's simply passing the time with me. God knows what they're murmuring to each other right now: "Sweetheart, my little monkey, how much I love you!" Maybe I'm not the only one he calls his little monkey. He could be using it for all his ex-es. Though I'm quite short and somewhat stoop-shouldered, I still don't resemble a monkey. I know I should stand up straight. I have to get used to standing up straight. I was near-sighted when I was young and used to bend my face over my notebook to see it up closer. For this reason I'm stoop-shouldered. My mother would always tap me over the head with a melamine plate to warn me: "Don't stoop!" If she'd taken me to a doctor instead of hitting me, he would have diagnosed it as near-sightedness and I wouldn't have had to bend forward but could have stood up straight. Maybe then he wouldn't call me his little monkey. Actually it doesn't bother me. I like it even. Let him call me his little monkey—I have no gripe at all, but I don't want him using it for others or calling his ex- his little monkey on the phone. Then there wouldn't be anything special about it anymore. How can you use the same pet name for everyone? If you use "My little monkey," for one, you must have something else for the others: My little devil, My cupcake, Sweetie, etc. No, Sweetie's no good. It's much too ordinary. It has to be more imaginative. He must have found something already. Because he's a creative person. Unlike me. I try and try, but the only thing that comes to mind is "I love you." Nothing else. I'm ashamed even to admit it. I know it irritates him. He's right, of course; he expects more pleasant things from me, but I don't have the inspiration. It's child's play for him. I wonder what he's saying right now: My rainbow, My chick-pea, My monkey nut! I could kill him! Do him in with one blow. I'll kill him instead of committing suicide. I'll take the iron bar out of the bedstead—it's already so loose that it creaks when we make love, spoiling everything—and I'll stand behind the door with the iron bar and strike him—whammo—when he opens it. Whish—a painless end. It's really a good idea to take the bar out. Maybe the bed won't creak anymore. That distracts one. That's all you take in. Screech, screech, screech. Even the people downstairs must hear it. How disgraceful! On top of that, it doesn't creak in harmony with your body rhythm. You slide forward, that is, with no sound at all. When you just start to slide back, screech! It's a real pest.

Luckily I've thought about the iron bar. I wish it'd occurred to me sooner.

The doorbell's rung!

There's a knock at the door. There's a knock at the door. He must be back. All I'd have to do is to sock him on the head with the bar. I'm not even dressed yet. Like this in my robe—without a sash. Once I raise the iron bar, my whole front will be exposed. Very indelicate. I'd feel disgraced. What if I held the robe closed with one hand and lifted the iron bar with the other? If I couldn't give him a heavy enough blow, I'd really be in hot water. He'd then lunge at me, shouting "you nitwit!" I wouldn't be able to make a peep. I couldn't explain anything. It'd be utter ignominy.

He's not at the door. It's the maid. "This isn't a very convenient moment; no need for today, thank you," I said and sent her away. She made no objection. Of course she doesn't mind less work. She cast a questioning glance at my hair and left. I really must dry my hair. I'd rather not get sick right now.

I think I'd better talk it over with him. Calm... calmly. Without pushing the panic button. Talking it over is the key to everything. One must be able to explain oneself to the person opposite. You must explain what you feel, why you feel that way, the reasons behind it, any slights of behavior that have piled up in the past, the attitudes acquired through the way you're brought up, the traumas of your childhood and the great misfortunes of your life. Only, I don't have much to say in this respect. I had quite a happy childhood. I grew up in a small neighborhood, in a house with a garden. I'd spend the whole day outside running and playing. I was hardworking, too; my grades were always good. My teachers liked me. My parents were unassuming middle-class folks. I don't ever remember them seriously quarrelling. Then nothing important happened during my junior high- and high-school years. In high school all my classmates were either leftists or rightists. They fell into opposite groups. They'd get all involved in zealous discussions. They'd get up early in the morning to paint slogans on the school walls. Sometimes they'd stop us in front of the school and say, "No school today." So we wouldn't go in; we'd go back home. Sometimes they'd converge and chant "Combat till liberation," "God damn fascism" or "God damn you." No, not the last, but still they were that infuriated. Sometimes they'd even quarrel among themselves, not simply with exchanges of words, but black eyes and cracked heads. Afterwards they all disappeared. All were sent to prison, and some died. I always looked on from the sidelines. I never meddled in such affairs. I was no honor student, but I never had to repeat a year. I didn't even have to repeat my freshman year. Moreover, I was admitted to university the first time I took the entrance examinations. Maybe the department wasn't my first choice, but who cares anyway? I was in. I graduated in four years. On schedule. Then I found a job. What more could one want?

Why then am I in this state now? If I can't rationalize my distress to myself, how can I explain it to him? Anyway, at least I have to try. Maybe I shouldn't go into so much detail and simply skip my childhood. Because that part could be boring. I've always dreaded giving boring speeches. Once I was asked to deliver a speech explaining the factory's overall quality management concept. All the workers dozed off. One even snored. I saw the worker next to him poke him. With the fear of being pulled onto the carpet, the snoring worker had propped his eyes wide open and tried to collect himself. I could tell how soundly he'd been sleeping by the amount of saliva he had in his mouth—enough to make chewing movements. But this is a different story. It has nothing to do with the concept of quality management. Here we're talking about me. My feelings. My own hurt pride. The deep sorrow of one who's been duped. An E.Q. never appreciated. A heart thirsting for love.

Can you imagine! He has the impertinence to leave me alone in the hotel room with my hair soaking wet and go out to the phone booth to call his ex-. All right, my hair is dry by now, but the important point is that it was wet then. If it hadn't been wet, I could have said, "I'm coming with you." Then he wouldn't have been able to call his ex-. We'd have gone out for a little stroll. Nothing unusual would have happened. We'd have come back to the room and made love. But now all the fun's been taken out of it. I don't have the stamina to speak, let alone make love. Now perhaps I should start from there. I could say, "With no stamina left, things will never work out! Little heartbreaks may end up as wounds much deeper than one could ever imagine. These persistent trials kill all of one's enthusiasm." I might even go so far as to try intimidation. I could say, "If you go on like this, you'll lose me."

Then what if he says "I don't care." Then I wouldn't be able to take it back. How could I possibly say "No, no! I was just kidding, would you ever lose me? If you want, go and call whenever I've taken a bath. It won't bother me. It's no big thing." I'd better forget about intimidation. Maybe it isn't a good idea to talk at all. Instead, I could just pull a long face so that he'd realize what was going on. He just has to. I'll not utter a single word, and he'll understand. If he asks a question, I won't answer but just avert my glance. I'll look out the window abstractedly. In fact, I could pretend to have a stomach ache to get some attention. If necessary, I'll even throw up. I'm sure he'll look after me then and ask what's wrong with me. What's crucial then is the answer I give. It must include some aggression and at the same time an accusation. Of course it must also disclose my dissatisfaction with the situation. It must also express my love for him. It must be brief and concise. It mustn't be a tirade. It must be right on target. A direct hit. A direct hit with the first blow. That is, my answer. Perhaps I'd be better off answering with a question. For example, I could ask, "Are you pleased with what you've done?" Expressing oneself with a question is always effective. Not only do you free yourself from responsibility by not making any judgments yourself, but you also make your partner say everything for you. Clever, isn't it?

Now just what do I expect him to say?

It's high time I got dressed. My terry robe would water down the situation. I shouldn't be wearing anything special, though, either. He must think I've put on whatever's at hand. He shouldn't notice any anomaly at first. Then what I say will make a stronger impact on him.

I could have a magazine in my hand. No, I can't, because I don't have any. I could pick up a book. Only, the one I've brought with me is entitled *The Man of My Dreams*. No! That would never do! He'd think I was trying to give him a message and it would create a very false impression. The best thing is to forget about reading. But if I'm not doing anything, he'll think I've been waiting for him. I have to be busy with something. What can I find to do in a hotel room? Obviously I can't wash windows. Anyway, I needn't exaggerate. It doesn't have to be a hard or a difficult task. An easy everyday task. Such as swathing my face with cotton wool, buttoning buttons or playing with a thread dangling from the hem of my blouse. No. These are all signs of mere uneasiness. The ones who play with the threads dangling from their blouses are those who harbor secret grudges that they just can't seem to get off their shoulders. They're like bombs about to go off.

He opened the door and popped in. That meant I must have forgotten to lock it after the maid left. He didn't say anything. He started to rout through his suitcase for something. Having found it, he started applying some cream to his face. Taking a deep breath and gazing out the window, I asked, "Where have you been?"

"I told you, didn't I? I went to the phone booth," he replied. Then he took a close look at his face in the mirror. Moving his mouth from the left to the right he began examining his pimples. Doing my best to keep my voice from trembling, "Whom did you call?" I inquired.

"My mother," he answered. He then turned to look at me. I didn't know how to conceal the stupefied expression on my face. "Your button's unbuttoned," he said, and I blushed to my ears, not with shame but uneasiness.

"Why didn't you call her on your mobile phone but went outside?"

Stripping off his t-shirt, he replied, "It needs re-charging now, doesn't it?" Correct. He'd left the charger at home. I'd forgotten.

"Yes," I said. "You're right." Turning his back to the mirror, he inspected his muscles for a short while. Modestly, as if just having a look at his moles. Then he looked at his face once more. Leaning towards the mirror he looked again at his pimples. He gently squeezed one. Then he took his shorts out of the suitcase and laid them on the bed. He took off his trousers. There was only one thing to do! I went up to him and hugged him. He hugged me, too. Then we made love—screech, screech.

Translated by Lütfiye Kozacıoğlu and Jean Carpenter Efe
"İnce Hesap," *Hepsi Hikâye* (2001).
Istanbul: İletişim Yayınları, pp. 7-17.

AYFER TUNÇ

A Small Well

It was a season when the sea was rough. The gray clouds in the sky above had little by little settled inside me. I felt uneasy. My head was aching and what felt like a fist pressing down on my heart wouldn't let up. I couldn't breathe. I didn't know what it was that might help me sleep more comfortably, peacefully, and feel a little of happiness inside.

I was with my friends. I felt, however, very peevish and tense. They were in a similar mood. All of us were trying to show a false happiness. But it was no good. Our faces, even if managing the pretense of a smile or a momentary ray of joy, would fade to their old expressions with a single blast of wind or a crash of the waves. We had come here to enjoy the fall, but actually we were playing cards, watching the rain and the rough sea the whole day long. Evenings we'd do nothing but drink. As I drank, it was as if the fist upon my heart was growing and would suffocate me. My head was swimming; my insides were swimming. Furthermore, we'd run out of words. There was nothing left to talk about. Therefore, we were each left on our own. And because we were left on our own, we got bored. We got angry—furious even—and fought with each other. It never occurred to any of us to alter the situation and shove off. Maybe all of us had thought of it but didn't dare do it.

One morning I woke up and thought about how we would play cards or fight with each other over trivial matters all day long at the seaside coffee house. The sun never showed its face. Why should I do this? Why should I sit here and be bored? I couldn't stand it. I got up and decided I wanted to leave the place. While my friends were sleeping, I threw the few belongings I had into my little bag. I left the hotel without even leaving a message and boarded a bus that was passing by.

I didn't know where to go, but that wasn't important at all. Maybe what I wanted was to be all alone, or maybe I was running away from my friends. I wasn't sure of that, either. But I wasn't thinking about why I did it. I hoped that if I saw places I hadn't seen before and talked to people I hadn't met before, my distress would wither away. The bus was traveling as if it were swallowing up the road on this frosty morning. Again it was cloudy. The sun was determined not to come out. I decided to do whatever I wanted. I would get off wherever I felt like it. I'd die if I wanted to or I'd sleep if I wanted to.

The bus entered a small village and stopped. It was a tea break—but it wasn't that kind of typical gas-station café where they fill the tea glasses only half-way. It was just a small tea house. I felt strange, but I knew it was nothing more than the combination of the weather and the confusion inside me. In fact, I tried to make myself believe that it was so. I got off the bus and sat down on a wooden chair with crooked legs. I asked the waiter for a tea. The sea was rough and my insides were rough. Then I suddenly realized that I liked this village. I could stay here a little while. I could have a rest and pull myself together. The waiter brought my tea. It isn't really right to call him a waiter. He was one of the village boys. His hair was short and he didn't even have a mustache yet. He had a short-sleeved shirt on. He didn't speak at all; he kept busy bringing tea to the passengers. The bus driver washed his hands and face at the tap in front of the tea house. He wrapped the handkerchief he'd dried his face with around his neck. I shivered when I saw him do that. The passengers drank their tea without a word. The driver's assistant announced in a rather loud voice that the bus was about to leave. The passengers paid for their tea and got back onto the bus. Drinking his tea without haste, the driver waited until everybody had boarded. When everybody else was on the bus, he looked at me. Aren't you getting on? he asked. No, I said. I'll stay here for a while. As you wish, he said. He got up, climbed into the bus and started the engine. In less than a moment the coffee house was empty. I looked around. The weather was clear but cold. There was nobody in sight. The sea had become wild. I sat alone on one of the chairs in front of the tea house. I thought for a moment that the sea would swell up and swallow me.

I drank another glass of tea. I told the boy waiting tables that their tea was very good. Yes, it is, Sir, he said. One who drinks it once drinks it again. If you're cold, sit inside, he said. No, it's okay, I said. The owner of the tea house came out for a moment, leaned some of the chairs up against the tables and went back inside again. I paid for the tea and got up. I wanted to stroll about a bit. I went down to the beach. It was only ten steps away. That southwest wind was blowing. I walked along the seaside paying no heed to the waves splashing me. The village had a small beach. The houses of the summer residents were deserted. Everybody had gone. The signboards had been removed from the boarding houses. There was no one at the beach. The fist weighing heavily on my heart was still there.

A hotel at the end of the beach caught my eye. It looked like a clean and new place.

I thought I might stay there. Taking my time, I wandered towards the hotel. I entered. Nobody around? I called out. In a moment I heard steps. A pale thin 25-year-old woman with a dreamy look in her eyes appeared. Without a word she went behind the desk. Do you want a room? she asked. Yes, I replied. I want a room overlooking the sea. The woman, looking at me dreamily, handed me the key to my room. Second floor, she said, the room at the end of the corridor. I was again struck by that dreamy look in her eyes. Did she only look at me like this or was that look always in her eyes? I didn't know. I found the woman's eyes, fair complexion and slender build appealing.

I went up to my room and threw my bag onto the bed. I opened the door to the balcony. And then I wanted to go outside and inhale this heavy, sultry air. Nothing except the sound of the waves could be heard. The waves were crashing against the breakwater because of that wind. I went down to the beach, wandered around, and then went into a restaurant overlooking the enraged sea. The restaurant was almost closed up. Only three tables were left for tardy holiday-makers like me. Was it the effect of this southwest wind that everyone was so silent or was it the sorrow over the summer's end that had settled into them, I didn't know. Nobody was talking. Only the most necessary things were mentioned. Sometimes a reluctant conversation was started up: a short conversation with short sentences. I sat down at one of the outermost tables. A young boy resembling the waiter in the tea house came up. What would you like, Sir? he asked. Bring whatever you have, I said. But be quick, I'm very hungry. I wasn't actually hungry, but I wanted something to dawdle over. A meal would be a good pretext. Okay, said the boy and left. I looked at the sea. The sea was gray and writhing. The waves were determined not to carry even a single piece of rubbish. My meal came and I ate it.

When I left the restaurant, I walked along the shore again. My mind was left a blank. There was nothing inside me. I had no particular feelings. Neither distress nor tiredness. The fist had vanished but I had vanished, too. I wasn't concentrating on myself. There wasn't even the slightest hint of an idea in my mind. I had no sense of existence. It was as if I no longer existed. It was pure relaxation for me. Then it started to rain. Going back to the tea house where the bus had stopped occurred to me. I managed to reach the tea house before I got soaked.

The people there were as silent as before. From time to time they'd utter a few words among themselves. They said that the weather would be better in a day or two. We can't take the boats out fishing, they complained. Some of them were playing cards. Even having the right card didn't give them any satisfaction. The owner of the tea house served them tea without their having to ask. The boy was inside washing glasses. Two men, who I figured were retired, read newspapers. The conversation reached my ear but I wasn't interested. I kept staring at the sea.

I had been there a few hours when a man around my age came into the tea house. He said hello to everyone and sat down beside me. He said hello to me, too, so I said hello. You've just come today, haven't you? he asked. Yes, I said. How long are you staying? he asked. I don't know, I said. Till I get bored. What do you do? he asked. Nothing, I said. I have a shop; it runs itself. I have a souvenir shop, he said. But when the summer is over, the shutters come down. I didn't particularly feel like conversing, but his tone was pleasant. My name's Orhan, he said. I'm pleased, I said, and gave him my name, too. He had a friendly face. Fall, he said, is the best season for relaxation. Peaceful and without crowds... We talked a little bit about autumn, the fury of the sea and the sultry air. Then, like the others in the tea house, we spoke of fishing and the sea. I know nothing about fish, I said, and he smiled. Don't think I really understand fishing because I'm from here, he commented. No one in this village actually understands fishing, but they don't have anything else to talk about. What can they do? They'll talk about fishing all winter, he said. I decided that everyone in this village must have a fist pressing down upon his heart.

I talked to Orhan till evening. I opened up and began to enjoy myself. He told me scores of funny stories about the holiday-makers. I decided he must be the most talkative man in this village. You'll be my guest tonight, he said. I refused, but he insisted. I like you, I won't let you off tonight, he said. Let's eat together, but I won't be your guest, I said. So, then, we'll eat and drink together but pay our bills separately? Is that right? he asked. That's fine, I replied. All right, he said, however you like. We had one more tea. Let's go to İbrahim's Hotel, he proposed. Okay, I said. It was almost dark as we left the tea house. He wouldn't let me pay for our tea. I didn't insist. The rain had let up, but the sea was ready to swell again. Somehow, I pondered, the sea must hate this village and the people in it. It reminded me of a tethered dog ready to mangle and maim those in front of it if its chain should break. Perhaps such things came to my mind because I wasn't used to such a sea.

At a slow pace we strolled down to İbrahim's Hotel. What he called İbrahim's Hotel was the place where I was staying. This is where I'm staying, I commented. Good, he said. It's new and clean; you'll be comfortable. Then he added, looking me straight in the eye, They have a special service here. Whoever visits once comes again. I smiled. Although I had no idea what he meant, Very good, I said.

We went into the restaurant. It was getting dark. There wasn't a soul in the place. We sat down together at a table by the window. Not very fancy—it was an ordinary place. I realized that the distress inside me had dispersed completely, but that now I was in a vacuum. Everything was flat; there were no curves or up and downs. It was better here than where I'd come from, anyway. Orhan handed me a cigarette, I took it and we lit up. İbrahim will come now, he said. We smoked in silence. The sun had set, and the lights of the restaurant were switched off. I could see how wildly the sea was attacking the shore.

Then suddenly the lights came on. İbrahim had arrived. He was disabled and walked with a crutch. He was a swarthy man of about forty-five with deep wrinkles in his face. His appearance suggested neither kindness nor cruelty. He seated himself at our table. He welcomed me. Thanks. Is it your first time here? he asked. Yes, I said. You'll like it here, he promised. You'll come again. I hope so, I said. What would you like? he asked. I don't know, I said. Let Orhan suggest something. Orhan ordered fish and rakı—and appetizers for us till the fish was ready.

İbrahim called out "Leyla!" in a deep, rather harsh and impatient voice. He called only once and then turned back to us. We started talking. He commented to Orhan that everybody had gone, the whole seasonal crowd. Have you closed up your shop? he asked. Orhan said that he had. Not long after İbrahim called out, the woman with dreamy glances showed up. I understood that the name of this attractive woman must be Leyla. She brought rakı and ice and some appetizers on a tray and served them without a word. She put some cheese and melon on a plate in front of İbrahim. She filled his glass with rakı from a different bottle. Orhan said okay to the woman. We could help ourselves to the rakı. The woman left. I noticed that she hadn't been looking at Orhan or İbrahim in the same dreamy fashion. There had been no such expression in her eyes. But when she turned her glance on me, I seemed to find little sparkles in them. I ascribed it to my imagination.

Then we started talking. The sound of the trees that were being blown about by the southeast wind and the sound of the waves, too, roared in my ears. I couldn't see the sea because the lights were on inside. But I felt that its sound had turned from the howling of a furious mastiff into the whimper of a poor and lonely dog. I had Leyla on my mind for some reason. Her beautiful eyes, her incredibly fair complexion at such a summer resort, her straight and slender body. Was she İbrahim's wife, I wondered. Orhan asked me if I wanted some music. No, I said. It's fine. Okay, he said. As soon as we'd finished our rakı, Leyla entered. She filled our glasses and left without a word. Insofar as I could draw my attention away from Leyla, I joined into the conversation. It was an ordinary conversation which carried no pedantry or arrogance, and in which everybody was an equal. We talked about the people who came in the summer, about fishing and at times loneliness. They didn't ask me questions about myself. They asked me ordinary questions about the city I lived in, questions easy to answer. I answered them because they were not prying.

Our rakı ended towards midnight. Leyla came and filled our glasses as if she'd been watching us from a secret hiding place and seen that we were out of rakı. İbrahim passed his glass to Leyla. Leyla filled it from the other bottle. İbrahim looked at me and indicating Leyla with a nod of his head, asked: Do you want her to dance? I shivered. No, I said. I don't like dancing women at all. Some like it very much, he said. They ask for it. Leyla dances very well. I came eye to eye with the woman. I could see a mist of shame pass across the woman's eyes. She averted them and disappeared. All the pleasure of the conversation went astray, and that fist came and settled upon my heart again. İbrahim wasn't aware of my uneasiness. Then the rakı was finished; the fish, the appetizers, the fruits, everything had been devoured. I'll pay, said Orhan. No, I said.

What was our agreement? You can pay the next time, he said. No, I said. We'll share it. It's on me this time, said İbrahim, but I insisted. They had no choice but to agree. Orhan paid the half of the bill. I told İbrahim to add mine onto my hotel bill. Fine, he said. Orhan stood up. I'd better be off, he said. All right, I said. I thanked him. He left. İbrahim and I sat down for a while facing one another. Then I stood up. Are you going to bed? asked İbrahim. No, I said. I'm going to walk around a bit. Okay, he said. Leyla wasn't in sight. The table hadn't been cleared, but İbrahim switched off the lights, and we went out. I'm going to retire, he said. Good night. Good night, I said, too. He went up the stairs. The sound of his crutch on the stone stairs clattered in my ears for a while.

At some distance down the shore, a street lamp was still burning. The waves were about to reach it. I approached the lamp and leaned my back against the pole. I looked at the sea. I listened to the sound of the sea, which resembled the crying of a wild animal. I thought of Leyla. She was a beautiful woman. I won't say very beautiful. Just one of those women who enter a man's mind and don't fade easily away, even though at first glance he might not have considered her a particularly beautiful woman. I smoked two cigarettes with the southeast wind blowing through my hair and then went back to the hotel.

I found my room keys on the desk. Assuming Leyla and İbrahim had gone to bed, I took the keys and went up to my room. The door was open. I had locked it, I remembered that clearly. I decided that since there was nothing to steal, it really didn't matter. I went in. I took off my jacket and hung it up. I went to the bathroom and washed my hands and face in ice-cold water. Then when I re-entered the room I saw Leyla.

She was lying on my bed. Through the darkness, the light of the full moon now and then emerging from behind the clouds would fall upon her. She had stripped, and her face was turned towards the window. I couldn't have been more surprised! I approached her; she turned her face to me. She looked at me with those same dreamy eyes. But this time it was as if she had an offended and somewhat pained expression. I took off my clothes and lay down next to her.

She didn't speak at all. She didn't utter a word. Her body was so hot. I felt like a person swimming in a warm sea on a cold day. As soon as I would separate my body from hers, I felt cold. The sound of the sea was incredible. I made love to her despite the fist on my heart. I kept telling her how beautiful, how passionate and how amorous she was. She didn't say anything. Weary, I fell asleep.

When I woke up I thought I had seen a dream. Leyla was no longer next to me. There I lay, naked. I felt very awkward—as if a joy were fighting with the fist inside me. For a moment the joy would gain control and then the fist would gain control. I was about to go nuts. I got up, I washed my hands and face and left the room right away. Leyla wasn't behind the desk. I went into the restaurant. There was nobody there. I sat down at a table. I was angry and at the same time I wasn't. I both craved Leyla and hated her. I was confused. After some time Leyla came up. Without saying a word she put the tray she was holding down onto the table. There was a breakfast on one plate, on another there was some toast and a tea glass. She poured some tea into the glass. I tried to catch her eye. But her eyes wouldn't meet mine. She flew away. I didn't touch the breakfast; I drank my tea and left.

I felt weary. The sea was churning again with the same fury. The southeast wind was still blowing. I was about to go crazy. What I had gone through was so strange. Who was Leyla? What was her relationship to İbrahim? Why had she come to my room? Why had she made love to me as if she were very fond of me—as if she were in love with me? I didn't understand it.

I went back to the same tea house. I sat down at a table facing the sea. I hoped Orhan would come. I would sound out him and try to learn something about Leyla. The owner of the tea house appeared. Would you like a tea? he asked. Yes, I said, a strong one. Okay, he said. He went. He brought my tea after a while. He left a *simit*, one of those yeast rings covered with sesame seeds, on the table. You haven't had breakfast, he said. I haven't, I said. How did you know? I asked. It's always the same, he replied. I didn't understand anything. I drank my tea. My heart was beating hard. I felt awkward. Just awkward. I couldn't understand it, or pin any name on my situation. I bit into the *simit*; it was warm and fresh. It did me good, and I finished it up.

Other than myself there were only the two retired men. They were reading newspapers near the sizzling hot stove. Once or twice I came eye-to-eye with the owner of the tea house. He smiled at me and got on with his work. He was drying glasses. After a while Orhan came in. Good morning, he said, and I said good morning. He sat down at the table. I thought he seemed aware of my awkwardness. Yet there was no difference in his behavior or glance. I asked, Would you like a tea? I would, he said. My voice vibrated with excitement. I looked at the owner of the tea house. He came immediately. A tea for me, said Orhan. Do you want another one, the man asked me. Yes, I said. Okay, he said and left.

I wanted to ask Orhan about Leyla right away. Yet I couldn't bring myself to broach the topic. The owner of the tea house brought our tea. He didn't bring Orhan a *simit*. I looked at the man and said: The *simit* you brought me was very good. He smiled and said, I know. I sat there with Orhan for a while without speaking. I was waiting for an opportunity to ask about Leyla; I couldn't ask about her outright. He leaned back and looked at the sea. The sea was seething mad last night, he said. Yes, I said. It would be better to say I couldn't sleep because of its noise. So I lied. The sound of the sea had come into my ear so gently while I was caressing Leyla's hot body. I'd liked it. Then I'd slept soundly. The sun had already risen when I awoke. He looked suspicious, as if he didn't believe me. Did Leyla come to your room last night? he asked. The tea stuck in my throat. I had a coughing fit. I was unable to think. I was about to choke. When I came round, I looked at Orhan's face. How did you know that? I asked. It's always the same, commented the owner of the tea house from a distance. With a grieving face, Orhan looked at me. Leyla never misses those like you, he said. Stop talking nonsense, I said. She's İbrahim's daughter, he said. She doesn't go to everybody's room; she goes to whomever she wants to. She started this years ago. When she was in high school she was tall and willowy. Whoever looked at her once looked at her again. All of the men in this village were in pursuit of her. Yet she likes strangers, he said. The first time she sleeps with someone she doesn't charge him, he said. I plugged my ears. In time you become addicted to her and then you pay her. A pain shot through my head.

I was trying to digest what I was hearing. İbrahim opened the hotel recently, said Orhan. Next summer it will have been two years. At first he had no customers. But because of Leyla he has regular customers now. They come in the winter, in the summer, on Tuesdays, on Saturdays, you never know. They come for Leyla. Leyla does all the work in the hotel. She dances for whoever wants her to. She dances so beautifully, he sighed. But she never pays any attention to us. No man in this village has ever touched her. Even though there are a lot of rich people in this village. If she'd say yes, there are men who could bring the world to her feet. She plays hard-to-get; she insists on strangers. She goes silently into strangers' rooms. They say her body is like silver. Especially in the moonlight... That's what they always say...

It buzzed in my ears. I shivered. I drank the rest of my tea and rose to my feet. How much is that? I asked. Nothing, he said. Next time you pay. I won't be back, I said. You'll come; it's always the same, he said. They say no, but they come again, he said. There was incredible pain on Orhan's face. I looked at him with hostility. I took some money out of my pocket and left it on the table. The owner of the tea house smiled. I expected him to say it was always the same, but he didn't. Yet, he looked at me that way.

I walked to the hotel quickly. All this was impossible. I wasn't so stupid as to interpret her looks in the wrong way. Hers were eyes that looked only at me that way. One couldn't be that mistaken. I went to the hotel. There was no one at the reception. Leyla wasn't around. I felt that the fist inside me had turned into rage. I was in a terrible state. I went up to my room and packed my things with trembling hands. I stomped down the stairs. İbrahim stood opposite me, smiling. I wanted to hit him, but my eyes fell upon his crutch, I couldn't. Did you sleep well last night? he asked. I clenched my fists. How much is the bill? I asked. Are you going? he asked. Yes, I said. I'm going. I can't stay here any longer. As you wish, he said. How much is it? I asked again in an angry voice. You can pay the next time you come, he said. I won't come again, I said. Are you sure? he asked. His voice had a teasing tone. Yes, I said. My voice was like the hissing of a snake because of my anger. Okay, he said. He went behind the counter, his crutch tapping on the stone floor. He wrote something on a piece of paper and handed it to me. I took it and paid. I left the hotel without a word. I didn't want to look at the hotel as I walked from the beach towards the main road. I couldn't help looking back at it. I saw Leyla. With her eyes that gazed dreamily. Maybe I didn't see them. I reached the main road and got onto a bus.

I wanted to go back again. I very much wanted to. I wanted to feel the unbelievable heat of Leyla's body and see her eyes. I would have gone if I'd been sure that she looked only at me that way. If only the owner of the tea house hadn't said it was always the same! To spite the owner of the tea house and all the men in that village, I've never gone back. My mind was hooked on two things. Had it been Leyla at the window when I looked back on my way out, and did she look only at me that dreamily? Afterwards, I resigned myself to living with the fist pressing down on my heart.

Translated by Hande Özdemir and Jean Carpenter Efe
"Küçük Kuyu," *Mağara Arkadaşları* (1996).
Istanbul: Yapı Kredi Yayınları, pp. 93-102.

ÖZEN YULA

One Last Word for the Sake of Health: Treachery in the Near East

A one-man show.

An actor or an actress depending on the choice of the director. [The English translation is written for an actor.] It should be performed continuously without an intermission. All decisions—including interpretation, decor, staging, and music—are left up to the director; intonation, pronunciation, mimicry, identity and elaboration of the character, gestures and the considerable stress necessitated are all left up to the actor or actress.

The character in the play is both "nobody" and "everybody."

Only, this play is not a play of anger. That is, the play is not only a play of anger. Therefore, no matter how much the director and the performer take the truths expressed in it under their wings, they mustn't nourish anger within themselves. Only if they control the anger will everything be calmly explained and grasped by the audience. Violence is in the essence of the play, not in the expression. The expression is ordinary. Like life.

* * *

I've saved my parents from your grasp.

Before that there was another person I loved very much. I've saved my lover, too.

I'm left behind.

Will it be better?

God knows how much you understand now from these moanings of mine. What meanings you attribute to each of them. Pretty soon you'll be sticking a plate of food in my hands.

Strange days these are. Suddenly a strange straight signal is coming; it penetrates my head like a buzzz. There is nothing but that. Only a buzzz.

And the cracks in the ice. Sometimes. Rarely these days, though.

From now on I want to speak in simple words.

Puritans, chastity, orthodoxy. I wish they weren't separate words. Let them be only one word. If only they weren't afraid of themselves. If only they wouldn't ruin my life.

Dionysus, Apollo.

Narcissus, Morpheus, Hypnosis, Orpheus.

The fire of youth. Lies or mistakes, nonsensical legends of life.

Commercials.

I never asked for any of them, not a single one.

I don't like the deep blue sky just before the morning dawn. As a child I used to love it. I don't anymore.

My room used to smell of linden blossoms in the deep blue of the morning as it absorbed the redness of the summer dawn. Not anymore.

What a great number of promises I had... once...

I have to meet someone's somebody or other. Go out for a meal. It'll be in one of those luxurious cafes lined up on a slope—or in a foreign restaurant. In one of those elite, but not always sweet districts. Districts subjected to the stiletto-heeled slippers of eager Barbies already past middle age, who moan to the simulated screams of a clean-shaven gigolo who has penetrated his Barbie and is counting his minutes. Districts subjected to the brand-name shoes of elderly business men with pacemakers in their hearts and senility in their heads, with enough passion concealed in their palms and enough love in their loins to take on a teenager four times in a row in their bachelor apartments, districts that despise their own soil. Districts that make us take to heart the concept of secrecy in the modern world where lies belie themselves and mistaken misconceptions mingle.

Barbies, teenagers, dates. I don't want such foreign concepts anymore—don't need them, either.

From now on I only want simple words. Like a word that's like the word itself. What use do I have for more than 300 useful words? With 300 words we can communicate more easily. As the number of words decreases, we'll all understand the same thing from the same word. What very easy and clear communication might be established among us! Please don't tell me this is sick reasoning. Besides, let's forget this bull about the richness of our language and the depth of our culture. 'Cause you don't really know either the language or the culture well enough. Everything is fake. There are a slew of counterfeiters among us. Here you have an example used in your own language. You can just wrap it up and keep it. It might do some good. You can take it out and use it in hard times: counterfeiter.

For example, I don't want the word simulation. I don't want a priori, a posteriori, demystify, conceptual approach, hygiene, or circulation.

Protect me from the books and looks of intellectuals. I'm aware of their cosmic power. Protect me from it. They're worse than wounded wild beasts. Protect me. From them, wandering in the written lines they worship, comforting and kidding both themselves and me, protect me!

Protect me from those who yield to daily life. Protect me from those who have nothing in life but their cunning and base intelligence, from those lowly who rewrite the unwritten rules of life to apply even to others who want nothing to do with them.

I don't want chaos or cosmos.

All I wanted was a modest life in a protected place. It would have been a larger place than what psychoanalysts call the mother's womb, but it would have been a smaller place than most of the accursed houses in this world. There would be no need for a living room and a *salle à manger*. There would have been no need for hot water running from the red tap and cold from the blue. Everything would have lived its own life in that small place, and I could've mine—or could *have* lived mine. Sometimes sloppy expression is a necessity—a person should be able to slur words and be understood.

I don't want to jump about in my speech. I don't want to stutter nonsense. You're right; my thoughts don't follow any finely defined line. I may twist my tongue. I might play around with particles and articles. However, when you consider that I haven't spoken for months, this speech of mine is miraculous. You know I've been silent. I've been silent for months. I was like fasting with words. Verbally fasting. I didn't complain about it. However, you wouldn't leave me alone. For whatever I wanted, you expected me to make a sound. Only then would you give it to me. I wanted water? First I should make a sound to clarify that I wanted water. Weird moans would come out of my throat. You managed to give meaning to those moans. I didn't have to make any effort. But then I understood what you were after and tried to go along with you. I'd make the sound you were expecting to hear. And you'd give me what that sound symbolized in your life—you wore me out. And how! You almost made me hate myself.

Hhhhhhhhhhhhhh.....   Hhhhhhhhhhhhh..... Hhhhhhhhhhhhhh.....

Like that. Then, suddenly...

I wanted to speak and something let me speak. This morning, all at once. I think it came from inside me.

I don't want the word psychoanalysis. Nor the word anti-psychiatry. No need.

Is what we call time anything else but God? It heals every wound.

Cosmic power, huh? I don't need that, either. Let them stick all their weirdy-weirdo words up their ass. Just give me simple words.

I don't want to speak about projects, either. What a great number of projects people have. Because they're always producing lots of projects, there's no time to produce anything else. I don't even want them to mention projects to me.

However I, too, have produced projects so as not to go on living what I'd been living through, so as not to do what I'd been doing. There's project on top of project in this shitty region, and discipline on top of discipline. Nothing is ever realized. If I had ever gotten on with them, you can be sure I wouldn't have lived through what I have. There wouldn't be anything left for me to tell you. I'd tell you what I wanted to do with them, what I plan to do, even the things that I haven't yet been able to do. None of them will ever be realized. All of them will mingle with my molecules and scatter throughout all the universes.

I don't want to use the word molecule, nor the words atom, universe, or physics. They may exist, but not for me. Universes full of black holes are the metaphor of this world. Everything disappears in the end. It's never ever found again. It disappears in the world's black holes and mingles into infinity. Whatever this infinity of theirs is! As if this infinity is something different from what they call nonexistence!

I used to see the city lights. I used to see those far-off places where the city ends. The landscape, those huge hills on which they've erected transmitters, the roofs they've decorated with satellite dishes. Lives hidden behind the lace curtains of the tall apartment blocks, and peeping toms who wonder about other people's lives. I knew that lives and cities had borders.

These I didn't want. I understood what I saw, but I didn't want to understand. These were forced upon me.

I didn't want any of them. What did I want, anyway? I don't know. To list what I don't want, however, comes easier to me now.

Perhaps I have to do this because my whole life long I've never known what I wanted. I've only known what I didn't want: That's all.

I always have to pee. Whenever I drink even a swig of liquid, I have to throw it out. Are my kidneys working too well—or is there a problem with them? A disease or something.

Do they give out first of all? Before the eyes, the heart, the brain...Do the kidneys rot first?

I don't want any medical words.

Oncology, gastroenterology, orthopedics, pediatrics, cardiology, endoctrinology, microsurgery, more and more... I don't want any of them.

I don't want to be a chip at the end of a kaleidoscope. I don't want to be a piece of mica attractive only for its color, having no meaning at all on its own—nor a stamp nor paper nor cellophane nor plastic. I don't want to be a mandolin pick, a guitar string, the key on a piano.

They made all my friends into chips. In my head they've installed a kaleidoscope that they call life. Sometimes when I turn my head quickly, I see them randomly. It seems they don't have any meaning on their own. With them all together and yet so scattered, it's like a fuzzy picture of my past. It's like they hadn't ever lived, like they were parts of a fictional past.

In the Near East children mature early and die early. They take their place in the kaleidoscope at once.

The number of the dead is increasing. I always look at the city lights.

I always stand apart from the living, remembering the dead.

They all want me to sleep with them. Both the dead and the living. The dead have died pleading their cases, the living are living to plead their cases. Now they want me to sleep with them. I can't even sleep by myself, let alone sleeping with you. I don't want to: That's all.

God is a necessity. Especially in these circumstances. Among disasters, mythologies, penal colonies, stories that we keep inside and here in the Near East, God is a necessity. A great necessity.

I have betrayed you all. I've done every forbidden thing. I've eaten every fruit. Apple peels have wedged between my teeth, mulberries have melted on my tongue, strawberries have stuck in my throat, fig seeds have filled the gaps between my teeth. I have watered the fruits of my insides well and I have betrayed you.

But I have never been able to recapture the taste of the fruits of my childhood.

Treachery is not easy.

You think first before you betray, very rarely does it happen on its own. Then what they call your conscience oppresses you.

Treachery should not be underestimated. Each betrayal paves the way for another, cultivates it and throws it into the soil like a seed. A betrayal is like a person.

As I'm sure you are aware, there is treachery limited to one's life span, but also another that lasts throughout history. Should you bring an instance of the latter to your tongue, you're as good as gone. Because those who've been betrayed—although generally aware of it—don't want to hear of it, and in every one of those betrayed lies a potential assassin.

Treachery is generally either fate or coincidence. People must learn how to submit to coincidence.

Treachery harms both the betrayer and the betrayed. That's why it's so magnificent and has its divine side.

Treachery will be avenged by everyone in a different way. That's why it's so exciting.

Treachery leaves people face to face with themselves. That's why it has a devilish side.

You weren't worth betraying; it happened anyway. I have betrayed you. Both sadly and happily.

First there was treachery. Then lives composed of three hundred words.

I haven't given you my word for anything.

When some power was absorbing all my energy and my feet kept getting colder, I didn't have a single word for you.

Your feelings of belonging somewhere were very powerful. While I somehow sensed I just didn't belong here. Yes, I too once wanted a place to call my own. I've even told you about it. But I just mentioned it as something that I knew would never be.

We were all going to go. My soul was a nomad. Destined to nothingness.

The time of departure was very critical, though. Our time of arrival wasn't our choice. We all had the freedom and opportunity to select our time of departure.

The soul has always been a nomad. It never belongs to any one place.

Whereas you wanted to feel a part of the places you somehow selected or where you were born. You've achieved that much, too!

They told you you'd give your life for those places. And you have.

Who knows what you understand from my groans now and what meanings you attribute to each of them!

Once I was a believer, but I don't want to believe anymore. What are we heading towards?

You've always written glorious histories, but the history of the crippled hasn't been written yet. Nor that of the scarred. Nor that of the blind, of the deaf, of those committing suicide, of those anonymously assassinated, of the children and of those involved in incest. No history of the animals and their world of feelings has yet been written. Hold on, my friends!

We're the children of a cruel world. The history of cruelty is unfairly and falsely unfolding. Give me a date, Dear God. Let it be free of fate, of nightmares.

Let it be untouched by a cruel God.

Please be patient. There's so much built up inside for me to explain. Patience. The most popular approach throughout the Near East. You haven't come this far easily. Always with patience. That's why I ask a little bit more patience from you. It's no big deal for you.

In my nightmares I find myself in a classroom. I'm in an elementary school. One of your schools. Battleship-gray. With a few highlights of light blue and a few of orange on the outside walls, but...

The pupils, the teachers, the basketball hoops are all battleship-gray.

I'm in dread that it will be my turn. The teacher's asking who broke the window. One by one the teacher is calling us all to the board. In numerical order.

Everyone has a number. We're all comprised of a few numbers. That's all we'll be when we're grown up, too.

At the bus stops, in the university halls, in the barracks, in hospitals, pay lines and insurance agencies, we'll all be just numbers.

On the internet, in the web sites and search engines, we will all be just aliases. Aliases searching for information. Each of us a bank account number ordering goods from far-away places. Each of us a card.

Just a series of numbers arranged in a row.

Stop pretending you aren't aware of this!

When they turn our heads to the south and lay us out next to each other on slabs of marble or wood according to the traditions of these lands, we'll then be a line of letters.

Isn't it high time we stopped overestimating the things we don't know and the things we've tried but failed to understand?

No one claims to know.

None of the children, I mean! I broke the window, though. They know but they aren't telling. Each child who claims not to know takes his place next to the others in front of the board. The room smells of chalk.

Somebody once said "We must do away with all the elderly." Was it that fascist Marinetti? If he were alive today, he might change his mind and say "We must do away with all the children."

He was a futurist, a fascist. I don't like those words either.

They've shit into our mouths with words that I've no use for.

Children are cruel because they're rotten seeds. So, why don't these kids tattle on me? Do they expect me to confess? They want me to suffer even more. This is a nightmare. Remorse is enough to kill a child. I think it was that day I died for the first time. On that afternoon in that autumn city.

Do you like underground music? Glam-rock? Punk or post punk? Isn't it time to hear *Bon voyage*? Do the concepts of *la maison* and *le cabaret* comfort you? How deeply are you into paranormal events? Do you deliver the occasional manifesto?

Yeah, right! Is now the time to ask these questions—in the midst of crises, cruxs, pressures, problems, destiny and vagrancy? I don't even want to use such words. They leave a foul taste in my mouth.

At that time I had a girlfriend. How I managed to fall in love at that age I don't know, but I did. Now it's her turn. When the teacher asks her who broke the window, she points at me—not with her index finger, but with her middle finger. Love seeks betrayal. Ancient knowledge passed into my genes let me sense this long ago. Love is betrayal. Betrayal of yourself, even more than that of another.

Until morning I thought about her. A battleship-gray girl. Her father was a police officer. At the end of that year, he was appointed to a coastal city. They left. I never saw her again. Now I come across her from time to time as a chip at the bottom of my kaleidoscope. She's still ten. Still wearing those thick glasses, still in a deep burgundy uniform. Slender, very slender wrists. It was the treachery in her I loved.

My cheeks are burning, my eyes and hands too.

Why must judgment be by fire?

This system teaches you to survive by concealing the revolt in your eyes and bowing your head in pretence of obedience.

I don't want so many words; I don't want any like utopia, proletarian, monarchy, oligarchy, autocracy, democracy.

My speech is rambling, isn't it?

Another time I was wandering in a large hall. I was confused. It was as if we'd been at war. It was a night of ceasefire in the middle of the war. It was a cool spring night. All the windows in the hall were broken. Parts of the curtains burnt in a blaze some nights before. Dark spirits were floating and flitting about. The curtains were like a flag. From what country I didn't know. An indicator!

I don't want to use that word, either. Indicator. It's always misused; it always sounds wrong.

At the far end of the hall, I saw the silhouette of one I'd once loved, whom I'd loved very much, whom I still felt passion for. She was the one who taught me that passion was an illness. That's why I did her in.

We'd gone for a walk in the forest. The weather was gloomy. We walked into the depths of the forest. We met a group of tourists. It was quite a while after we parted from them that we stopped for a break. For a long time—mentioning even the most minute details—I explained to her why I had to kill her. I couldn't stand the thought of being without her, but in the end I'd be without her. More important than that, I couldn't let her go on alone into this curse that's called life. That's why I had to see to it myself. She was gazing at me in disbelief. She even smiled. If I'd been in her shoes and someone began to go on like that, I'd have tried to escape. However, she was quite naive. She listened to me, laughed and said "OK, the next time we come here you can kill me." She thought I was kidding. When I brought the stone down upon her, she was about to drink from a spring there in the depths of the forest. Blood dripped into the water. She collapsed silently where she was kneeling. Trying not to look at her face, I buried her between two oak trees. I washed the stone off in the water. I left it in the very spot from which I'd borrowed it.

I loved her dearly. I loved her as you love the intellectuals. It was because of passion that I killed. No one ever discovered the crime. In the Near East, there are far too many homicides that remain anonymous.

It was years later that she appeared to me in the nightmare. I recognized her immediately. In fact, I'd never forgotten her form. I'd kept it aging along with me. I'd let her mature and put wrinkles on her face. Why wouldn't I know what she looked like now?

From her silhouette I begged forgiveness. It seems she'd already forgiven me because she realized that I'd saved her and sacrificed myself in her place, beginning to lead two lives. She was thankful to me for my bearing the burden of her life.

That's right, life in the Near East is notorious as a burden on the people. That's how it's supposed to be. Life has been intentionally complicated for the Near Eastern people. They exist only to suffer.

Symbolic, expressionist, impressionist, inflation... How cruel and how relative these words are, now aren't they? They should be destroyed immediately. New words can be used in their place. Or even better, let's manage with three hundred words. We'll understand one another more easily. Three hundred isn't such a small number after all, now is it?

The teacher now knew who'd broken the window. The teacher's eyes were very cruel. Eyes like snake's eyes. Everyone was looking at me.

I am a child, a child.

Our classroom was on the third floor. Thirty pupils all in uniform in a single classroom.

I had to get out of that room; out of all rooms.

I threw myself out the broken window. A sliver of glass at the bottom slashed my face. I released my body into the void. Behind me I heard screams. From the third floor I began my flight. I didn't fall, I flew. Everything below grew smaller and smaller. The winter sun was nearing my face. That the winter sun burns stronger, I learned that day. I could see the roof of the school. The snow on the tiles. The terrified expression on the face of my teacher looking out. I was flying toward heaven. And I could see all that was going on below.

But no one believed me. Only with difficulty did they bring me to the ground. Immediately they called an ambulance and rushed me to the hospital.

Lotus flowers, the phoenix, simultaneous, spontaneous, simulacrum. I don't want any of them. They're very fake and very cruel.

In every village, every town, and every city, there are uneasy souls, you know. Actually, there is at least one uneasy soul in every household. For this uneasiness there's no great or grand explanation. The only stipulation is existence. If you exist, you may well be uneasy. That's all.

How much our flesh loves this world, though!

Those who died in torture also loved the world... And those who were stabbed to death by their husbands... And those students caught in the range of fire by a man who suddenly rushed in while they were peacefully listening to the lecture even though they hated their teacher... Those who starved in a hunger strike for the sake of their beliefs did too... and those whose limbs were blown asunder by a bomb planted a few minutes earlier in the mall where they were doing holiday shopping... Those who used long sentences loved their world too... and those who contented themselves with very simple words. All of them loved this world.

Where are they now?

As their molecules mingle with each other and scatter throughout the universe, where are they?

You and I, where are we?

How many of us are there here on this stage-like earth? Or better, how many of us are no longer here?

They thought they'd survive through music... through science, through knowledge, through religion, literature, and culture...

How rich are your theologies! How rich your mythologies!

But the feet of each of you smell after they've been covered for a while, and if you stick your finger in your bellybutton you can pull out some lint.

It's for this reason I've loved you, but you won't remember me long.

I've passed through cities with all shops shuttered up and painted with indelible graffiti that will not be easily wiped off. Endless strings of letters on every one.

I've passed down wide avenues. Signs, advertisements, billboards. Every shop has a name and is full of signs and advertisements; there are billboards one after another. We've dirtied ourselves with letters. With speech and writing.

We've established language—thousands of languages. Now with communication viable, we've chosen not to communicate. Our minds have become confused.

Does it seem to you that I'm talking too much without saying anything?

How strange, I have the same feeling, like I'm not the one speaking. Someone else has written my script.

Sometimes I open the door of the refrigerator and sit in front of it for hours. Winter or summer—it doesn't matter. With snowstorms blocking all the city streets, there I am in front of the fridge. With the sins of the city covered in white, there I sit on the cold kitchen tiles... I know I'll someday be a part of that chill. I won't feel it. I'll cool down until I become the cold itself.

I look at the refrigerator. Empty. Only the edge of one bag protruding from the vegetable bin. From the refrigerator you can understand a person's loneliness. I take out the bag. It's tied up. When I open it, *bulgur*—cracked wheat—scatters on the floor.

An ingredient of the most popular dishes in the Near East. I leave everything as is. Some grains cling to my legs. I get up and pull back the curtain. In the distance there are far-off city lights and just outside the kitchen window flakes of snow as big as walnuts.

Everyone talks big; it's all bullshit. Talking too much is very characteristic of the Near East. Bombastic phrases. Though the tradition of outward silence backed up by an official excuse is also very common in the Near East. Fake, immoral silences. Traditions borrowed from the Middle East. Short meaningless phrases are becoming even more popular now in the Near East. A new way of communication. Like trying to place yourself in a different class by distancing yourself from your own. Impossible expressions. Now we've begun to borrow from the West as well. I've adopted such an attitude, too. As if I did anything different.

The Near East always adopts the wrong traditions. The snow falls in huge flakes.

A snowstorm, disaster!

Why do I persist in this? What is this strange impulse? Is it because the middle class has melted like structures of ice? Why am I telling you all of this?

The world's been put into a refrigerator, maybe for that reason. Because you're not aware of it.

If I'd push myself a little, I dare say I might like you. If I tried a little, I think you might like me. But I don't want to. I couldn't care less about either.

Some nights I take ice cubes out of the deepfreeze. Sitting on the tiles of the floor,

I build all kinds of towers with twenty-one ice cubes. It's not easy, of course. Especially at first. They'd slip all over each other and fall. One night I bought a packet of flour. I dusted the cubes in flour, then put them on top of one another. It worked... at last. I built a tower of Babel with twenty-one ice cubes. The first principle of architecture is to distribute the load, and the second principle is the ground. My ground was slippery, the equilibrium was at the very edge, the load was centrifugal. How would I have known? The tower collapsed.

Are you bored with what I've been talking about? Or what you think I've been talking about? Don't you talk all day long among yourselves about things a thousand times more boring? Like what shall I cook tomorrow afternoon, I got it for a pittance from the market, but it won't make a good stew, where have you put the remote control, is that you, we have guests coming this evening, we won the match, have you ever seen the likes of this? Come on! Open your mouth, the boy doesn't even say a word; he and his girlfriend aren't on speaking terms, how many times must I tell you that's my glass... and the like.

You're the ones who attribute meanings to my moans. There are strange expressions on your faces. Who knows what you're getting from what I'm saying?

Pop-art, op-art, minimalism, cubism, fauvism, constructivism.

You'll say he's just talking nonsense again. Yes. No, I don't want these words. What do they mean? Everyone says something different when you ask. I don't want them.

Whether it's the right or wrong time now to say so, I don't like the word conjuncture.

Power games, strategy, planning, optimization, maximization... I'm sick of them. What need is there for them in a world where the very next moment's insecure?

Literature's just there to tease us. Like the theater, like cinema, like music...

Consider that in each city of the Near East women are dying every day. They hang themselves, swallow agricultural pesticides, shatter their brains with their fathers' or husbands' guns. Unhappy women live behind the curtains of this city. They suffer so much. While the waves from the antennas offer us different lives. Fake loves, playboys, playgirls, dollars, artificial hearts...

References, CVs, cult, kitsch, camp.

We can string them along one after another. These words I can't seem to make my own. I don't like them.

I told you before, you know. I've betrayed you, and some betrayals go unpunished. You can build an entire life on betrayals. I'm aware of this now. Only too much so. Whatever "only too much aware of something" might mean!

Treachery... There's a tingling in the word. It will sap the strength from any words it's sandwiched in between. No matter what sentence you use it in, it will be the word that stands out, the word that remains in your mind.

Treachery.

In the colors of the sunrise, birds used to sing in the branches of the trees outside my window. From the warblings in their throats I'd learn of the coming daybreak. I'd turn off the lights. As the day brightened, I'd try to go to sleep,

I used to avoid sleep. Such a deep sleep had been contrived for us that some of us just had to stay awake. It's not insomnia I'm talking about. Just staying awake, rejecting sleep. Like keeping watch. I'd think of that old tale. The hero cuts his finger and rubs salt in the wound; the pain keeps his eyelids from falling shut. Like in that story.

Now, when I listen to a nursery rhyme, my heart is iceeey.

Now, when I listen to a trip-hop video, my heart is iceeey.

Now, when I repeat over and over phrases composed of words used time and time again, my heart is iceeey.

It all started with a nightmare. On one of my sleepless nights, I had a new nightmare.

I hear a crackling in my heart. My heart skips a beat. I begin listening to my subconscious. There's a crackling in my blood. It's as if shreds of cellophane are flowing in my bloodstream. They don't hurt, though. They flow along, clinging every now and then. While I ask myself what this might be, a terrible pain suddenly pierces my heart. Thinking "I'm dying, I suppose, what else can this be," I realize that I can still stand on my own two feet. My blood's still flowing. But my heart—it's turned to a chunk of ice of the same size and shape. That's why pain sizzles inside.

The mold of ice is strong. Stronger than I am.

I feel no more pain. It flows on and on inside me; I flow on and on inside.

I remember how afraid I was. I was afraid because I couldn't feel any pain.

You're mistaken. If you shrug this off only as a nightmare and say it will pass, you're mistaken.

When I came to I was on the floor. I was writhing on the bare tiles. I felt that a transformation had begun. My heart was getting cold. And truly... it was turning into a mold of ice.

It's never passed. It's been with me since that day. That ice hasn't melted and now I have a chunk of ice in place of my heart.

Now, when I see people being killed, burned, trodden upon and tortured on TV and see others being led out from dank cells with their hands and feet tied, I feel a fine crackling in the ice. But the flesh deep inside me doesn't bleed or sear the way it used to, nor does a cloud of razor blades rain upon my heart.

Now, when I read newspapers and feel taken in, manipulated, asked to hate or to worship someone else, I no longer hate those responsible for what I see on the sheets of paper like I used to. There's only a crackling in the ice.

Now, when I see those so good at being peevish—when I see them act as if they were different from other people, I'm no longer upset. There's only a crackling in the ice.

Ah, if only you knew how I've struggled not to like you all!

Your faces are like a windowpane after the rain. Something I can't see through clearly. Steamed-up like. It's raining cats and dogs, and I've become soaked under the heavy rain of time. How dry you are in your houses, in your homes, in your rooms!

It has been quite a while since I've silenced my inner self. There's just a signal in my head. A buzzz.

Leaving doesn't help, nor does coming back...

To die you can leave, come back or stay where you are. I've chosen to stay... to the end. My soul has decided to go. I have decided to stay.

To stay in the Near East.

The Near East...

Here where all children grow up sick because those who bring them up are sick.

The young mature without hope. Hopes are invested in iron and steel.

Because I am saying this, I must be sick too. Otherwise, what difference would there be between me and the Cretan who said all Cretans are liars.

But...

If you cared about me it wouldn't be like this.

You loved me the wrong way. Because they loved you the wrong way.

You loved the me that you created in your mind.

You loved your father, and it's him you see in me. You love him again.

You loved your mother, and it's her you love in me.

You adored your little brother. You adore your sibling in me.

They showed their love by handling you roughly; they've injured you. You, whatever they've taught you, whatever you've learned in life, that's what you've done to me.

If you had been able to love me properly, if you'd really liked me, I never would have been like this. With my head confused, my heart iceey, my brain in a tizzy, my mind with a buzz, I wouldn't have to walk down the charred streets of cities in ruin.

You loved me because you wanted to analyze me. You loved me so much you've dissected me, loved me until I have no defenses left.

You loved me as in the old Turkish songs—waaay from the depths of your heart—belting them out together till your neck muscles bulged, never bothering to stay on key.

Ah, you! You yourselvezzz loved me by creating terror. You taught me that love must kill.

You loved me until my heart grew iceeey.

I have come to hate many words since that day.

Pre-modern, modern, late-modern, hi-tech, post-modern reincarnation. I couldn't learn to love such words.

Vandalism, imperialism, communism, capitalism, mandates, patronage. No way could I like them.

Whether I like them or whether I don't, these words still exist. Only I have to avoid them.

I used to take long walks by the sea. On the horizon there'd be rowboats—and sometimes ships. On the strand there'd be bags washed ashore, and carrions of seagulls among a litter of plastic bottles and sometimes dead fish floating by and baby turtles. The wet face of the sand. You know water's always stronger than fire, air and earth. The original betrayal was that of the earth by water. Although it seemed weak, in truth it was the strongest of all.

Water's as transparent as glass, as a mirror, as the moon. All images are transparent anyway. And images betray their originals.

I'd like to have been water. It wasn't my fate, though.

I always feel as if I'm missing out on something. You know, like putting off things that I can do any time but never getting around to them, never accomplishing anything.

Standardization, panic-attack, manic-depressive, anxiety, paranoia, schizophrenia, neurosis, psychosis, psychosomatic. These words make me sick. These are words that categorize us, belittle us and force us into uniforms. We desperately need to get rid of them.

Treachery... the most powerful word.

You might have betrayed your lover, your wife, your husband, your children. You may have betrayed your principles, your beliefs, your values, your hometown, your country, your language, your body, your religion, and possibly even yourself.

I have betrayed you. You can betray me.

We might have liked each other, though.

Grotesque, absurd, arabesque. I don't want these words. If you'd help me in fact, how many more words we could have come up with—who knows? There are so many words we don't like that we could discuss their uselessness for years!

It's difficult to climb a mountain without any equipment; it's quite impossible. It's very hard to cross an ocean swimming alone; it's quite impossible. But why should it be impossible—or even difficult—to exist as a human being?

My parents were very old. This and that complaint would arise in their aged bodies—older even than their home. High blood pressure, palpitations, asthma, paralysis of the left arm... so on and so forth. Some nights after they'd gone to sleep I'd go into their room just to listen to their silence.

One day it suddenly happened. I don't remember quite how it happened, though. However, I clearly remember that it terrified me. All my friends began to call me. Their parents were all collapsing. This illness bit appeared all of a sudden that day. They were all rushing their parents to hospitals. I thought the whole generation had decided to sacrifice themselves for us. I was not so sure of it, but this must have been the reason. The explanation comforted me. The idea that my generation, too, would all suddenly fall ill and pass away was comforting to me.

How strange! You don't even know my name. I don't know your names. It's better this way. No one knows the names of real heroes anyway. Only those in the limelight are known. Those on the marquees. The celebrities. What about the people who made them celebrities? No one remembers them. It's better like this, I mean that we don't know one another.

Or—yes—as if we exist in virtual reality. We don't know one another's faces or one another's frames. We have nicknames. We chat artificially under aliases. It smacks of the stage, doesn't it?

Nuclear family, traditions, time payments, obsession. We must immediately rid ourselves of these words. They are trite. They complicate a simple life, making it incomprehensible and confusing—addictive words.

What was I saying? Oh, yes—it was as if the old had all decided to depart on the very same day. I rushed home. My parents were there. My father was silent, lying in bed. My mom was silent, resting her head on the kitchen counter. I rushed them to the hospital. There was a potent smell of gas. I'd arrived just in time.

The phone didn't stop ringing. All my friends' parents were being rushed to the hospital one after another. It was an awful day.

Later, we all decided that our parents' falling ill on the very same day was merely coincidence. That comforted us. Of course it had only been my mother's carelessness, but anyway...

The Near East is founded on coincidence. You know that because you've experienced and witnessed it. We owe even our existence to coincidence.

The climate in the Near East changes from west to east. In the west and southwest the climate is temperate. It gets harsher as you go eastward. There's rain in the north, snow in the east and fickle weather in the west. Even the climate in the Near East is coincidence.

I'm a prisoner of the Near East. You are prisoners of the Near East.

The Near East imprisons us whether we like it or not.

Much later, one night I decided that I must be rid of them—I mean my parents. One of the distinguishing characteristics of the Near East is this: You're always under surveillance. Family, neighbors, friends, teachers, colleagues, your neighborhood grocer, the shopkeepers all around, then the official and civil institutions—they always keep you under surveillance. As if it is for only this that they exist. You're not a gift to this world; this world's a gift to you, a favor you have to pay back. You should bow to their control and live silently and carefully: a harmless creature. Otherwise you're isolated.

Paradigm, protest, performance, personnel, stock-exchange, transaction volume, speculative aims. We must eradicate these words immediately. Three hundred words are enough. Then we'll understand each other better.

One night, I went into their room, listened for their regular breathing and then turned on the gas. Before, remember, they'd been rushed to the hospital for the same carelessness. They were breathing perfectly normally. They were peaceful—in the best phase of their sleep.

The graveyards of the Near East are places where lives converge. Everyone there is equal. Tall, thin, sad trees called cypresses grow there. That's why there's shade in the graveyards. As you go east, however, the cemeteries are more barren. A grave is like a life, you know.

There people cry, reminisce, calm their souls, wonder why they've struggled so in vain, and reconsider the necessity of their passions. In their memory they recreate the good and bad deeds of the deceased—and they talk to the dead, they chat on and on. They suffer and feel relief. Pain yields to peace in these shady gardens.

I've said, you know, my heart was iceeey. I could only feel joy for them. To be honest, I relived two childhood memories. But there was only a crackling in the ice. That's all. In fact, five or six friends who'd come to the cemetery were surprised at this state of mine. I gazed around with glazed eyes. They'd been old, forgetful. They'd left the gas on, that's all—that's all.

I hope they're comfortable now.

The Near East is merciless, you know.

Then an idea suddenly dawned on me. I belonged in those peaceful domains. That is to say, it was time that I should be taken to such a peaceful domain.

What I remember after that is the bridge. The wind was terrible. It was hard to stand upright. But the wind felt good to me. It was as if I were listening to a full and beautiful voice that I hadn't heard for a long time. Down below it was very, very black. From my perch high above, I could see the lights of ships that were passing. From immediately below there were other lights and sounds.

Macro, micro, mega, meta... I don't want these words. I am convinced we must get rid of them.

What percentage of you likes me? What percentage of the population believes in reincarnation? What's the percentage of bribery lately? What percentage of us believe in fidelity, in love? What percentage is convinced that ethics has been corrupted?

Since our lives are based on percentages, I hope you know the answers.

Don't even bother to ask what else I hope for. Never mind.

Right now, however, there's this issue of treachery. What are we going to do about it? Treachery's somehow like the sterling silver candy dish on the big coffee table in the parlor. Offered to our neighbors with respect.

There's some treachery in nearly everything. For example, ever since you arrived I've been repeating words you must get rid of. They'll echo in your mind whether you want them to or not. As you think some of them will come to mind. While I say that we should get rid of them, I'm handcuffing you to them. A ball and chain. This is treachery.

Then...

You've left your homes and offices and come here to make me talk. My speech is far from theater; it's close to life. Here and now we stand far outside anything that might be called a play. In one sense we're a part of life as it plays itself out in the Near East. And this is a betrayal—treachery when you really look at it.

You have been betrayed so many times in your lives that my treacheries seem like needles in a haystack. How they've sacrificed you! Isn't it a pity?

And you, you yourselves have betrayed others so many times that this treachery of mine fades in comparison.

You've betrayed your partners by having relations with others. In bed you've betrayed the person whose flesh is merging with yours by dreaming of another. This is treachery.

My whole life long you have taught me treachery. You've made me an expert. However, there's still that crackling in the ice when I see what an amateur I am compared to you.

The history of the Near East is a history of treachery. I have told you only one tale of treachery. Whereas it's what you've taught me my whole life long.

You've betrayed me by sticking bottles up people's asses. You've betrayed me by torturing people or leaving them to starve. You have betrayed me by leaving children on the streets, little children whom you nurtured on turpentine and glue. You've betrayed me by beating your wives, by bestially raping your own sons and daughters, by killing in the name of age-old customs and massacring in the name of art. Behind masks, you've treacherously committed every immoral act there is in the name of ethics. I no longer believe in you nor in your so-called ethics. You've betrayed me with your contrived wars. With the money spent on them. By depriving people of education… By leaving the suffering to die… By leaving the brains in your hands untrained, by driving intelligent young people off to other countries… By polarizing the populace toward power politics… trusting in shallow thought… eliminating the colors of the rainbow in the name of consistency… You've betrayed me with dirty money from abroad whitewashed in the ski resorts. You must pay for this. It is the penalty of treachery, and you owe it to me. It is in spite of you that I've lived this life.

They've ruined our lives. They've ruined the lives of many before us. They sacrifice one generation for the next. The winners have always been the old. The old, whose hearts and brains are spent. The old, trembling with ambition and living off the flesh of the young. And we watch them win. We've watched them win, waste, and wither our lives. Their ideals have won out. I should congratulate them one by one. But this doesn't mean that history cannot change. History changes, too.

I find myself in a place where each concept involves another and another. A place where each tries to eradicate the other. A place with impossible precepts, a place where conflicting concepts represent nothing more than a chain of order and command.

You are about to leave. You're returning to the treachery called life. After one or two drinks, you'll watch a paparazzi program and forget what I've said here. Some of the words I want you to get rid of will stick to your collar. They're not so foreign any more. They're your words. They won't hurt. Don't worry. That's all. That's all!

If you ask me, I have saved my mother and father from you. As well as the innocent lamb I was in love with.

The people below wanted to talk to me. Why was I there? They wanted me to come down to them. There was solution for every problem in this world. I might solve my problem if I'd just tell them about it. Then a car stops. Someone I recognize from television calls up to me. He says I'd better come down. He promises to help. The wind is strong up here. I take a deep breath, then release my body into the darkness. Now I'm in the embrace of the dark. Even though I used to be afraid of heights. What a wonderful thing this height is, though. It's like freedom. Maybe that's why I used to be afraid of heights. Because I'd been frightened away from freedom—because longing for freedom had turned out to be a crime.

If only I hadn't snagged on the iron grating... I wish I could have felt the "concrete impact" when I hit the water. I wish it had been the last thing I'd had to learn. I wish I hadn't been left a loser, a survivor with broken bones.

It was my silence with which I actually betrayed you. By seeing what all you'd accomplished—what you'd done and done in—and remaining silent, I was betraying you.

Now I am betraying you in a more active way: by not remaining silent. By not remaining silent I refuse to be one of you. I'm now speaking in the name of all those who have been silenced. In the name of all those fed up and no longer on speaking terms with you. In the name of those kidnapped, lost, killed and done away with surreptitiously. I am betraying you by speaking in the name of all those, civil or official, who are obliged to remain silent. By speaking in the name of all intelligent and civilized people, I am betraying you.

In fact, I am betraying you by telling you things that you already know very well.

Now there seemzzz to be an endless crackling in the ice. Something's happening inside me. As if there's movement under the ice. It's as if my iceeey block is splitting down the middle. Am I freeing myself of it as I speak, or what?

Am I getting rid of the Near East, all of you and your treachery, or what?

Now then, I've gone over everything to the last detail. I've cast out all that's been inside me for months. For months you've wanted to make me talk. Am I recovering now, or what?

Or would you prefer to see me silent and depressed, with a fixed glance? Like a poor illegal Romanian worker, longing for his homeland and cursing his new life? Silent— and watching the days turn to nights and the nights turn to days with as much passion as I felt for casting myself from the heights?

The body has healed itself, but what about the mind?

Me oh my! Is it better now that you've saved me? I selected my date of departure. But you stopped me. If you'd just left me where I fell!

Is it better now that you've turned me back from the gates of death?

Is it better now that you've made me speak?

Yeah, if I could just leave off this meaningless moaning and groaning, if I could speak straight, I'd explain all of it to you.

I'd expose and betray all of you. But for months only meaningless moans have come from my mouth. And you guess what I'm saying by attributing your own meanings to my moans. You feel sorry for me. In a little while you'll feed me, believing that my moaning is for want of food.

What have you made of these recent moans of mine? I really wonder. I wonder whether any two of you interpret them all the same, or whether my complaints have said something different to each one of you?

I want to talk but somehow I can't seem to manage.

From the day of my attempted suicide it's been like this. I go on moaning. I think I'm speaking but I am not, I know it. Only meaningless moans come from my throat.

Ah, if I could really speak! Splashing and plashing so, purling and gurgling. Like the rivers of this land. Like the waters so much stronger than the soil.

You're gonna get up and go, but I'll still be stranded here. On a stage resembling the Near East.

This is the price of my treachery. I accept it.

Will things go better?

After how many more generations?

When?

(With strange moans from the throat, the character goes on trying to explain something. Gradually the moans lose all semblance of speech. Darkness. In the darkness his moans continue for a while.)

Translated by Jean Carpenter Efe

"Şifa Niyetine Bir Son Söz: Yakındoğu'da İhanet," *Jartiyer, Kırbaç ve Baby-Doll'ün Ötesindekiler: Hayattan Apartma 21 Kadın Portresi* (2001). Istanbul: Doğan Kitap, pp. 129-159.

İNAN ÇETİN

A Story of Separation

There is no such thing as great misery, great regret or great memory. Everything is condemned to be forgotten. Even the greatest loves. This is the bitter truth in life and this is what makes it beautiful.

ALBERT CAMUS, A Happy Death

Whatever happened, it happened because of that photograph album. If I hadn't taken it out from where I'd hidden it years ago and looked at it, none of this would ever have happened. As if the devil had tempted me, in that deathly still night something came to mind, and I took it out of the dusty bookcases.

The brightness on the wall, unaware of anything until that moment, suddenly shifted to reflect and linger upon the hopelessness in the words of the unknown lover: "Our paths separate."

I used to hate this sentence with a passion. I would dance around these three words like a moth around a light. As I'd approach, both the light and the words would disappear.

As I moved away and sat down on the edge of the bed, again that brightness and the three words appeared inscribed in a large font: "Our paths separate."

It was unbearable. I stretched out face down on the bed. For ages I waited for the light and that ill-fated sentence to disappear. There was not the slightest sign, however, of any stirring. Then I realized that she was in the room, too.

In actuality, she couldn't really be there. Therefore the light and the sentence didn't really exist either.

Experiencing some difficulty in comprehending this, I stood up and walked towards the light. I went nearer, nearer, and nearer, and suddenly both the light and the three words disappeared. Face to face with the unknown, I turned in panic and ran to the window. My mind was chaos. I decided it was nothing more than a trick of my mind. The light and writing didn't really exist. If they were real—and they were still on the wall—then the unknown lover had to be real, too, and that was impossible. Because she lived only in dreams and couldn't escape from that world of dreams.

Then when I looked up and saw her reflection in the window, I was ready to swallow my tongue. From my feet upward, I sensed the blood draining from all my vessels.

The woman behind me right now was the woman of my imaginary world, into which no one else could enter. No! In no way was she real.

As if to prove that she was real, she took off her green coat and, brushing her hair back from her forehead, she smiled.

"Here I am back again," she said; she moved her hand up my spine, and touching the hair at the nape of my neck, "You weren't expecting me, were you, but here I am back again."

I felt a tingling in my head I'd never felt before. I was speechless. There was absolutely no movement in my body other than that of my mind. The fact that all my senses had lost their functions in the face of this unbelievable phenomenon brought ridiculous thoughts flocking to mind.

Nevertheless, one of these ridiculous thoughts was a reality. This thought had brought her to mind. First I'd remembered the colors in a flowered skirt that reached to her ankles; then those three words: "Our paths separated."

The voice that had rung in my ears for a while then trembled in the furnishings and died away. With each step she took towards the door once the voice had faded away, mysterious and awesome realms opened up. I stood staring in wonder as if my eyes saw nothing.

How miserable one can become. When he feels hopeless, how in need of shelter. She was continuously walking towards the door. Nonetheless, I expected her to stop and say something, to gaze long at my face and then smile, blinking her sad and squinting eyes. The door was coming closer, closer and ever closer. The expectation inside me continued to build up.

I watched her feet without missing the slightest detail. Suddenly she was glued to the floor as if some force had stopped her. Here's where she turns back, I said to myself. So I wasn't wrong after all. She's going to turn back and gaze long at my face and then smile, blinking her sad and squinting eyes. She'll say, "Because I love you, I'm not going." She'll run to hug me, she'll kiss me under the chin, kiss my hair, my forehead, the tip of my nose, my cheeks which are blushing with happiness, she'll kiss and kiss…

Her right foot lifted again, then after it the left one… Actions and thoughts followed one upon the other. Just as the hope within me began to fade away, she stopped dead in her tracks.

My inner voice spoke up: This time she'll turn back, surely she will.

She took another step with her right foot, then slowly again with the left... It was at that very moment that all my hopes were dashed. With great pressure, hopelessness collapsed on top of me.

I looked at her reflection in the window, her straight chestnut hair, her black eyes, her eyebrows in the shape of arches, her slightly turned-up nose... It's she. No, that's impossible! This couldn't be real! I rubbed my eyes; when I opened them, she was still there.

"Why have you come back?" I asked.

She made no reply. She looked at me for a while as if she hadn't understood the question, then she took a step backwards to sit down on my bed. She unbuttoned her blouse, took it off, and threw it on the bed. Folding her hands on her knees, she drew her tongue across her lively lips like a shy and innocent little girl.

"I'm sorry, I'm really very sorry," she said. "Everything happened because of that storm."

My heart was beating fast. If it is she, I said to myself, here she is, thus in fact the union of abstraction and reality... If that's the case, what exists in thought but not in reality actually does exist, and why can't we realize this? This means that what exists and what doesn't are two halves of a whole...

I was caught up in an endless game. Every question was at the same time both real and unreal, serious and ridiculous, and so it went on until I was startled by a cry down the street.

With my arms leaning on the windowsill, I was questioning myself whether this nonsense was a result of longing. Or an outcome of my loneliness and merciless over-sensitivity?

I turned back, and there she was sitting on my bed again. A smile appeared in her eyes and spread across her face, where a slight, hardly visible ironic expression then flickered.

"Aren't you going to take me in your arms?" she asked in a whisper.

My breathing became panting, my heart beat faster and faster. I leaned my head against the window; I closed my eyes for a moment and stood there a while.

"I'm sorry, I'm really very sorry," she apologized. "I feel cold." She put the blouse she'd thrown on the bed back on, raised her face and gazed into mine for a long time. Then, taking hold of the sheet at one end, she yanked on it. She wanted to tell me something but, like someone who didn't know how to go about it, she was looking for any excuse to procrastinate.

She bit her lips, casting her gaze downward, and said, "Being together after centuries is unbelievable, isn't it?"

The more she talked, the more confused I became. I didn't know what to say or how to act. She, like a statue on the other hand, watched me from where she was sitting.

"Cen-tu-ries?" was all I could say. I was about to lose all faith in myself. My voice, hoarse and unbelievably weak, threw me off kilter.

She stood up and walked towards the table. Just as she was about to leave, she complained: "You don't remember anything. How weak your memory is."

She touched the photograph album on the table. She fondled it as if fondling a baby. I was becoming really upset.

"What are you talking about?" I yelled.

"I'll help you recall everything," she offered. "Do you have a cigarette?"

I nodded. "They're on the table," I said.

She rose to her feet, took a cigarette from the pack and lit it.

"It was centuries ago," she began, her eyes nearly overflowing with tears; brokenly, she coughed and then stubbed her cigarette out in the ashtray.

"Listen carefully," she said; she waited until she'd begun breathing regularly again and then repeated, "Listen carefully, I told you, sweetheart, if that storm hadn't broken out…"

I was going through a kind of a mental depression, discontent. I commented, "Are you trying to tell me a fairy tale? Go ahead then, I'm fed up with the truth." She looked at my face with something almost like pity. Her gaze wandered about the room, then returned to me, and she eyed me from head to foot.

"Years ago," she said, "there was a city called Harput. I was the daughter of King Sky. You were the boy of the shepherd Sun. One winter day the weather was so warm, clear, and still that it reminded me of spring heralding the promise of summer. That day I'd awakened early and gone out for a walk.

"As I passed in front of the castle, I saw you on your knees. In front of you was a turtle, its head and feet pulled inside its shell. You fondled it; you stroked it for a while, kissed it and played with it. First the turtle poked out its head, then its feet. It was smiling. I can't explain what a great happiness it was to see a turtle smile."

"Come on, now!"

She continued as if she hadn't heard my words.

"I'd fallen in love with you. This coincidence must have been the will of God, but it was a hopeless love. Until the dream I saw."

"Dream!"

"Yes, the dream, the only way for us to come together was to make that dream come true."

"You can't be for real! You're not real at all!"

"I'm here, and because I'm here I'm real; because I'm real, what I'm telling you…"

"You're out of your mind!"

There was a period of silence. There was the same complete silence outside as well.

"That night," her words continued, "there was a fog blanketing the clouds. There couldn't have been a more ideal night for a dream to come true. You were saying that foggy weather is good for the wolf. The only thing you had to do was to dress in my clothes and walk into the palace.

I was afraid. If things went wrong and they caught you, they'd execute you in the public square.

However, this was our only hope to come together. After that night, the fate of the city changed too."

A horrible shiver passed through my insides. I was stunned. An hour or two passed. I looked outside; a puppy was running up the street, it stopped now and then to bark and then continued running. All of this is a lie, I thought. The cry I heard wasn't real, either.

"Sooo," I said in a scornful tone.

"I know that you're curious, sweetheart, but only if you remember, can we get to the bottom of this."

"Don't tell me what to do and what not to do!"

"Calm down, my love. Try to remember that night; it was after that night that everything happened."

At these words, she changed position and put her head between her hands.

"Everything is a lie, isn't it?" Like a suppliant I asked.

"I placed the decapitated head of my father in the coffer with my own hands," she went on. She raised her head; she was crying. The tears that ran down her cheeks dropped one by one onto her bosom.

"Your father's decapitated head? What are you trying to do?"

"Nothing, sweetheart. I just want you to know why I left you, that's all."

"I think I'd have to be an oracle to understand what you're telling me."

"Not at all. I'll tell you everything in the greatest detail."

"No, no, I don't want to hear it."

"You should listen to me, sweetheart… A white-bearded man had told you in a dream that the only way for us to come together was for you to decapitate the king and place his head in an embossed coffer and bury it under the giant sycamore."

"I cut off your father's head, put it in an embossed coffer and buried it under a giant sycamore, is that what you're trying to tell me? Even the birds would laugh at this."

"Yes, that's what happened."

"Then we came together."

"I don't know, maybe it's taken this long for us to come together."

Suddenly everything changed. Silently I kept repeating her sentence: Maybe it's taken this long for us to come together.

I was lost in complete chaos.

"That night," she continued in a voice soft and clear, "that accursed night, the storm broke out. It was raining, pouring like a river from the sky onto the earth. It went on for days—hundreds of people died. If it had continued any longer, not a single creature would have survived. One day the old man with the white beard had once again visited you in your dreams. He asked you to put the head into the grave, and if you hadn't done this, the storm wouldn't have died down. He'd said though that if you put the decapitated cut head in its place, it would be impossible for us to come together."

"But then…"

Suddenly she rose to her feet. "There's a recompense for every price paid," she said interrupting me. "In return for this, the storm died down, but the time for our separation arrived. Look how you've forgotten everything. How soon!"

I realized, however, that great loves could never be forgotten. I didn't have the courage to look her in the face. I looked for her reflection in the window; she was gone. Outside, there was a silence deep enough to drive one insane. The photograph album slipped and fell from my hand; I bent down and picked it up, and turned the pages quickly.

Scarcely legible on the center page was: "Our paths separated."

Then I fixed my gaze upon the wine bottle standing on the table; the telephone rang. I rose to my feet. Who could it be at this hour?

Translated by Burçe Kaya and Jean Carpenter Efe
"Bir Ayrılık Öyküsü," *Bin Yapraklı Lotus* (2003).
Istanbul: Alkım Yayınları, pp. 65-73.

MÜGE İPLİKÇİ

The Ramparts

We arrived at the Topkapı Ramparts. There was a flag to welcome us. That flag, faded a tone or two, was gently billowing atop the ramparts in the sweltering July sun, a symbol of our miscalculation. You were absent-minded as usual but very self-confident! As a person claiming to have known this city for years, you'd crowded me into one of the shuttle-buses in Eminönü and said to the driver, "Here's two fares to Topkapı." That self-confident aura of yours still persisted when you glimpsed the flag on top of the Topkapı Ramparts; afterwards you added in a mechanical tone, "Topkapı Palace or Topkapı Ramparts, it hardly makes any difference." With the arrogance of children from a decent family, at first we advanced among the pushcarts of the street-sellers from which the wailing notes of Müslüm Baba songs emanated. Unless we take your contemptuous attitude into account, it was obvious that we were both in total distress. However, I can easily say that later we ran off the track. You'd shown me various publications and tricks of the trade that could be defined as noxious, and said, "Look, there's a good side to everything," as you bought several old *Playboy* magazines. One of your friends was collecting the old issues of *Playboy*; he was going to do some statistical research—in fact these magazines had a political aspect. There *were* serious articles inside; they were worth reading. "That's why they sell so well," I commented half naively, half in jest. "If you don't know, don't speak up," you'd scolded me. At that point the flag was flapping wildly atop the ramparts behind us... It was continuing to ridicule us. You were being a nuisance. That was the essence.

This hasty sketch was of course not what I had dreamt of as the tourist sights of the city. This present vision was fragile and vulnerable; moreover, our major problem remained unresolved. How would we get to Topkapı Palace?

According to you, it was really very easy. In short, it was a trifle. The main issue was whether we would drop into the nearby Russian bazaar where we could buy cheap silverware, binoculars, salt-shakers and even those Matruşka dolls. While I was still asking where Topkapı Palace was, you took us to a counter full of binoculars—and even a telescope—and succeeded in exhausting the man with your capacity of some ten words recalled from your elective course in Russian.

In the end we took to the road with binoculars hung around our necks, having looked through the telescope once and seen a hollow, colorless dream. Your mind was still in the heavens.

"I wish it were night so we could see the moon and this-and-that through it... Once in Taksim Square a man set up a telescope like this one when there was a full moon—not like this one actually, maybe five times—or ten times bigger. The passersby paid a good deal of money to gaze at the full moon. With *Biz Heybeli'de* playing in the background, my God, he was both sipping his *rakı* and enjoying the night. At that very moment I stood before the telescope, looked deeply into it and saw spheres with weird and fascinating surface features—not the moon, perhaps one was Venus—or no, Mars. I turned to the man. What're these? I asked. He could have cared less; he just nodded. Meanwhile, I was listening to the song, smelling the anis and hearing voices from the people in the queue, complaining, Come on, you've been gazing long enough! In fact, I didn't mind their fuss because I couldn't even bring myself to speak after seeing those fascinating features. Hey, hold on, I've discovered something, you godless souls! As if we're in a bus queue! If it had been any other time, I'd have turned around and shut them up; I couldn't get a word out. Everything aside, I felt broken-hearted. You'll never be able to go that far, I told myself. With such a short look, you'll never catch that moment out there. That I'm sure of. I felt awed. Do you know what happened then? Something you wouldn't—nobody would—ever believe happened. Amidst those come-on-brother complaints, the Heybeli Island song, the horns of the cars, those landscapes should I say on Venus or Mars—let's say on the moon, or maybe it was another planet—perhaps I became giddy or my soul was too involved with the concept of remoteness, I saw a woman dancing in white. She was dancing, really dancing, with bare feet, her hair streaming in front of something resembling a strange gramophone I'd never laid eyes on! This was an indescribable dance. A beautiful dance. She'd fling her skirt high, then wrap it around her, a woman on a remote planet, shining in the darkness, as if she might be pregnant."

"Does that bus go to where we're headed? Look, it says Beyazıt on it..."

"It's no problem, Ergun" he said, immediately returning to his adventures with the telescope.

That night he had been haunted by the paranormal. When he arrived at his bachelor flat, he'd found the door open, and rather than turning back, he'd entered his rooms;

just at that moment, the electricity had gone off and he muttered, par for the course! Then fear began to arise; he took out his flashlight and went round the house like a thief. In the rays of his flashlight he could see the place had been ransacked, all drawers in his bedroom gone through. It was just as he'd been leaving the bedroom... Bewitching eyes were gazing at him from a window in the apartment opposite. The full moon was very bright. It was stronger and even more compelling in the dark, he said. At that moment he'd heard the barking of several dogs in the street onto which his living room faced. Perhaps it had been only one dog. He couldn't be sure. However, it had been such a bellowing that anyone who heard it would surmise that all the dogs in the neighborhood were rising in rebellion. He'd quickly gone back into the hall to catch his breath—actually, he collapsed. A little while later he'd gathered himself together and once again gone into the bedroom, as if coerced by some mysterious power. Simultaneously he stiffened and began to pray for the electricity to come on. And then their eyes had met. With hers rimmed in black and her face a paler shade of white; in a nightgown like a straightjacket—yes, he'd even been able to see that—there she was in her bedroom on the third floor of the building opposite... At that point the electricity had come on only to go off again—as if somebody were playing a game with him. The pursuer would constantly change. First she was 'it' and then he. Amidst the flashing of the light he'd noticed that she was swaying like a pendulum. First right and then left...

"I was terrified, to say scared to death would be an understatement. With the electricity constantly flashing on and off, she swung from left to right. It was as if her eyes were peering into my heart. Between her building and mine there was a large open space. In the daytime eight or nine cars would park there in a single row; judge the distance from that. From so far I could easily make out the purple under her eyes. It was unbelievable how her eyes surrendered to me, full of meaning where I expected only a blank stare.

There was a point between us where the light was broken. I was aware of that. But I don't know why such a thought should have stirred me so deeply. I do believe it was the curtain fracturing the light. I mean it seemed like that to me. Then many aspects of the breaking of light crowded into my mind. Of course, camera obscura is the simplest of all. However, it gives the basic principle. You know, there is a candle, and the projection of the candle is a reverse candle. However, it is in fact the same candle, my dear Ergun.

The candle.
The point was not the light, but the candle. Namely, myself. In fact, she and I. I may have to explain it further.
You have the candle in mind, don't you?

The candle, that's what's important.

I felt as if I'd seen the reverse of my own image. It was as if I were receiving not only my image, but the future as well. Don't think I had minutes to spend on this. It was only an instant. I don't know if this has anything whatsoever to do with my being burgled or my looking through the telescope that night in Taksim Square. I'll never know. However, my feelings were fugitive. Was it at all possible not to have noticed that person in the apartment opposite? I lead a rather lazy life. I admit this. Nevertheless, there are times when we receive urgent messages from our own lives. Moreover, this wasn't the first time for me. Of course, the idea of just pondering this wasn't good. Why altogether? Receiving such a message, hosting such a message on my own. Calling these consecutive incidents coincidence, going on living as if nothing had happened...

I didn't speak of this in the police station when I went in the next morning. While interrogating me, the man—looking at my metallic hair—commented: 'You look like a foreign film star, but who? I can't make out who. What *was* the name of that film?'

'Could it be *Metro*?'

'No, not that one,' he said.

'Are you sure? The star of *Metro* had hair like this, too.'

'No, not that one,' he said obstinately. 'What was your real name again?'

'Servet Gerede,' I answered."

It was at that point we clambered into a taxi. Around my neck hung a pair of Russian Zenith binoculars. We want to go to Topkapı Palace, Servet told the driver.

OK, he agreed. To Sultanahmet.

That's right, Servet confirmed. He started to hum the soundtrack from *Metro*.

A city exasperated by the oppressive heat passed by the windows of the taxi: a few sycamore trees, some swarthy-faced men and wearied women, the silhouette of the 4.8-earthquake centered in the Prince's Islands that was about to occur as we toured the palace, the lunacy that would gradually take Servet into its grasp in ten years' time, my inability to visualize the reflected image of myself even in reverse, and the theme song from the film: *Life Is a River*.

Translated by Hande Öztürk and Jean Carpenter Efe
"Kalenin Bedenleri," *Transit Yolcular* (2002).
Istanbul: Can Yayınları, pp. 129-135.

MÜGE İPLİKÇİ

You Are Without Me

I saw a nightmare the other day. A man standing in front of me. He was so kind as to tell me his name: Mr. Prank. Mr. Prank was his name.

Mr. Prank didn't know his P's and Q's. He didn't know his P's and Q's at all.

He was trying to pull down his pants even while he was speaking in a preaching tone about what we consider really grave matters, saying: "Forget it… Forget everything. Give up living life in search of that special muse. Forget all your grave obsessions with life because life is too short…" Luckily, I'd closed my eyes.

Then Mr. Prank suddenly turned into Snow White with her taffeta dress filthied and stinking with the dirt from all those years. And I'd thought he was a man. You know that *Snow White* film with Little Ayşe, that's who it was. Yes, it was Little Ayşe, I'm sure. Then I heard Mr. Prank's voice: "The princess here with her make-up all smeared is actually destiny itself that's been put through the thousand-and-one hoops of fortune." Then, poof! He came out of the princess. Again, Mr. Prank. Little Ayşe is standing there as well. She smiles sweetly. Meanwhile, Mr. Prank is soberly asking me questions. In this, he reminds me of my middle-school teacher: Come to the blackboard. Solve this equation.

Would you like to speak to him?

What would you say to speaking to him?

Come on, do something crazy for once, take a spin on the wheel of fortune!

He doesn't pay any attention to my saying stop, don't, I'm an elderly woman, what's more there's my heart condition, my high blood pressure, my high cholesterol, my anemia; despite my fierce resistance, I'm ashamed to say, as you may guess, he goes inside me. Not the way you think, not like that at all. Never! It was something else that this Mr. Prank did. I'm ready to open my mouth and speak. But no. It's impossible.

Someone else inside me speaks on my behalf. The voice is mine, but it's not me speaking. However, as to the wishes it makes, they're all wishes that have long been in my mind.

Meanwhile in front of me—or should I say us—is, oh how should I know, Little Ayşe, Destiny, Mr. Prank's designer, I don't know, one of them looks me directly in the eye and murmurs sweetly: You mortal! Do you believe in the virtue of going away?

I do, I say. Supposedly I do. I've never left for good before. I've yelled and cursed at everybody else for leaving, but the truth is, you see, I've never gone away in the true sense of the word.

I do, I say.

Supposedly I do.

It seems I do.

Since you do, then wish from me anything you want!

Wish for anything you want!

My answer is clear, it seems to be clear: a journey of the self.

"Whaaat?"

"A journey of the self."

"A swift one or a pausing one?"

"A pausing one." (It seems that Mr. Prank is protecting my heart.)

"One reaching an end or not reaching an end?"

"Not reaching an end." (But how, Mr. Prank?)

"One teaching a moral or one not teaching a moral?"

"NOT TEACHING A MORAL." (But why not, Mr. Prank?)

"Okay, but then why in the world do you want to go on this journey?"

"To get myself out of the way." (What a cruel Mr. Prank, what a crude Mr. Prank.)

"Wait a minute now, it's not that simple."

"Still, I'd like to try." (I'll get back at you someday, Mr. Prank.)

"Stubborn! At least tell me this much: dead or alive?"

"I've been dead this long, so let's make it alive now." (Smart-ass, Mr. Prank.)

"Comprised of absence or comprised of a beginning?"

"Neither one. Let it consist of a journey. The story of a wandering traveler, a slave of death." (Mr. Prank, you'll get yours!)

"Take this then—a prank which will get yourself out of the way!"

(What shall I do now, Mr. Prank?)

It is the moon as well as the lights in my mind that brighten my way. Scattered cars pass me by—in a thin stream, flowing by in thin lanes.

Did you say it was two in the morning, the you who were passing under the train bridge—which you? Your face, your hands, your ankles and your eyelashes. All the corridors in your life. In one of these corridors you wanted to laugh strangely and perhaps nonsensically. For example, your middle uncle, about to reach the seventieth rung on the ladder of life suddenly remembers that you're his niece and then stops speaking to you because you haven't been asking after him... The nights of your life; and yet another light, a pair of headlights, brights, you were unwarily ensnared by the brights of a yellow taxi. Your uncle's wife must have a finger in this, for sure. "Look," she's probably said, "look, does your niece ever call you? That mother of hers, who's supposed to be my sister-in-law, constantly reproaches you because we made her take care of Mom. And what about your niece, does she ever call you, did she come to the engagement of our own dear son who's supposed to be her cousin, her own cousin, did she even bother to come, did she bring even one piece of jewelry to our daughter-in-law..."

As much as the lights in my mind, you too are in front of me. You, passing under the train bridge in the middle of the night. A very young and handsome man, for some reason you've pictured him in a trench coat with the collar slightly turned up, quite a smart young man... you've dragged this man along with you. You were searching for a park in Toprakyer, tugging at his sleeve. This is a repetition of a chorus for those who've heard it or assume they've heard it: This waaay, no no, that waaay... It was neither this way nor that way. The park had been lost and was never to be found again; even if it had been found, that young uncle wouldn't have been there; even if he had been there, he wouldn't have been wearing the trench coat; and even if he'd had it on, the times of the Toprakyer playground had become history. So is or was the problem of this uncle? No. If a problem has to be sought, it must be sought in our disappearances in the present.

As much as the lights in my mind... You are there, of course you are. Within the passage of time, pick out any period you like, your being suddenly dumped on the pretext of made-up excuses. Or those you've dumped maliciously. Your hair damp from the recent drizzle. And red. You, you, you. Oh, how much you are like me. Just a while ago you were at the gas station in Toprakyer. Under the green fluorescent light of the BP station, you'd asked the night tank-watch, "Do you have a cigarette?" You were a frog princess in that phosphorescent green. And red. Then suddenly those brights... Those ominous bright headlights. Damn your past and damn your future! You're a funny one, time-tripping with your curses.

That you in front of me, don't be angry with the taxi driver. Never mind his honking that scares you to death. Never mind his splashing fast through the puddles under the train bridge, the tires and the water and the horn and your hair's being washed with the underbridge waters. Look how pretty you are: the lady of the underbridge waters. And red. Smile; nothing is worth being discreet about.

Smile. Smiling's hardly enough; laugh out loud. Never mind your uncle in the trench coat coming home empty-handed with an expression that implies "you're to blame" and then still more: If one settles for a crow as a guide in life, and… is what happens when someone trusts you, etc. Laugh now like a three-year-old child. What would change / have changed if you'd said that this was all a labyrinth and what's more that it wasn't a game? The park had vanished between the greenery and the blue of the horizon. It was no child's play to find it. Moreover, no game is ever as innocent as one imagines.

You as much as the lights in my mind, the bricks under the bridge like the lights in my mind, the fairy tale of how the "underbridge" street urchins shall be saved and transformed into good kids, the movies with Little Ömer and Little Ayşe and the childishness that begins with them running as far as the cheap pink *Nolamaz Nüneyt* romances—transformed into glimpses through rose-colored glasses—well-meaning but always well-meaning—with the reality of today sold out long ago… Whatever these fairy tales actually represent to me, as much as they have, you too have disappeared into thin air.

What was it that you were searching for that day in what you called the playground?
What was it that you were searching for that day in what you called the playground, tell me.
The swings, a boyfriend in a trench coat, and now, the slide, a naughty niece, your uncle's fiancée that you began to envy even at that age, the Little Ayşe movies your uncle took you to, sometimes with his fiancée, your occasionally catching them cheek to cheek or in one another's arms and turning your head away to the other side—lip to lip or perhaps one lip inside the other—darkness, the knowing looks of Little Ayşe, your hope to see action-comedy films turned down…
What was it that you were searching for that day in what you called the playground?
What was it that you called a game that day?
The game that day was murdering your uncle. Games take on the magical spell of life from their strict rules.
What you were searching for that day in what you called the playground was your future. It was your boyfriend in his trench coat who left you in the middle of the night. Hasan… It was your boyfriend whom you'd already left long before. Yes, this Hasan. And the game was over.

You, as much as the lights in my mind, your escapes… You've just slammed the door and gone out. If it had been a spring evening, your name probably would have been "I encountered you one spring evening," but on an autumn night one stop before the Toprakyer gas station on the train bridge that leads to Tozkoparanyer, do you think it will be chiseled in history after some hero called "everything-inherent-but-not-in-use-for-anything"? Your uncle's wife was right; you should have taken something gold to your cousin's engagement party. Moreover, rather than submitting a blank ballot in the last elections, you should have given your vote to one of the rightist parties on the left-hand side of the ballot, you shouldn't have been angry with the NGOs and admitted that they too were in search of some goal. You should have said, "Then again, then again…"

The woman looking at the bricks, the woman now so wet and red, the woman the shadows dimmed and muffled—then start from the beginning, a bouquet of lights, the rain on the streets, the slippery roads, did you say it was two in the morning, why this hour, I know you like to be on these strange roads at night, an unfulfilled backwater that best suits the city people, one third of whom are out of their minds. Luckily, the moon is on your side. Actually, why bother to lie, you're not very fond of the moon either. Hold on a minute, this you in front of me, even though I can't see from here—your face, your ankles, or even your eyelashes; tell me the truth now about this trench coat, where did you get this very symbolic, tattered, oversized trench coat? You are as much as the lights in my mind. That's why you'll never pull the wool over my eyes with your tales of the "Invisible Citizen" with such sweet concern.

Translated by Sevinç Ener and Jean Carpenter Efe
"Bensizsiniz," *Transit Yolcular* (2002).
Istanbul: Can Yayınları, pp. 120-127.

ASLI ERDOĞAN

Wooden Birds

The door of the room opened suddenly and a red head burst in. Dijana's voice, breathless and impatient, was heard, "Come on now, Felicita! Shall we be waiting for you all day? Get that big arse of yours out of bed. You're dead inside, woman, dead."

The door was shut as quickly as it was opened; the antiseptic smell of the hospital corridor, Dijana's shrill voice and superficial but hurtful mocking remained outside.

Filiz, whom the lung patients called "Felicita" ("Happiness"), was in reality an extremely pessimistic, reserved and embittered person. Her status as a political emigré, her Ph.D. in history and the volumes of books in her room had rendered her a not-so-endearing intellectual in the eyes of the patients. "Ah, that Felicita of ours," Dijana would say, "I'd rather read a book on oncology than attempt a chat with her. She hardly ever opens her mouth." That dark and withered Felicita of ours! She was in the nick for two years in her country: Felicita, whose head was buried in books, who had not managed to learn to speak German without an accent in all these ten years!

Filiz got up from the bed very slowly. Her long-lasting illness—pneumonia in both lungs and chronic asthma—had taught her to use her strength sparingly. She would yield to the whims of her body that whined and begged continuously.

For the first time in eight months she was to leave the hospital premises. On the roll of patients in the recuperation phase who were granted the two-hour Saturday leave this week, there was also the name "Filiz Kumcuoğlu." Dijana, who had turned the hoodwinking of the nurse on duty at nights and the pinching of the patients' files into the greatest adventure of her hospital life, had been informed on Monday of this development. She had prepared "a big surprise." THE AMAZON EXPRESS! Filiz deserved to participate in the secret of the third-floor patients and embark upon the Amazon Express. In truth, Filiz had absolutely no expectations whatsoever. At the very most, they would go to the only settlement in a radius of thirty kilometres, T. village, and have a glass or two. Perhaps they might meet the village lads or the male patients of the men's sanatorium, as spent as themselves. What else was there to do in the midst of the Black Forest?

Filiz remembered all of a sudden, just as she was leaving the room, a story she had heard at least twenty years ago and then buried in one of the unfrequented recesses of her memory. At the beginning of this century, the consumptive female patients of the Halki Island Sanatorium would go in secret to the woods at night and make love with the consumptive male patients. Pale-faced women in white nighties, ordained to die, walking with torches alight in their hands... She had not believed the truth of the story, but found it poetic and tragic. Poetry had long forsaken her life; her personal tragedies had so multiplied that like parasitic plants they had drained the sap of her being.

Get out of the double-glazed door! Turn your back on that sombre, frowning, gray sign, "T. Hospital, Unit of Lung Diseases" and looking neither left nor right, walk fast. To the line where the gigantic shadow of the building terminates. And right there, pause at the boundary of the empire of the sun, hold your breath and slowly take that single step, the single step that shall lead you out of the shadow. So that even the frail northern sun warms your back all of a sudden and you convince yourself that you can erase your past completely! Let the sun play little games in your hair, let the woods be attired in raw colors, let the lineaments of the world be obliterated and let truth be transformed into pure light.

Filiz recalled Nadezda, who dreamt she would fly up into the skies if she but raised her arms, the unhappy Nadezda of Chekhov's "The Duel." She felt like a Chekhovian heroine. She might perhaps be transformed into a bird there and then, but only a wooden bird. An inanimate, helpless, ridiculous bird whose wings were not for flying but only for emitting mechanical noises. She was filled with a painful fervor. She wanted simultaneously to laugh and to cry, to live and to die.

"Come on now, Felicita! You stand frozen like a mummy. We're late."

Gerda's contralto voice, thick with smoking and tuberculosis, joined Dijana's. "You'll miss the Amazon Express!"

The group that met in front of the garden gate consisted of six women. "Three foreigners, three Germans. Three with tuberculosis, three with asthma," classified Filiz on the spot. "The Germans all have tuberculosis, we of the Third World, asthma. Quite the contrary would have been expected." Martha and Gerda, two tall and stout blond Germans, had managed to remain strong and hefty in spite of tuberculosis. (In fact Gerda was not very tall, nor could she be called blond, but Filiz's eyes, insensitive to personal details, saw the two women as identical and placed them as representatives of the working class in the small community.) Filiz was a little wary of the physical strength of these women, of their crudeness and their determination in defending whatever was to their benefit, but at the same time she secretly envied them. The third German was the twenty-year-old Beatrice, skinny as a totem pole, cheeks sunken, an introvert ex-heroin addict. This girl, with her chestnut hair cropped short, her wistful eyes that seemed to be always looking for something she had lost and her adolescent body that resembled a withered tree, made Filiz sad. The playful red fox Dijana had a finger in every pie. She cared for nothing, didn't get annoyed at anything. Except for being called Yugoslavian instead of Croatian. And Graciella from Argentina...

At the sanatorium the only patient as ostracized as Filiz, perhaps even more so, was Graciella. The very sight of this woman, distinguished by birth and wealth and unanimously described with epithets such as "elite, graceful, cultured" amongst lung patients, was an example of the dry humor of life. She was about one hundred and fifty-eight centimeters in height (shorter even than Filiz), dainty and of a slender build. With her straight fringed hair, her "Marlene Dietrich" eyebrows, which she shaped without fail even in hospital, and her almond eyes that had at once both a warm and an icy expression, she had acquired the appellation "Evita." She was the pet of the doctors and the nurses; they treated her like a rare, fragile antique vase. In any case, she tended to leave the impression that the whole world should treat her with care and consideration. Filiz, however, had sensed the hardness in the perfect lineaments of her face, which resembled a feminine china bibelot. Graciella had a smile that inspired fear in people. She reminded Filiz of her pleasant, ladylike primary school teacher who had worn a scarf every day and turned into a first-class torturer the moment she entered the classroom.

The first time Filiz had seen Graciella, she thought she was a visitor who had entered the patients' canteen by mistake. She was at a table for one by the window; she was wearing a straight black velvet skirt and a shirt with eye-catching buttons open down to the breast-line. Between two attractive boobs glittered a heart-shaped necklace. High-heeled and buckled "tango shoes" and nylon stockings provided the final touch. Amongst patients with greasy hair, wandering about in tracksuits and sandals, she looked like a rare tropical flower. Be that as it may, Dijana, editor of the hospital gossip news, had noisily entered Filiz's room one day and disclosed a secret.

"Did you know that the Argentinian Evita is just like you?"

"What do you mean, 'just like you'?"

"A political émigré, that is. Imprisonment, torture and stuff. That's how her lungs had it. Her ex-husband was a diplomat. Both came of wealthy, well-established families and had influential friends. But then the man provoked someone and an order for his arrest was issued. Within two hours he vanished into thin air. Leaving his wife behind. For two months they tried to make Graciella talk, but they couldn't get from her the whereabouts of her husband. Perhaps she didn't know. Would you believe it of that frail woman? One should not be deceived by appearances."

This was a devastating blow for Filiz. It was as if her deepest afflictions were being made light of and Filiz K., with her personality and history, had been rendered worthless. In her own ego she had created a mythological heroine of herself; she could sustain her life only by believing in this heroine. The memory of her awful past was indispensable as a proof of her existence and had acquired a sacred niche in her soul. But that snob of a woman had spat in the face of her icons. What right had she to claim possession of the same tragedies as the strong, daring and principled Filiz (that's how she would describe herself) who had paid the price of her convictions? And in the name of a love felt for a base man with a paunch and a couple of mistresses, too!

The group of sick women was walking along the narrow tarmac road which meandered like a gray snake down to the T. Valley. Right at the start of the journey a mitotic division had occurred. The group of pioneers consisting of Dijana and the two large Germans was engaged in a light chat. A Saturday chat that moved from one topic to another, topics that interested Filiz not in the least. The doctors were thoroughly criticized—the food in the cafeteria and the coffee were condemned, along with television programs, a comparison of Banderas and Pitt and so on… The Germans defended Banderas while Dijana, who admired the German race, was for Pitt. One or two memoirs pertaining to the pre-hospital period… In the factory where Martha worked four years ago, one of the female hands had been found naked with her throat cut. Gerda also had in her stock a few tales of murder; she recovered one such from the deepfreeze in order to warm it up and present it. As for Dijana, whose family lived in Bosnia, she said not a word about savagery; she hid behind a silence that gathered more and more like an avalanche.

Not having at all decided where she belonged, Beatrice walked alone. She was listening to her inner world. She was trying to take in, without wasting a single drop, this extraordinary September afternoon, the emerald green valley that lay before her, the couple of hours of freedom. She seemed happy, and happiness on this ruined young face was for some reason even more poignant than a grimace.

Filiz had fallen in beside Graciella and was trying in vain to discover a topic for conversation. The silence between them was long and thorny.

"Seeing you on the Amazon Express is quite a surprise, indeed."

"Why?" inquired Graciella harshly. In her eyes there glittered a cold flame which was a reflection of the anger which, like ore, had been hidden inside her for years. "They did not tell you where we're heading, did they?"

"No, they conceal it as if it were a great secret."

"It is truly a great secret, the Amazon Express. (A mocking, calculating tone, a smile like the mark of a scar.) Even you will be amazed."

"Perhaps we're going to the village?"

Graciella placed upon her lips a long fingernail painted with a cherry-red varnish. "Hush," said she, like the nurse in the "Be Quiet" poster in the hospital.

Filiz had neither the courage nor the desire to keep up the conversation. She devoted herself to getting the utmost enjoyment out of the trip. She was outside, after eight months, walking in a fairy-tale forest, inhaling the air, placid like water, pure and delicious. This very air purified the past of all its squalor as it filled her exhausted lungs.

A loving, generous sun, an infinity of green that stretched to the horizon and the ordinary, simple, gorgeous happiness of walking as much as she liked without any barriers... Without any closed doors confronting her... The iron-barred doors of prison wards, the hospital doors with the room numbers written on them, soundproof and with the hinges greased... A healthy person could never comprehend the illimitable pleasure arising from exercising one's legs freely and carrying one's body. Filiz perceived the incomparable scent peculiar to the forest. This scent, not sweet and domestic like that of the newly-mown hospital grounds, was crude and earthy and made one dizzy. Perhaps it was the odd silence that made Filiz's head swim. The T. Valley was spread before her like a thickly-knotted green carpet and the hills were blinking, as it were, behind one another's backs. In the valley deepened by the light of fall, sun and shade were engaged in an interminable battle to claim the land. The crucifix of the village church shining like gold could be seen in the distance. "Everything is so bright and carefree that it hurts," she reflected.

Beatrice, her palms full of wild strawberries, approached the party of dark-haired women. She must have solved her identity crisis and resolved to belong with the "aliens." The tragic bond that drew those two ex-prisoners to each other was pervading and swallowing Beatrice too, like the web of a poisonous spider. Heroin had taught her solitude, despair and ruin, and although the youngest, she was the most intimate with death. She had carried death in her half-child body. The others had struggled to believe in life, hold on to life, be a part of life and they were still struggling, but she, as early as sixteen, had rejected life. Heroin, prostitution, jaundice, tuberculosis... She had received consecutive mortal blows, but each time, had pulled herself up like a boxer at the count of nine before the knockout bell sounded and went on to receive the blows.

"Would you like some wild strawberries?" (No, neither does.)

"Last night there was a program about Argentina on television. Did you watch it?" (No, neither had.)

"It showed Buenos Aires. An extraordinary city. So sad! Reminds one a little of Berlin: the architecture, the cafés... There's a district full of houses the colors of the rainbow: Elbakar—"

"El Boca," corrected Graciella. "It means the mouth. The birthplace of the tango."

"Yes, yes. El Boca. The district of the marginals, painters, musicians."

"Apparently it's now full of pickpockets and vendors of souvenirs."

"Do you know how to tango?" burst in Filiz.

"No, I'm not from Buenos Aires. I'm from Mendoza." (For some reason Filiz was sure this woman was from Buenos Aires and could dance the tango perfectly.)

"Mendoza?"

"On the border with Chile. A city at the foot of the Aconcagua."

"Aconcagua. The highest mountain in South America." (Compared to these Germans, even a heroin addict is well-educated!)

Silence. The labored conversation terminated all at once, as if cut with a knife, as if the three women had nothing to say to one another. "Look, look! See that loop on that low branch?" Beatrice failed to control the fervor in her voice—the two middle-aged women stared amazed at the nondescript piece of rope. "A dwarf might well have committed suicide here," continued Beatrice, with a poisonous imagination inspired by her twenty years and the heroin. But immediately remembering that her companions were extremely short, she blushed. Nobody, however, had taken it personally.

When the group of women left the road going to the valley and turned west towards the sheer hills covered with thick woods, Filiz began to grow suspicious. They were not going to T. village then. Perhaps like school kids or prisoners, they had picked a secret corner of paradise for the Saturday license. But if such were the case, they would not have to check their watches every so often and hurry on. "The Amazon Express!" Did they mean the rain forests or the legendary women, expert hunters and warriors, who had cut men off from their lives the way they had chopped off their right breasts?

They were no longer walking along the wide and sunny tarmac road; they were proceeding in a single line along a path covered with shrubs and tree roots where the vegetation did not allow for easy passage. The forest journey had commenced for real. Even the sun was now clad in green. A journey teeming with thorns, underbrush and beds of fern which, after warning the unfamiliar travelers lightly at first, was growing increasingly more aggressive; a journey teeming with brown butterflies that fluttered hither and thither among the branches, shy mushrooms that hid in shady nooks, and autumn flowers. Pearls of rain dripping down the leaves, the saturated, sticky moss on the tree trunks, the refracted colors of the daylight... Streams that continuously intercepted the trail: the vital arteries of the forest... Seductive paths that revealed no clues as to their destination...

Filiz had always lived in big cities; she did not know the forest. True, she had been in a sanatorium at the center of the Black Forest for the last eight months, but there, too, the forest had remained inaccessible; it remained abstract and mysterious. At night, the darkness that descended before her window like a dark bird and the roars that accompanied her nightmares were a huge mute sentinel that prevented her from going out and returning to her real life—whatever that was. But now, having entered the very core, the very heart of the forest, she saw it truly for the first time. This was more than a meeting; it was the sudden encounter between two beings that had been unaware of each other's existence. That's why it had a shattering impact on her. Before her was a simple, primitive, magnificent spirit, like that of the ocean. Having directed her out of her dusty and parched nutshell of a world, it was making her listen to the vibration of a completely different plane of existence. The forest had a savage and multicolored throb, beating like a pulse. It was covered with shades, contradictions and shiverings; a vibrant and misty air was spread over its secrets like a sheet of tulle. Trees, trees, trees... Ancient, venerable, proud, tall, profuse, commanding trees... They were as somber as if they had born witness to each and every miracle and crime on earth. Older even than time... They had struck their roots deep; in their journey that had as its goal the sky, and only the sky, they had made enough progress which showed that they had not been blown here and there randomly.

When they slowed down at the foot of a steep hill, Dijana pulled Filiz aside.

"This is not quite the time, but," she paused a few seconds trying to regain her breath. "We must get together tonight. Well, I wrote Hans a letter."

"Have you posted the last letter I wrote—we wrote together?"

Filiz realized how breathless and thirsty she was when she began to talk. Her mouth was so parched that she had difficulty moving her tongue.

"Of course, that very day. No reply yet. Let me see, it's been nine days. Must have been delayed in the post. Besides, Hans is a little slow."

"You do believe he'll reply, don't you?"

Lightning struck in Dijana's amber eyes. Her face was covered with rain clouds. "It's not that I believe it. I can sense it."

About a couple of months ago, returning from the medical director's office, Filiz had seen Dijana in one of the phone booths on the ground floor. Grasping the phone with both hands, she was talking and at the same time crying without a pause. At first she thought Dijana had received yet more terrible news from Bosnia—it was in one of these booths that Dijana had been informed by a deep voice at the end of a line frequently cut off that her sister had passed away in Bosnia. Fortunately it wasn't so this time. Dijana's last boyfriend, Hans, the tall blade, was more than fed up with this consumptive ruin of a woman with noisy breathing, bags under her eyes and his dreary hospital visits. The two women had jointly written five letters to Hans, but Filiz's sensitive and impressive pen hadn't helped, and no reply had ensued.

"If I were you I'd put him out of my mind at once."

Filiz was aware that her attitude was fierce and merciless, but she was extremely tired. She was wallowing in sweat and terribly thirsty; the veins in her over-strained legs throbbed. She had no more resources left to deal with Dijana's problems.

"You have a heart of stone!"

"There are bound to be a few stones in my heart, too. Alright, let's have a go at making him jealous then."

"What, in the midst of the forest? Were men, and not cones, to drop from trees, perhaps!"

"We could insinuate that there was a romantic prelude between you and one of the doctors. And we'll pick someone with attributes quite the opposite of Hans's. 'Long and slim, the fingers of the surgeon,' 'walks in the forest on moonlit nights' and so on."

Dijana smiled; she had at once recovered her customary joyfulness. She had indeed an extraordinary smile that could completely transform her disproportionate face. She was touchingly simple, sincere and unaffected. Filiz thought she had never before seen an expression that spoke so directly of happiness.

"I want him back." Her face was beginning to cloud over again. There was a tremor, a vague plea in her voice. It was as though if she could but prove that she really wanted Hans, divine justice would send him back to her. The dark shadow that hid behind her ebullience and nonchalance revealed itself only at moments such as these. Dijana would hide her true self in extremely secret passageways as if it were a monster that should not be allowed the sight of daylight.

"He'll come back, I'm sure," said Filiz, in a peremptory tone, quite pissed off. She enjoyed neither telling lies nor discussing men. She did not believe in love; she no longer remembered whether she had loved or not once upon a time, prior to the thirty-three days she had counted off in a cell full of blood and screams.

"Dijana! Dijana!"

"Yes, what is it?"

"We're very late! We won't get there at this pace. We must take the shortcut."

"Just a minute. I'm coming over to you. Let's see how we're doing."

With uncertain steps she ran towards the Germans. Filiz suddenly felt Graciella's red-hot eyes upon her. She turned; two pairs of eyes met, suffering, ardent and profound. A communication that could not have been expressed in words was immediately and spontaneously established between them.

"If you care for a bit of happiness in this world, you must be transformed into a little girl skipping and hopping hither and thither."

Graciella's face remained completely unmoved. Did she understand? No doubt she did.

"Have you ever heard of the Brazilian Paolinho?"

"No, in truth I know almost next to nothing about South American music."

Suddenly Graciella began to sing. This was a miracle, something unexpected, amazing, moving, extraordinary... "Vida e bonita..."

An unbelievably sad, silky melody that struck one's heart. A piece of music that could simultaneously give one both pain and happiness, that drew one closer to both death and life. Filiz's eyes brimmed; she gulped in order not to cry. She would not cry in front of others, nor would she sing, even if they pointed a gun at her head.

"This is what the lyrics mean: Life is beautiful, beautiful, beautiful... It's full of grief and joy, but still beautiful... Don't be ashamed of wishing to be happy... Paolinho was born in the streets, suffered from poverty and died of tuberculosis at the age of thirty-three. I explain all this so that you don't turn up your nose at the song."

"If someone who has hit the bottom of a chasm tells me life is beautiful, I suppose I ought to stop and lend my ear. But in order to truly appreciate this music, one needs to have suffered a different kind of pain."

Dijana interfered. "Listen, Felicita, we have to take the shortcut. We have very little time left. Will you be able to stand a mountain path that all in all takes twenty-five minutes but is absolutely killing? How fare the bellows?"

"They have not started complaining as yet. But I don't understand this. What are we late for?"

"It's the very essence of the matter that you don't know where you're going until you get there. You have to decide right here and now whether you're coming or not because we can't leave you here on the middle of the mountain. You'll appreciate that we can't cart you on our backs either."

"I'm coming. I don't quit half way."

"Come on girls, Felicita too is with us! Women's Brigade! Forward march!"

From every quarter rose screams, jokes, commands. "Come on, the Amazon Express! Here we come!"... "Avina!"... "We may die, but we won't give up!"

"Oh, my God! What hysteria, what tomfoolery!" thought Filiz. "And now we begin to play soldiers. A bunch of half-mad tubercular women. All we need is bells!"

Raising hell, screaming and shouting, the crew of women took to the mountain path. The inhabitants of the forest fled, the birds grew silent; nature quietly moved aside to make way for these boisterous, clumsy and selfish animals. Dijana, who knew the trail well, proceeded swiftly in the front like an Indian pathfinder, determining the route and discovering the tracks. Immediately behind her could be discerned the wide backs of Martha and Gerda. Backs that were strong, that did not give in, that trusted only themselves... With clumsy but firm steps, they crossed the mountains; they broke branches and bushes, when necessary, opening the way like trailblazing tanks, raining commands on those behind. Beatrice climbed like a wildcat that had managed to break free of its cage. With her long agile legs and mountain boots, and above all her youth, she was as supple and at ease as a mountain goat. In fact she frequently paused to lend a helping hand to her black-haired companions in distress.

Filiz spent the forest journey of twenty-five minutes sweating profusely, trying to hold on to thorny bushes and roots, looking in a flurry for firm stones upon which to place her feet, nearly passing out in panic and anxiety. She kept slipping and falling on pine needles and stumbling and floundering over roots. The bushes escaped from her hands, leaving pink marks, the branches rained harsh smacks. Her muscles, grown limp through long disuse, began to tremble like a diapason and in place of her legs there seemed to be two aching hot water bottles. The shivers that made her teeth chatter wriggled like cold snakes on her sweaty back. She was soaked to her underwear and could not relinquish the thought that it was fatal for a lung patient, especially one who had been granted permission to go out that very day, to perspire so heavily. Moreover, her lungs emitted that terrifying wheeze known in the hospital jargon as the "shift bell." She rained curses upon herself for having joined this adventure and jeopardizing, for nothing, the health she had recovered with immense difficulty. She was about to cry out of exhaustion, regret and desperation. Seeking refuge in her personal God, whom she resorted to only when deep in trouble, she implored devoutly, reciting prayer after prayer.

Like all things terrible, like bodily pain or imprisonment, the journey too finally ended and Filiz, raising her eyes from the path, could look around to see where she was. During those dreadful twenty-five minutes when each subsequent step to be taken was a matter of life and death, she had wallowed in her own body and fear, taking no interest in her surroundings. But now, breathless with a tightness in her heart, blinking her eyes that burnt with salt, she could see that they had reached an extraordinary place.

They were on top of a very steep hill, wound, as if with a gigantic fish net, with bushes, tree roots and scrub as tall as men. Forty or fifty meters below flowed an angry river, frothing and roaring in fury, dealing endless blows to the rocks it had carved out in notches. A path bedecked with purple flowers that resembled large carnations was embroidered, like delicate needlework, across the face of the cliff along the horn-shaped visible slice of the river before it cut a sharp bend to disappear in the rocks. "The path of purple dreams," reflected Filiz.

"We shall descend from here, Felicita. You've got to be very careful."

Filiz stared in amazement at her companions. They all looked devastated. Their faces, turned a livid hue, were sweaty, muddy and full of scratches. Their hair and their shirts that hung loose from their trousers were thoroughly drenched, and their nipples conspicuous. They had fallen many a time and had cuts all over. What were these women after? Wherefore all this struggle, danger and injury?

"Look, I've had just enough! Running through the forest like maniacs was not enough and now we have to go down the chasm! What's going on?"

"Don't be a spoilsport," hissed Dijana. "You promised to follow until the end."

"I gave no such promise."

"Let her do as she pleases." It was Martha. No. Gerda.

"Felize, please try a little harder. Believe me, it's going to be worth it." It was Graciella.

"Come on, Filiz, please." Beatrice held her arm, pulling it gently.

"Come on, girls! It's three twenty-three! Seven minutes to go!"

The group instantly forgot about Filiz and started moving, like an acorn rolling downhill upon a single flick. Drawing upon the last dregs of their strength, the women, holding on to branches, stones, anything they could lay their hands on, often sliding on their bottoms, holding hands to lend one another support, were descending to the river. A single false step meant being torn to pieces down the chasm. Filiz too became a link of the chain, without even thinking. She had bowed down to the transcendent power that had called her and joined in the journey along the delicate, sharp and slippery border between life and death. Danger had stimulated her, whipping all her sensations. She was full of a sensation akin to sexual desire. She loved life exquisitely at this very moment, feeling deep inside the joy of existence. What she held in her hands was not a stone or a bush, but the stupendous wounded heart of the forest, of the world, of life. A tree that had bent almost parallel to the stream crossed her path. It had released its squid-like roots in the hard rock and with perseverance, stubbornness and determination succeeded in growing upon this sheer hill. Its shadow fell upon the chasm. It offered Filiz one of its tired limbs; for a brief moment, for the duration of a brief moment before each continued with her makeshift journey and life, they held hands.

After a descent that was akin to crossing hell from one end to the other, they had reached a completely different world. Trees eager for friends, dreamflowers and all traces of life had vanished from sight. Here there were rocks and only rocks, terrifying, cold rocks... They were much larger than seen from above. They stretched up to the sky like bright sable daggers. And there was also the terrible noise of the river, its anger for no reason and for no cause... Filiz felt she was upon a stage; the company of marionettes had broken loose and picked upon this spot to enact their mysterious parts.

Before Filiz's eyes, wide open with amazement, Dijana sat upon a rock the size of a double bed and struck a pose peculiar to third-rate porno magazines. Bending her knees slightly, she opened her legs sideways in a V shape and placed her hands on her crotch. On her face she had put on a "pre-orgasm" expression enraptured with sexual pleasure. And Martha was lying with her profile to the stream, one knee pulled to her belly, her head pushed back and her hands clasped at her nape. On her face too there was an identical sordid and whorish sexuality for sale. Gerda exhibited, in the crawling position, her magnificent arse. Beatrice was standing with one foot resting on the rocks, bending forward with her arms hanging down. She had placed her cheek on her knee, as if leaning on the shoulder of a loving and passionate man. She looked at the water with dreamy blue eyes. Confronted with this mind-boggling sight, Filiz sought, as a last resort, Graciella, but she had long since joined in the game. On top of a sail-shaped rock, she was standing, alone, immobile and half-naked, like the statue of a goddess. She had stripped off her shirt, and resting her right hand on her waist, slightly arched her breasts. Her posture reminded Filiz of a pigeon: She was natural, innocent and fragile. Between the two blackberry-colored nipples, there were stripes of seared scars hiding behind her silver necklace. She had her eyes fixed on a point in the sky. The slim fingers of her left hand wandered upon her half-open lips taut with thirst. She just seemed unable to speak and give tongue to her intense and excruciating passion. Her whole body, grown thin and elongated, was transformed into an arrow aiming at the sky. She was ready to launch and hit the target. Filiz found herself in an incredible dream from which she could not wake up; even in dreams there would be more meaning and internal consistency.

"Felicita, come on now, give us a pose, go on. Find something amusing."

Filiz continued to stand as rigid as the Sphinx. She could comprehend nothing. Gerda's accurate watch struck three-thirty. At first nothing happened. For a minute that was heavy and dissolving in mists, the women waited, almost without breathing, stuck in those ridiculous, farcical, and strange poses of theirs. And finally, a canoe was sighted amongst the rocks. Four young men, four young, healthy and robust sportsmen belonging, as could be read from the emblems on their life-vests, to the rowing-team of the H. University seventy kilometers away, pulled on the oars with all their might, waging a superhuman fight not to be torn to pieces by the sharp rocks in this narrowest and most dangerous pass of the stream. They sighted the women. Where they saw them every Saturday.

"Hey, forest nymphs! You again? We'll call upon your village today!"

"Girls, open up a little more, won't you?"

"We'll park the canoe and come back. Don't you disappear anywhere!"

"Redhead, what good is it if you don't take off your trousers?"

The women offered no replies; they were not even giggling. They were rigid and frozen, more silent even than marionettes.

Whistles, screams and coarse but not totally indecorous jokes... A few reckless words on Beatrice's thinness, Dijana's naughtily exposed crutch, Gerda's bottom, Graciella's naked breasts... As for Felicita, she just stood there immobile, striking her own pose, petrified with amazement, thinking, remembering and feeling nothing, unable to remove her eyes from Graciella's breasts and scars proffered to the whole world. At last, when the canoe was about to disappear from sight, Filiz's arms slowly rose to the air. Like the wings of a wooden bird that had long ago forgotten to fly, they spread sideways, pausing and with difficulty, but immediately exhausted, closed upon her head. Like broken wings they collapsed upon each other. Graciella's voice, coming from a totally different world, was indistinctly heard amidst the fury of the stream and the screams growing more and more distant. "Vida e bonita..."

Two warm drops rose in Filiz's eyes and trickled down her cheeks, leaving traces like a muddy yellow stream. The canoe had long disappeared and the women were left all by themselves amidst the forest.

Translated by Nebile Direkçigil
"Tahta Kuşlar," (unpublished short story).

MURAT GÜLSOY

My Life's a Lie

My name's Fırat. Fırat Saner. I live in Flat 12, Block B, Basın Housing Estate. I work for a publisher. I'm in charge of the storeroom. I'm thirty-three. Single. My name's Fırat. But recently, other people have stopped believing this. They're laughing at me. "A lie—your life's a lie," they tell me. I try to put them straight. I talk about myself at great length. At first they listen to me, eyebrows raised, with a condescending look on their faces. But then they just say "rubbish" and walk away. I feel like running after them and pleading, but no, I can't bring myself to do it. I'm not an important person—that I accept. All the same, to be denied existence just like that touches my honor. Everything has its honor: a stone, a tree, soil. Nothing can be denied existence. Nothing can be denied existence, so long as it exists.

The first person to break the news to me was Bahri Yücel. Last year he came to pick up his book. Such an impatient man! He had actually wanted to go and fetch his book from the printer's but, because he'd argued with the printer earlier, he had to wait until his book reached the storeroom. He'd been sticking his nose into the business of the guys at the printer's, moaning "Look, you haven't cut the cover straight," "The picture's faded," "Print it again." Well, the printer got worked up. They're irritable people to start with, printers. Our job's straightforward. Packages of books arrive. We count them. Then we repack them and start the distribution process. We run a straightforward and calm storeroom. A total of one hundred and eighty square meters. Apart from me, two other people work there. They've been getting uppity, too, all because of this Mr. Bahri. Madness is contagious!

I always felt that Mr. Bahri was a bit odd. For one thing, he doesn't behave like a man in his fifties. When he appears at the top of the stairs, you think for a moment that a tall white-haired aging primary school kid has just entered. Lop-sided, as if weighed down by his school bag. That bow-tie... The obligatory cookies in his bag... (I don't know where he gets them; they're awfully tasty.) He'd heard that his book would be coming out on Friday. We in the storeroom didn't know anything about it, but he'd found out from the publisher and dropped by. Well, we served him tea, sat him down; I call the publishing house, but they pass the buck to the printer's, so I call the printer's and the man there says, "We can't get it done today. Out of the question!" Friday's the most chaotic day. It's the day when all of the payments and allocations are dealt with. While pleading with Dursun Efendi over the phone, I watch Mr. Bahri pulling over packages into the middle of the room to create a small tea-table. I feel sorry for his predicament. Noting his frayed jacket sleeves, his stooping body and his enthusiasm, it really gets to me. This man with a bow-tie, I think, is actually an overgrown child living in a world of his own. I tell Dursun Efendi to send twenty books over here no matter what. We settle on a large bottle of rakı as compensation.

Eagerly I rushed over to Mr. Bahri to pass on the good news. When I announced that his books were on the way, he gave me the strangest look. As if he hadn't heard what I'd said. For a while, neither of us said anything; Mehmet and Burak stopped what they were doing and looked up at us. "Tea," I said. "Bring the tea." The tea arrived, and a glass was placed in front of Mr. Bahri. But like a primary school child puzzling over how to do his homework, he remained silent. The way he was staring at me was getting on my nerves. The man was a bit odd, that's true, but still he was the only writer who occasionally showed up here. Even if it were only once in a blue moon. Authors of all these other books I sometimes see in the paper or on TV, but none of them know me. Only Mr. Bahri. If it weren't for him, it would gradually cease to make any difference to me whether these packages contained books or detergent. Maybe I liked him. Even if I felt sorry for him, I certainly didn't feel I was being disrespectful towards him.

I couldn't wait to eat the cookies, but as long as Mr. Bahri kept on staring at me, all I could do was sit there, motionless. "The thing is," he eventually said, "your life's a story."

"I don't understand," I said.

"There's nothing to understand," he replied. "Your life is a piece of fiction, a story, a lie—all made up," he commented and started laughing. I was just about to pity him even more when I noticed Mehmet and Burak laughing. They were laughing at me! Annoyed, I left the room. Inhaling deeply on my cigarette, I tried to calm down. What made me most angry was Mehmet and Burak.

"You bastards," I thought to myself. (I like the word "bastards" so much—a keepsake from my dad). "You were hungry, I gave you work and fed you. When you pinched books, I didn't say anything, as I thought you were reading them. Then, when I found out that you were selling them, all I did was warn you; it wouldn't be right to threaten your livelihood, I told myself." Just when I was grumbling to myself that no good deed goes unpunished, the books arrived and I managed to get rid of Mr. Bahri.

He signed his book "To the hero of a story, my dear friend Fırat." On his way out, he added: "Don't be sad. We're all dying to be the hero of our own story. Look at me. I've been trying like mad for years, but I'm still playing minor roles in other people's stories." After that, he said the strangest things. He was well-intentioned. I could see that. But this didn't stop me rushing to the restroom after shaking hands with him. I gave my hands a good soapy wash. I was convinced that Mr. Bahri had been infected by a Chinese virus that caused madness.

Then this madness began to spread.

At one point, they were banging on in the news about an epidemic causing insanity; it was apparently spreading from China to the rest of the world. For nights on end, I followed this news on the talk shows. According to experts, the epidemic was a consequence of the unequal division of labor in the globalizing world. Labor was so cheap in China that anything that had to be produced at minimum cost was being made there. Everything from textiles to electronics, shoes to watches was coming to us from the Far East. If we looked on the back of any object in our house, we would be sure to see *Made in China*—or perhaps *Taiwan*—or the stamp of some other country in the Far East. An epidemic that had started in that part of the world was spreading everywhere via these products. People had begun to panic. Chinese restaurants all over the world were putting up their shutters. Nobody wanted to go anywhere near them. For some reason or other, at the time I didn't consider the possibility that the epidemic could reach us here. I thought that—as usual—the experts on TV were out to frighten us. I was quite sure that they were out to put the wind up all those people who weren't being lax on hygiene and health. But you see, the news had turned out to be true! And now I see the epidemic spreading rapidly around me.

The day after the incident with Mr. Bahri was a Saturday, so I didn't leave the house. From morning till evening I zapped between TV channels, looking for news about the epidemic. There was nothing except news of the war and show-business. Now the experts were waiting with baited breath to see how the markets would react to the war. They seemed to have forgotten all about the epidemic. How about you? Do you remember it? Well, maybe you do have a vague recollection of such news appearing at some point. Of course, it's been quite a while; it all began back in May last year. To be honest, if Mr. Bahri hadn't come out with all that nonsense, I'd have forgotten about it, too. The last I heard about the epidemic was a week ago. Now there were other things on the agenda. The more I heard about them, the less interested I felt in the epidemic, and by evening I'd lost all interest in it whatsoever. It terrifies me to think of what all else I might forget in the same way. Perhaps what you need to do is keep a diary. But those hundreds of events would hardly fit into one person's diary. With the weary and bleary mind of a man who'd spent the whole day in front of the TV, I was just about to surrender to sleep's sweet embrace when temptation struck. "Get up and go for a walk," I said to myself. I thought I might be able to relax. Because it was spring, there was a lot of work to be done in the storeroom. The best months are July and August. Then there's practically nothing to do. We open the storeroom door as well as the back windows. While outside it's hot as hell, inside we're wandering around in our jackets. Watermelon and cheese for lunch. One day last summer Mr. Bahri had dropped by. It was clear that because his books didn't sell very well, they'd printed them during the off-season. He made a big thing about not wanting to eat any watermelon. He'd only have some if the seeds were removed. I did my best to get rid of them, but he stuck to his guns. The seeds would stick in his throat, he said. We had a good laugh at that, Mehmet, Burak and I. Now they're all laughing at *me*, the bastards! At the very thought of them, I decided not to go out. That weekend I didn't feel up to meeting anyone.

By Monday morning I'd forgotten about everything—Mr. Bahri, the virus and all that nonsense. I thought life had returned to normal. But then, on my way to the store, a few people I didn't know said hello to me. And when I went into the corner grocery near the storeroom, it all started again. I was going to buy some cigarettes. As soon as I stepped into the shop and nodded hello, the grocer's face lit up.

"Brother, we're all right behind you. Good luck!"

"What do you mean by that? Why should I need good luck?"

"We've heard you landed the lead role in a story."

"What story's this supposed to be? Where are you getting all this crap?" I shouted and turned on my heels. But I knew where he'd gotten it. The virus had spread to the grocer's. I was scared stiff. Out on the street, I cleaned my pack of cigarettes with a wet wipe before opening it. I decided to buy some disinfectant as soon as possible. When I arrived at the storeroom, then, a nasty surprise was awaiting me.

On entering, I found Mehmet sprawled out on some boxes.

"Where's Burak?" I shouted, waking Mehmet in the process. He obviously wasn't at all perturbed about having been caught sleeping. He stretched and yawned, "I was having such a nice dream!"

"Listen sonny, where's Burak? And what were you doing asleep? Is something wrong? Are you ill?"

I was beginning to suspect that they'd caught the virus too. And maybe they hadn't washed Mr. Bahri's glass well enough. They didn't care much about cleanliness. And here was the result.

"Me? I'm fine. But how are you? How's the story going?"

When he saw that I didn't reply, he began in a soothing voice. "There's nothing to be sad about. This is as far as we go, and there's nothing we can do about it. Obviously, your work here's over. We'll see you again some time. Well, actually, maybe we won't. I wish you the best of luck in your story. Thanks for everything."

I wanted to tell him that he was speaking rubbish, but I'd run out of steam.

"Where's Burak?"

He looked around as if he didn't know who I was talking about.

"Burak?" he said. "You're right; there used to be a Burak here, too. I don't know. This must be as far as his role goes."

It occurred to me that, as the person in charge of a storeroom with a staff of two, both of whom had gone mad, what I should do next was to call the publishing house. But I was worried that the people over there might have gone mad, too. I wasn't in any state to take another blow.

I went out, and began walking down the street. Mehmet reached out his hand to shake goodbye, but I didn't touch it. "You stay here," I said. I had to get away before I too became infected by the virus. I panted my way up the hill. As soon as I started down the road, I noticed everyone looking at me. It was as if everyone was frozen in place. The cars weren't moving even though there wasn't much traffic. Drivers, passengers, children—all of them were gawking at me. I hastened my pace and headed for the local hospital. I could see people waving at me from afar. Schoolboys were pointing their fingers at me, giggling. I started to run. I couldn't bear everyone gazing at me with love and compassion. In one breath I told the hospital receptionist everything. Presumably, what I said didn't make any sense. "The new virus, huh?" said the receptionist, and called over a few nurses. I was about to pass out. They laid me down on a bed.

When I opened my eyes, I saw the face of a doctor standing at my bedside. In a self-confident voice she said hello. I smiled, weary, yet relieved.

"How are we feeling? A bit tired, right?"

"Well, yes."

"Okay, it's all over now. Now you're going to tell me the whole story. There's no need to rush. Slowly and calmly."

I began to tell her what had happened. That the virus from China had crazed everyone around me, one by one—first Mr. Bahri, then the grocer, so on and so forth. From time to time I'd ask exactly how it was possible to contract the disease. Whether it could be passed on through a glass of tea or by shaking hands. I got no answers, for she responded to all my questions with other questions.

"What makes you say they've gone mad?"

"They start to say things that don't make any sense."

"Like what? Hostile things?"

"No, I wouldn't say hostile. But they're making fun of me. Mr. Bahri started it all. It's as if they've all agreed to say the same thing; every one of them tells me that I'm the hero of a story. They say my life's a lie. That's the kind of bizarre stuff they come out with."

As if struggling to find the best way to put the question, the doctor drawled, "W-e-e-ell now... What if I were to tell yo-u-u-u... that you really a-a-a-re the hero of a story? W-e-e-ell, what would you think then?"

She began testing me. Asking questions to determine whether or not *I* was mad. Questions like "What's your name?" or "What day is it today?"

"What else could I think, doctor, except that the virus has got hold of you, too."

"Just one more question then. Why does the idea of being the hero of a story disturb you so?"

This I hadn't expected.

"What are you trying to say?"

"Tell me about yourself. Tell me who you are."

"My name's Fırat. Fırat Saner. I live in the Basın Housing Estate. It's Thursday today. I work for a publisher. It's May. I'm in charge of the storeroom. I'm single. Thirty-three. My name's Fırat. Recently people have started telling me I'm not real. To my face. "Your life's a lie," they say.

"And what about your youth, your childhood, your family? Where were you born, for instance?"

I was confused. The storeroom appeared before my eyes, as if she'd asked me where I worked. But she'd asked me where I was born. Then I became angry. What did this whole thing have to do with my childhood, my family, or anything else for that matter? At the same time it occurred to me that I might have lost my memory. I closed my eyes. I believed I was all alone in a world gone mad. How long could I bear it? I began to pray. "Dear God, if this is only a story, please let the doctor and the hospital vanish before I open my eyes." Though my eyes were tightly shut, I could still smell the doctor's perfume, wafted around the room by the draft from the window, slightly ajar. She took my hand. I opened my eyes.

"I'm a doctor. My duty is to cure the ill. But you're not ill. You're the hero of a story. There's a life for you to lead. Do you understand?"

Her voice was soothing. All I wanted was to hear her voice. I felt as if the great wound opened inside me was being healed by some medication oozing from her voice.

"So what about the virus? Are you saying there's no such illness? Hasn't everyone gone mad?"

She smiled.

"There's an old fairy tale, a story that takes place in a small kingdom where the people had always lived very happily. There comes a time when some poison finds its way into a river of the kingdom. One by one, those who drink the water begin to hallucinate. The king forbids his subjects to drink the water and orders his vizier to guard the palace. For a while the situation remains under control, but when the people can no longer bear the thirst, they run to the river and drink, and the madness spreads until one day all the people, save for those in the palace, are stark raving mad. Then the water reserves in the palace begin to run out, and all but the closest friends and family of the king go crazy. With every passing minute, more and more people join the ranks of the insane. The vizier appears every hour on the hour to warn the king that the water reserves are running out and that the people can't take it any longer. Then the vizier disappears for several hours. While the king is eagerly awaiting news from the vizier, the door opens and the vizier enters, followed by a huge crowd. They immediately pounce upon the king. There is grief on the faces of the vizier, the queen and their close friends in the court. The king still hasn't understood what's happening."

"Why are you telling me this story?"

"Well, you're in the middle of a story like this. This world is here just for you alone."

As she spoke, her voice rose. "Everything, all of us, this whole hospital," she said, and pulling the curtains aside, "these streets, this city, all these people are here for you!" I must have made her angry. Perhaps she was trying to tell me that I was being selfish. I didn't understand. I was confused.

"You're not going to keep me here, are you?"

"Keep you here? Quite the contrary."

Getting to my feet, I asked her, as if requesting permission, "What should I do?"

"Go and live your life."

I was pleased that I wasn't ill, but I was also sad because there was no cure for my plight. I had no choice but to head straight for the storeroom. Mehmet and Burak were working. I was glad to see them. Everything seemed normal. But they weren't happy to see me. They glared at me with fire in their eyes. Mehmet, the more enterprising one, boldly demanded, "What are you doing back here? What is there here for you to do? Why have you come?"

I was taken aback.

"What the hell are you trying to say?"

"Your work here is supposed to be over."

I went on staring into his eyes. Shaking his head from side to side, he opened one of the boxes he had finished packing and pulled out a book.

"This isn't a real storeroom. Look at this."

He began to rip empty pages out of the book he was holding, one by one. At first I wanted to leap upon him to stop him. But then I realized how pointless that would be.

"Whenever *you* come here, you'll find us packing these books. There's no point in it. Don't you get it? This is only a space designed to look like a storeroom. But it's not actually a storeroom. There's nothing inside the books. And have a look at the covers—there's nothing on them except small gray squares. Like a pattern on the binding. Look here, just look; there isn't even a publisher's name! Do you know the name of the publisher? Do you? You see, you have nothing to reply because I'm telling the truth. Don't come back again. Go and live your life. You'll be better off, and so will we."

I wanted to calm the waters.

"Come on, just forget it," I said. "Don't get all worked up about this kind of thing. Have we got any tea?"

It was Burak's turn to cut in:

"Mr. Fırat, sir, your story doesn't belong here any more. I admit, it may well have started off here, but it's fulfilled its purpose here now."

The storeroom that Burak was indicating with such a shrug of helplessness really did look run-down and deserted. Everything was covered in dust. Conversations like this are upsetting indeed. Aware that they had no good answer, either, I asked, "So, Burak, if my story isn't here, where is it then?"

He shrugged his shoulders again and replied, "I don't know. That's something you should know."

"Well, what would you do if you were in my shoes?"

Now Burak was taken aback. He looked at Mehmet helplessly and stammered, "I-I-I d-d-don't know. I'd probably go in search of adventure. Maybe find a beautiful woman. Enjoy myself. Travel round the world."

I was becoming annoyed.

"Is that what you think happens in stories? It's obvious that you didn't read those books you stole. I should have fired you the moment I found out that you were selling them on the sly."

At which Mehmet blurted out, "I swear we never stole anything! Whoever said so was lying."

I decided on pretence of anger to end the conversation.

"Well, that *is* my story, if it's okay by you. I'm the protagonist in the story, aren't I? My story is here, in this storeroom, among these books. I don't want to hear about this again, OK? Or I'll show you the door! People are queuing up to pack those books you turn your noses up at. There are millions of unemployed people out there."

After that day, they haven't moaned once. They go on packaging—like automatons. They carry on packing those items which I too had begun to suspect might not be books. For a while, people like my landlord, my boss and the grocer tried to talk me round. Because I realized that their thoughts about my life were just part of their general madness, I began to ignore them. Then they too gave up trying to persuade me. They lost all hope in me. And I went back to my ordinary routine of storeroom-to-home, home-to-storeroom.

I don't understand people. I don't understand why they're so persistent. A few days ago, a young woman threw herself at my feet and began pleading with me. She said she was fed up with waiting for me, and that this endless wait was finishing her off, tearing her apart. It was the first time I'd ever seen the woman. I tried to explain to the poor soul. She didn't even listen to me. She was simply obsessed…

Sometimes I run into people like you who hear me through patiently till the end. The thing is, they don't believe in me. Some of them even laugh at me. Do you think what I've said is funny? I don't think so. You don't believe me either, do you? You're sure that I'm only a character in a story. How can you be so sure? Do you remember everything accurately and in all detail? Are you sure that everything around you is real? If you're looking for an example, you have one right in front of you. Me. I'm telling you all this. You think I'm not a real person. But as for you… you're living in a world of reality, aren't you? Well, then, how is it that you can come across an artificial, fictional person like me in your world of realities? God only knows how many imaginary things you've incorporated into your world of realities! But no, you know best! Well you're wrong, and you can't fool me. My name's Fırat. Fırat Saner. I live in the Basın Housing Estate. I work for a publisher. I'm in charge of the storeroom. I'm single. Thirty-three. A while ago people started telling me that I'm not real. To my face! "Your life's a lie," they say. I don't believe them.

Translated by Emine Deliorman and Jonathan Ross
"Hayatım Yalan," *Bu An'ı Daha Önce Yaşamıştım* (2004). Istanbul: Can Yayınları, pp. 173-184.

DENİZ SPATAR

The Scar

*To my American Indian
Spider Grandmother,
as the Goddess of Mind and Memory*

"Come on, say something! Say something!"
He was yelling in a voice much stronger than one would expect from a body as puny as his. Staring into his eyes, I remained silent.

"I called you early in the evening! I did! Some fellow said, 'She's gone out'!"

The man in the house had grabbed my arms and was shaking me. I was being shaken.

He stopped for a moment; I glimpsed him pulling his head back. His head then struck my face full force. I don't know how a head can be so hard. My feet were out from under me even before I had the chance to feel the salty agony in my nose, teeth and cheekbones. It didn't take too long; first my back and then my head smashed against the wall. I was just thinking that it would splinter into smithereens in a manner far more impressive than the animation in science fiction films when the clock fell onto my right hand, ricocheted off the bones and slid to the floor. While I was trying to understand what had happened, he wheezed and grabbed my neck in one hand and my arm in the other. Sticking his face right up against mine, he questioned me: "Where the hell have you been? Where the hell!"

Then I was hurled backwards once more and heard my head bang and grate against the wall. In such situations one better understands that there are a multitude of reasons causing the internal organs to act up.

Just as I was picturing the whole body of this man as strings of long white nerves, he left the room, clearing his throat. From the toilet came the sound of running water and his blowing his nose. "Disgusting man!" I thought to myself, simply "a disgusting man!"

I started to search for an empty space on the walls to gaze at. An emptiness that would absorb all my thoughts… I was trying not to see the paintings, the bookshelves, our pictures from "the happy days," the record player or the CD shelf.

Finally I saw the spider-web at one corner of the ceiling—and its landlady. First of all, the fact that the house had recently been cleaned came to mind. So my cleaning lady Ziynet Hanım was cheating me! She wasn't even cleaning the spider-webs off the ceiling! I was ready to cry. I felt sorry for myself, like every weak mortal I felt cheated. Everyone was stronger than I, and there they were pushing and shoving me around! With this idea I fell into an inner silence, deaf to everything. I began listening to my own ideas.

Then I realized I couldn't take my eyes off the spider and its web. I tried to look at the bookshelves, but I couldn't. A strange bridge extended between the spider and myself. It was spinning its net and waiting. A quiet, simple life. Do what you have to do and wait.

I wanted to learn more about the spider. It made no sound. It remained motionless on its web. Did the web have any voice? Perhaps with a breath of air it might create a tingling sound. This idea brought back my sense of self-pity. I took a deep breath as the thought passed through my mind: "There's no air left in this room, how could there be any breath of air?" Then I let out my breath again, making a strange "hopffh" through my nose and mouth at the same time. I gave up feeling sorry for myself. I was no longer able to think of anything other than the spider.

Minutes or hours might have passed. I don't know where and how the time flew. Stiffness caused a chilling pain to spread from the back of my neck down into my shoulders. The spider held still, I held still. I knew that the spider wasn't dead; it was alive though it was far beyond my comprehension how it could hold still for so long.

I've forgotten to tell you: Besides the chilling pain from the stiffness I ached all over. My nose was most probably full of blood and snot. Each time I took a breath I felt as if a hot knife was sinking somewhere into my back. A fine insidious wire was creeping from the end of my spinal column towards my loins, searing every spot it passed. My two front teeth were broken, and every time I'd open my mouth, sharpened points of icicles pierced into my brain.

Suffering through all this I must have cried a lot, but now I was only hiccupping. The fit of hiccups that shook my whole body wore me out and increased my aches. However, all this was physical pain. Once I'd glimpsed the spider, I felt no more pain.

My feelings of arrogance, honor, longing, self-pity, lust, anger, and betrayal—in short, all my feelings—were assuaged by watching the spider. As these calmed, they learned patience. Patience taught my feelings to spin a web. The web taught me how to wait. My feelings set out on a journey comprised of nothing more than waiting.

Only self-pity raised a rebellion. The spider web vibrated for a moment and seemed as if it would tear; the spider could hardly cling to its web. My heart leapt into my mouth. Just at that moment I realized that people who felt sorry for themselves sailed into an ocean of arrogance, dragged towards the depths by the winds of anger, inviting thunders of revenge and fighting in vain and finally pulling down into a whirlpool of nothingness. Thus I ceased to feel sorry for myself.

It was after this that an intensive lilac glow from the stillness of the spider began to flow towards me. I lay right where I was. The light flowed over me and finally surrounded me from my head to my toes. I shed my physical pains as well.

As for that man, he returned to the room at the best possible moment for himself and the very worst for me. He turned on the TV as if nothing had happened. I didn't care what he was watching; I was neither looking at him nor listening. Engulfed in the pleasure of the lilac hue, I'd fallen sound asleep with my eyes wide open. It was then he shouted:

"Stop your play-acting!"

The light emanating from the web faded slowly away. The spider came alive and the web vibrated softly. Suddenly I spied the source of the vibration. The spider had received the reward of its patience. A fly was caught in the web. God damn it! I'd like to have seen that moment.

Gently I pulled my legs up toward my stomach, wrapped my hands around my knees, and rested my head on my knees.

I heard him mumbling, "Freaking female!" I didn't look at him. I took a deep breath and touched the blood oozing from my split head and licked it.

He knelt beside me.

"Why do you act like this and drive me crazy?"

There was that softness that sometimes creeps into his voice as he'd conclude, "I'm a nice compassionate man." His head was keeping me from seeing the spider. I pushed his head slowly away to look at the spider. It was busy turning the fly over and over and wrapping it in the strands of its web.

A bone vice clamped my jaw. Shaking my head with his grip on my jaw, he exclaimed, "Stop this nonsense and come to your senses!" Indeed, he sounded more hopeless than harsh.

I felt my physical aches and pains once more and became angry. This time I shoved his head more violently. When he saw the spider, he began to kiss my hands and moan. "Please, sweetheart, don't do this to me!" I glanced at him to see what he was doing and whatever happened, happened at that moment. I noticed the fleck! Yes, that purplish scar on his temple. Unaware of what was happening, he was trying to smile. However, he looked disgusting!

The fleck was swelling and growing. After a while his pulse began beating in this scar. It was swelling and shrinking! It was at the surface! Slowly the color of the scar changed. The blue of a nearby vein mixed with reddish purple. The fleck became a dark purple protuberance. It grew longer and longer, reaching from his temple toward his neck. Then a multitude of extensions forked out from that protuberance. These spread swiftly across his face (but underneath his skin), over his forehead, cheeks, and the back of his neck. Some of them went under his hairline and disappeared among the strands.

I think he was still begging and kissing my hand. I, on the contrary, couldn't see anything but the vessel-like extensions all over his body and was shaken by great nausea. Here was a man in front of me whose vessels were protruding above his skin. The capillaries in his eyes thickened. He was so disgusting that I couldn't take my eyes off him.

I knew the story of the scar. Since he'd first told me, it had been stored in my memory encoded as "the story of the fleck."

Understanding! I didn't understand this man and his scar. He was a man of many strata. I was one of his strata, and I too consisted of many strata. We married as a consequence of a one-in-a-million chance when two of our strata happened to meet. From an outsider's perspective, I was a woman beaten by her husband. He was a man who beat his wife. We were living through a marriage packed with masculine chauvinism. After writing these sentences out line-by-line and considering the situation from the perspective of my strata, I panicked.

However, when I began to understand his sufferings, I could tolerate his... May all gods and the atheists protect and defend me! Was violence something to be tolerated?

Anyway, forget about me! The problem is this scar on the man's temple! The story is the story of the scar!

One night as we were working up toward lovemaking, I was just touching his body here and there when he pushed me away—and letting his chin tremble like actors do in the dramatic, exaggerated scenes of Turkish films—trying to let masculine honor shine in his eyes, "Stop! Stop!" he cried out with an exaggerated stress on the "p"s. I stopped. I silently swore at all those "p"s. I threw something on and went to the kitchen. I put on some tea.

When I returned to the bedroom, he was massaging his right temple and staring at the carpet as if watching a horror film there that I couldn't see. I handed him his tea without a word and sat down in an armchair some distance from him. I think those were the days when I'd first started to hate his face, which he always fitted out with mimicry as if it played a very important role in life. "What's happened?" I asked. He slowly raised his head, looked at me and said, "Nothing at all!" Then he continued to watch the horror film he was watching on the invisible screen on the carpet. Meanwhile, he was no longer massaging his temple; he'd begun to pick at his scar.

"Don't pick at it! You're going to make it bleed!" I said angrily. I'd learned myself that if he bloodied his temple, I couldn't sit there but would have to busy myself looking for tincture of iodine, hydrogen peroxide and cotton.

I thought to myself, I wish he'd stop scratching his forehead so that I can go to bed. But I couldn't leave him there and go to bed. Not because I was a good soul, but because I knew what would happen to me if I did such a thing. If I'd gone to bed, he would have come after me to say, "You turn on your ass and sleep while I'm in such misery." Then too, he had a foul mouth, and his cursing would sometimes make my blood run cold, brought up as I was with the good breeding of a formerly bourgeois family.

Still! Still he continued scratching his scar!

"Don't scratch thaaat!" I hissed, balling my fists.

"Did I tell you how this happened?" he asked. Okay, here we go again.

"I don't remember," I said nervously because if he had told me and I didn't remember, that would be worse. In such instances, he'd convince himself I didn't care for him, and this conviction would reflect onto me as minor sensitivities and major inferiority complexes.

"I hit it on the corner of the water tap while I was running after my mother. It bled profusely, and this scar was left."

"Reeeally?" I replied.

Without waiting for my own words to end—eh—I am flesh and blood after all, I lost my temper. Without thinking, I reached for his scar. Like an earthworm... Cold. I felt a great desire to grab a hold of, pull out, and then stomp on this strange, gleaming, cold "thing" full of twists and turns. I know how to restrain my compulsions; I held myself back. I touched the scar on my own temple to vent my rage upon myself. I massaged my temple. That wasn't enough, so I scratched my temple.

"Don't pick at it!" he said.

"I can't pick at it?"

"No, don't!"

"I can't pick at my own scar?"

"That's right! Don't scratch your own scar!"

"It's all about your scar, isn't it!"

Ah, my dear husband couldn't say a word. Leaving my own scar, I grabbed hold of the end of that protuberance thrusting out from his scar. He knelt down in front of me. As if paralyzed, he froze like a statue.

I worked freely. Through lack of care my fingernails had become rather long. I pinched the earthworm-like protuberance between the forefinger and thumb of my right hand. I began to dig at the scar as if picking a scab off a wound. It wasn't long until my little finger entered an icy cavity. My other fingers followed my little finger. I enlarged the cavity and then put my other hand in as well. Poor slimy, cold earthworm. I easily caught hold of one end. I drew it out from the darkness. Disgusting! Cold! Slimy! Earthworm-like! The more I pulled, the more came out. I remember hearing his metallic laughs. His voice saying, "It's spread to you too! Hah, hah, hah! It's enveloping you too," echoed throughout the room, between rapid successions of his loud creepy laughter.

What I first took out was as long as a hand-span. Cold. Slimy. Like an earthworm. I couldn't stop: I pulled; it lengthened. I pulled; it kept coming. I pulled, and the more I pulled, the more came out. When his laughter was interrupted by coughing and his voice became hoarse, I stopped and realized that there was a heap of veins lying like a Gordian knot in my lap. Therefore I must have to undo all the kinks one by one, putting the long strands into order, winding them tightly, making skeins of them and setting them aside.

One by one, I undid the knots. Patiently I put these extensions in order. Once all the knots were undone, I began wrapping them round my foot to make a skein. I wrapped and wrapped; holding onto one end, I made many skeins. No matter how many skeins I made, it kept coming as long as I continued pulling; my feet tingled and became numb under the weight. So I began wrapping what I pulled out around my left shoulder. Holding onto one end, I made skein after skein. Both my arms and fingers became numb. There still remained, however, a heap of strands in my lap. Cold. Slimy. Like an earthworm. How endless it was!

I felt weary. I tried to take a breather—the light faded from my eyes. I couldn't see. Colors and scents left me as well. I was gasping as I tried to breathe. I was lost in a dark void. For how many days, for how many nights? How should I know, I've said I was lost!

Ah, to wake up! Ah! The strong smell of salty breezes and green seaweed! Ah, the coastline of my city! Ah, the black cormorants that still haven't deserted the coast and their fractious neighbors, the sea gulls. The sun that rises again every morning! I've awakened from this nightmare, too. Like a child who's recently recovered from an illness, I'm hungry; I'll go out into the streets. I want to run and sweat and laugh till tears run from my eyes. Like a small child who's been ill for a long time, there's only one thing on my mind. The guy I love had smiled before he left me, you know...

He told me that he loved me but he had to go, you know.

Maybe he's come back, huh?

I must have broken out in a smile. Smiling, what great torture! There's a strange sensation in my face. It hurts! God damn it! My hands and arms are entangled. I'm struggling to free one of my hands from some cold, earthworm-like things. With great difficulty I touch my face. It's my forehead! Crackled and flaky, rough and red! As I try to move, something is gnawing at my flesh. If only I could open my eyes and see what's going on.

Bright white light. Oh God, I think I drank too much again last night. I don't remember a thing, though... What am I doing in this fishing net? I'm washed ashore on a deserted coast and... Of course! It's all my...

Translated by Burçe Kaya and Jean Carpenter Efe
"Leke," *Kopya Kadınlar* (2003).
Istanbul: Alkım Yayınları, pp. 29-38.

MURAT SOHTORİK

The Village Seen

"Why are they cutting down the trees?"
"They dirtied the tops of the cars."
"Is that why they're cutting them down, these imbeciles! Who the hell's idea was that?"
"I complained about them, Uncle. Did I do wrong?"
"You complained about a tree?"
"How would you know; you don't have a car!"
"Your 'cars' are the curse of this city. On top of that now you've gone and started cutting down the trees. As if your exhaust isn't enough…"
"Uncle! Now you're being insulting!"
"My boy, what if you'd park it 10 meters further on…"
"The customers are complaining, too. After all, it's my shop-front, why shouldn't I be able to park there!"
"Didn't you also drink your lemonade in the shade of those trees in the summer?"
"Is that a problem? We can put up an awning."
"You can wear an oxygen tank, too! You fool, these trees mean fresh air."
"Uncle, what difference does their little bit of air make?"
"Don't say that, either. Did you ever cut such trees down in your village?"
"Well, we did cut down trees in the village."
"What strange sort of village you must come from!"
"There is no village or anything left, Uncle! Everything's under water."
"What a shame! Why?"
"Because of the dam! They said the water would come, so we had to get ready to leave. Not just three or four, a whole wood it was. Pistachio was it, or walnut? Some sort of nut at any rate! My big brothers felled as many as they could fell. Like this, with an

electric saw. They didn't let me help! Sounds so much like a motorcycle, doesn't it?"

"The only motor I like to hear is that of a sugar-beet tractor. It reminds me of the coastal villages... You migrated to the city then?"

"First to the upland settlements the government had prepared. I remember that place better. Then of course, my brother and I escaped to the city. My parents stayed there, though."

"Did they get to like the new place, then?"

"Nope! 'Specially my dad... He still goes down boating on the river. Sometimes my mom worries."

"Worries about what?"

"That he's losing his mind. Because he was seeing things in the water."

"What did he see?"

"The image of the village!"

"Oh, the poor guy..."

"Like a reflection left on the water. He'd describe it as if it were real."

"Can you really see it?"

"Come on, "Uncle," you're an educated man. It's old age. He's become senile."

"Are you so clever, then? If only you could see it, too!"

"Anyway, "Uncle," see you later. It's getting hot here. I'm going inside..."

Lost in thought... I simply stare at the water. Meaningless, meaningless. My father insisted... We had to pass over the old village by boat. He cut the motor... Silence... The wake has died away. The surface is like a sheet of glass. We're simply drifting. I'm lost in thought. For a moment I feel his gaze.

"What's the matter, Dad?"
"Nothii-iing... What do you see, son?"
"Nothii-iing... What should I see?"

Why don't I see it? How come he can see it?

"Do you see it right now, too, Dad?"
"Of course I do..."
"What do you see?"
"First of all, the pistachios... All around... the stone houses, gardens in rows... The bed-frames—we used to sleep under the stars, you know that, don't you?"
"In the water?"
"Hey you, the big baths... I know your heart's still warm! The cave in the distance... You can't see it from here, though... Over there's the mosque... It's somehow different from all other mosques!"

"What's the difference!"

"Look, there's our homestead! The one with the best view. I'm glad we'd repaired it before the water came. Only the trees, I wish I hadn't had them felled."

"That's the reflection of the barren mountain, Dad!"

"That's our village, son!"

"The waters have swallowed the village, Dad."

"Over there, son, it's still there."

"It's collapsed by now."

"Nope! In perfect condition. Only, the trees..."

"You're dreaming, Dad!"

"I see it, son."

"Then... why can't I see it?"

"If you can't see it, then you can't, son."

"I was very little then, Dad. I can't even remember what the village looked like back then."

"If you believe in it, you'll see it, son."

" If I'd see it, I'd believe it."

A pause...

"What's become of the trees, son?"

"Which trees?"

"The ones dirtying the cars."

"I had them cut down! How do you know about those trees, Dad?"

"Good for you, son."

"I did the right thing. You're not angry with me?"

"Why should I be angry? You did what you thought best. Since you thought they were dirtying..."

"Only... that old 'Uncle' living upstairs!"

No comment.

" 'You complained about the trees!' he said."

"Do you regret it, son?"

"The trees give off clean air or something, he said."

"That's in the air, son... that's something you can't see either..."

"Dad! Dad..."

"What's up, son?"

"Look over there... You see that?"

"What, son? Do you mean the minaret?"

Translated by Zeynep Tüfekçioğlu and Jean Carpenter Efe
"Görünen Köy," *Fırat'a Karışan Öyküler* (2003).
Istanbul: Can Yayınları, pp. 133-136.

KARİN KARAKAŞLI

Days of the Flood in Zeugma

Under the Water (I)

I am a mosaic who has seen her day. They tell me I am a mosaic. Also that I hark back to ancient times. If you ask me, I'm actually timeless: the heritage of the past, the witness of the present. No mosaic suffers this much.

In those days they called me the goddess of the soil and the land. The whole community worshiped me. We'd hold festivals to celebrate our abundance. Back then the harvests followed one upon the other. The trade road passed through here. Now they're burying me in the waters, me and a piece of history. I'm not surprised, for the past here has always thrived on destruction.

So many people have come and stood looking down at me. I was their last glimpse before the disappearance. They're building a dam nearby. The ascent of the waters makes no concessions to an ancient city. Actually, there's no need for it. Who appreciates a few ruins and mosaics, anyway? Could those who don't appreciate life today possibly respect the dead of yesterday?

While I was still visible—ordinary and unimportant—a few archeologists and tourists fond of history would pay me visits. For some reason or other, as the time to disappear came closer, I was paid more respect. Once it was already too late to do anything, people came rushing and flocking to my side. I simply looked back at them.

Recently, thousands of people have come and gone. Rather than my face trembling under the insidious waters gradually rising, what they looked at was their own reflections. They gazed at what was appreciated only when it was about to disappear. What they were looking at was their own present.

Among all those visitors, it was the eyes of a local woman that touched me the most. Her eyes were dark green. She leaned far over the water. We came eye to eye; we paused eye to eye. Then, dipping her hand into the water, she touched me tenderly, as if stroking a friend. I shivered in the summer heat. She didn't tell me about herself; she just smiled, "Good-bye, my friend in fate," she said. She threw her scarf into the water, and across my face gently glided this colorful scarf with crocheted edges. We both watched the scarf. I felt as if the woman herself was floating from life together with her scarf.

I am weary of stares. So many civilizations have come and gone; yet these lands have never improved. It was as if each were in a hurry to wipe away the traces of the previous. I've always been here. I was the silent witness of the dead and the living. Neither when it was an impressive city nor a village left to its own destiny did I abandon this land. This was my homeland, the roots of which nourished and sapped my strength with sins and blessings. Perhaps it's the times I've witnessed and the sufferings I've brooked that are pulling me under. Little by little the waters cover me. It's now time to fall asleep. After all, we don't consider everything vanished that's no longer visible to the eye.

Above the Water (II)

Many strangers come here now. They come to see the waters rising and the ancient city sinking. I've been there, too. For me it's only a step away. For once, I wanted to see the places I lived through the eyes of a tourist. After all, the waters have swallowed up not only the old city, but my home as well.

We were forced to move uphill. Where my cool and comfortable home was, now only the wind blows. The water blows, I really should say. They put up a prefabricated house. They settled us in it. We live like refugees there. The sun beats down furiously. It's as if the water has handed us over to the sun, telling us "Do whatever you want—you're on your own now."

Or maybe these were the words of the bureaucratic system that displaced us. "Do whatever you want." Many knowledgeable and well-educated people came but weren't able to save the city that's been here for millennia. Who should care about a few miserable houses or their poor inhabitants?

The moment I saw her, I was frozen in astonishment. She was a picture in mosaic surviving from ancient times, but to me she was real. Her eyes penetrated me. I leaned over the water. I dipped my hand into the water and drew it across her face. I had nothing to say to her. Still, I felt as if we were chatting. It seemed she could read my mind with those large eyes of hers. There's nothing that would surprise this woman, I thought. There was nothing she hadn't witnessed over the centuries. I smiled at her. Moreover, I believe she understood what I wasn't able to say to her. Who knows how many others have looked at her and spoken to her over these thousands of years? She was a very wise woman. She could sense one's mood. "Good-bye, my friend in fate," I said slowly. Thank God there was no one else around. I was the only one to witness my foolishness.

Then I threw my scarf into the water. My man had given it to me. It was colorful, with crocheted edges. I threw it in anyway. There was no place for such a scarf in our box-like place. The scarf was a memory of our happy days. It shadowed the woman's face for a moment, then drifted away with the current. At least it had a place to go.

I've always watched things departing. The scarf and the passing years.

We said a fond farewell to each other. Time to go back to the place that is not home. Nights I sit in front of the TV. Something's on, but what I'm always seeing is our old place. The trees are rustling in the wind. I gaze at the Euphrates in the evening. Then all that I see becomes a dream.

Above the water everything is much more difficult. That woman will now rest in peace in the depths. Whereas my todays consist only of dust and sun. I wish the waters would swallow me up just like they did that woman. I could remain with her in the depths, at the very bottom. So that I could be forgotten, so forgotten as not to care about indifference and so that not a soul would ever remember me again. Just those eyes of hers... are enough for me.

Translated by Zeynep Tüfekçioğlu and Jean Carpenter Efe
"Zeugma'da Tufan Günleri," *Fırat'a Karışan Öyküler* (2003).
Istanbul: Can Yayınları, pp. 47-50.

ŞEBNEM İŞİGÜZEL

Fragments from Real Life for the Last Scene of a Movie

"Nothing can be more important than love."

Gidon Kremer

I. Out of necessity

We had to walk. This necessity made me happy. I hadn't been this happy for a long while, I thought. It's hot. Stifling heat one would call it—that's the kind of heat we're having. Not a single cloud in the sky. The blue of the sky is the prettiest blue I've ever seen. I don't like whitish blue. This blue has both dark and light hues in it...

The sky is not actually the way I see it of course. If you ask the person on my left, he'll say it is white, the one on my right will say gray. I personally think that if you take a careful look you'll see every tone of blue in it.

The street is awfully crowded. What are these millions of people doing in this city? Most of them weren't even born here; ask them and you'll find out that they came from the other end of the world. Why in the hell do they come here, I used to think angrily. One day I sat down and gave it some serious thought. I was born here, but what about my father or grandfather—why in the hell had he come to this city? I changed my opinion after that. God placed a compass in people's pockets, the needle pointed to this place, and so here they are!

What we call destiny is this compass. When the needle points to happiness, you're happy; when it points to death, you die; when it points to love, you're in love. One day we decided to get drunk. I told this compass story to those I was drinking with. I forget who exactly, but one of them said: "What if the compass goes askew?" "You'd go nuts in that case," I replied, and we all laughed.

I wish my compass had gone askew, too...

The weather is lovely. So are the women. Some are blond, some brunette; some are overweight, some skinny. Each one is pretty in her own way. There, that one walking in front of me... Her hair has such a pretty hue. And it shines with the sunlight falling on it. Even though she has a loose skirt on, one can tell she has round hips. She's wearing shoes open at the back; her heels are dirty. The girl coming from the opposite direction keeps lifting her glasses with her index finger. If I had a daughter, she'd be her age. She must be at least twenty. Think of a girl this tall calling me "Dad"! Too bad that nobody will call me that in my lifetime. I was married once. I wanted to have a child then. The girl I'd married was a student. She kept putting off motherhood until she finished school. She didn't take marriage very seriously anyway. At the beginning she used to feel very embarrassed when she introduced me to her friends. Then she started to educate me—if you could call it that! Books, movies, etc. Realizing that she wouldn't get very far, she left me as soon as she had graduated. I knew from the very beginning we would end up this way. I had the nerve to dream of fatherhood. In fact, I was nothing but a "necessity" in her life...

II. Life is sweet

Life is sweet... Thus he had pleaded with me when I killed him. Life is sweet... People like us can't tell the difference between what's sweet and what's not. If you had a job and you were in a good mood— like I am now—I didn't know that, looking up at the sky, you were supposed to say, "Life is sweet." The man I killed was like me too, but he had learned that life was sweet. At one of the court sessions, his wife and brother attacked me. The wife's screams still ring in my ears: "How dare you annihilate any living creature!"

Am I God, damn it! Why did I shoot the man? Why did I take his life? When he'd said "Life is sweet..."

III. Provided that you love mankind...

I could have become a different person. Reading or exerting one's brains isn't essential. Provided you love mankind.

We just drag through life, millions of people. Of all colors, of all languages.

Some of us are happy, some drunk, some derelicts, some idiots. We are at least alive... We see the sky, we know the rain.

Just now I thought of the transsexual who used to live in our building. He wasn't exactly a transsexual; he hadn't gathered the courage to have it cut off. He still sounded funny when he attempted to talk and laugh like a woman.

But he was more honest than any woman I have ever known. What's more, he liked me. In fact, he was in love with me. Once we were drinking and he insisted that we should make love. God forbid! I could go to bed with other faggots, but not him. Because I saw this kid in a different light.

He used to go up to the roof to feed the seagulls. With his bowed legs, I can still recall him walking slowly on the terrace in his high-heeled purple shoes. He used to think seagulls resembled him. He never explained why; I wouldn't be able to retell it the way he would have, anyway. One of his transsexual friends had one day said, "Our buddy's in love with you." That was no news to me.

I felt very sad when he was stabbed to death in the middle of the street. It was a drunken client who did it. At his funeral his mother kept sobbing, "My daughter, ah, my daughter!" I have witnessed so many deaths, in addition to being a murderer myself, yet I am still scared of death. In one of my dreams I was dead. It was freezing cold when I woke up. It was as if I were one step from the gates of death. Mother was there too; praying.

IV. Coming close to the end

Someone once told me that everyone feared death when the end was close. Each day we get closer to the end. Boats, trains, planes are continuously bringing down people. People are escaping, arriving, leaving, waiting. We are all approaching the end...

The heat is getting worse. I feel as if I have been walking for ages. I've passed through these streets with so many others... Years ago it was with Mother and my brother, who later hanged himself. First Mother died, then my brother. Now I'm all alone.

My brother was not like me. When he died, we thought he'd hanged himself for no reason at all. This wasn't the case though. When you get close to the end, you learn that even walking can make you happy, that life is sweet, provided you love mankind. He'd told me so before he hanged himself. At the time I didn't understand what he meant.

V. Very close to the endless end

"There is happiness at the endless end."

This he had written somewhere before he hanged himself. "He must be learning all this from the books he reads," I'd thought. Now, see, even I—a person who has never opened the cover of a single book—believe that there is happiness at the endless end.

We were on a trip. The bus smelled of rotten eggs. I was in low spirits. He seemed to be enjoying himself. He pointed to the down on the neck of the girl sitting in front of us. It was blond hair, not very healthy-looking. I don't know why, but it seemed I was looking at a rich wheat field on soft, tenuous skin.

After that I was in a good mood, just like him.

VI. Endless end

I walked past the sea. And the blue... The people, the faces as well...
And the streets I'd walked through years ago with my brother who knew there was happiness at the endless end...
I'm no God. Now I have learned not to kill.
Life is sweet. See, I'm saying this as well for the first time.
I should have married the transsexual who fed the seagulls. From him I could have learned everything that I now know.
This building is awfully depressing. I haven't counted how many times I've come here. The colors have disappeared. There are voices and faces.
"Our walk took us ten minutes." The security officer on my left says this.
Did it take ten minutes as well before they reached the verdict or was it longer?
"Execution by hanging."
Death, in other words. I turn back and look:
"Haven't you folks died?"
My mother, my brother, and the transsexual. The man I killed, his hands crossed on his chest, is smiling at me. He's wearing the bloodstained shirt which had nauseated me so that day.
I call out to the man I killed:
"You said life was sweet."
Those present, even the very serious-looking lawyer, were puzzled about who I was calling out to. They may have thought I was trying to escape the rope by pretending I had gone nuts. I, too, at first wondered if my compass had gone askew. Then I remembered that the needle had pointed to death.
As I left after the verdict I had to walk. This necessity made me happy. Then I thought of how I hadn't been this happy for a long time. It's nice weather, and hot as well. Stifling heat one would call it, that's the kind of heat we've been having. Not a single cloud in the sky. The blue of the sky is the prettiest blue I've ever seen. I don't like whitish blue. This blue has both light and dark hues in it.
The sky is not actually the way I see it of course. Ask that man and he'll say it's white. If you asked the convict inside whose compass is pointing to death, he would say gray... I personally think that if you take a careful look you'll see every tone of blue in it.
In the last scene, upon hearing his death verdict, the convict should turn and look back. In this scene his mother, brother, the man he killed and the transsexual should

appear. A blurred effect is necessary in this scene. (To provide the blurriness one should talk to the boy who worked as the lighting technician in the last movie: Now, what was his name?)

Translated by Suat Karantay
"Bir Filmin Son Sahnesi İçin Gerçek Yaşamdan Alıntılar,"
Hanene Ay Doğacak (1993).
Istanbul: Can Yayınları, pp. 94-100.

ALMİLA ÖZDEK

The Goddess of Fertility

Zeynep didn't know where she could pack her dozens and dozens of *üzerlik*s. Those that were little or big, those embroidered with floss or beads, those covering the walls in rows—showing the guests nothing but themselves—and those hanging in the corners like wallflowers… For years, without paying any attention to her mother's grumblings, instead of working on her dowry, she wove and braided countless *üzerlik*s, trusting that they would show their blessings when the time came. That's why she couldn't now dare to remove the *üzerlik*s and put in dozens of petitions instead.

Ever since people from seventy-seven nations started flocking to the region armed with strange equipment, Zeynep had been working on her *üzerlik*s more enthusiastically because the foreigners loved the *üzerlik*s she gave them, showing them excitedly to one another. Zeynep would go and watch them working whenever she found the opportunity. She was thrilled at seeing the bright colors of her *üzerlik*s popping up every now and then in all that sweat, dust and soil. However, as the number of newcomers increased, she decided she must fit her *üzerlik*-braiding into a schedule. As soon as her morning work was done, she would immediately sit down with her seeds and floss in front of her. While working on each *üzerlik*, she strove to create a different pattern; racking her brain over and over, she'd sometimes spend long minutes holding the seeds in one hand and the floss in the other. Sometimes, too, she'd strangely enough take it out on the seeds. She'd stick the needle straight into their hearts, squeeze them tightly on the string as if wishing to choke them. This kind of *üzerlik* she'd never give to strangers. She would hang them all on the walls of her room.

Then, too, Zeynep had this one *üzerlik* that she kept hiding from her mother in every nook and cranny. One night, as she was lying on the roof, the creation of this *üzerlik* had come to mind. An *üzerlik* that she would never give away, but that would remain in the memory of anyone who ever saw it and remind them forever of Zeynep. Before collecting her material, Zeynep considered for days what kind of pattern she wanted to create; she would gaze at the hills and mountains, wander in the gardens, and on the roof keep seeing this *üzerlik* in place of the stars. And eventually she decided what she wanted. First she was going to braid and embroider the greens; in this *üzerlik* there should be every tone of green; those looking at it should be able to distinguish each and every green, yet feel that they were seeing only one color. She was going to do the same with the blues as well, and then unite the greens and the blues on two sides; in the pool between them, she was going to emblazon all the colors she knew without rhyme or reason, a blinding mélange never before seen. Reds, yellows, purples and pinks... Not a single color should be missing. The cloth, Zeynep cut from satin and her dowry material; one by one she collected hundreds of seeds; as busy as she was, she collected the nerve to beg the neighbors for beads. She'd developed a passion for beads when she was small. Although small, she knew she wasn't a little kid—nor a boy, nor a woman. The day she first started stringing the beads for the *üzerlik*, she felt a pulsing of excitement deep inside; she suddenly cast them all from her hand.

Although she'd never dreamed that the petitions would challenge the *üzerlik*s, she didn't have enough space for both in the chests. For months her mother had made her write petitions regularly every day. Sometimes she would speak softly and say: "Oh, let's not bug the statesmen," and sometimes, infuriated, she would simply scald those statesmen in her petitions. The men of the village weren't any different at all; although they couldn't discuss the situation in the village coffeehouse—now under water, they wouldn't give up their habits entirely. They'd gather just at the water's edge and discuss the petition problem for hours, dipping their feet in the water for a second and then drawing them back. Who sent how many petitions where, what he wrote, how long it took for a reply to come, what it said... They'd discuss a single word for hours, each driving a different meaning from a reply probably written in two minutes by who-knows-what official.

Zeynep also had dreams in which the petitions, the *üzerlik*s and the Euphrates mingled together; in some of them she would be drowning between the lines of a petition, in some she would be taking up life in the depths of the Euphrates. Once these dreams became more frequent, writing petitions had become even more unbearable, but at the same time she didn't want to deprive her mother of this occupation and fray her nerves any further. After each petition was written, her mother would retire to her room and not come out for hours; all you could hear was a quiet rustling. Zeynep hesitated to disturb her, in part because she herself could use some peace of mind. She had no idea how she would take care of her mother once they moved into their new place; her mother's feet that were used to walking on warm, damp soil were going to freeze on the concrete floors. Zeynep had spread layer after layer of mats, but still the concrete didn't seem to care; the strange cold of that concrete would soak into one once and for all. Besides, her mother wasn't even aware that it was a village of concrete; all she knew was that they were moving away from the water and that they'd have to haul water to make their garden grow. Moreover, it had never occurred to her mother that their garden might never again be green.

Sometimes Zeynep wondered whether—in place of each petition written in this village—an *üzerlik* had been woven and braided, it wouldn't have brought the blessing of fertility with them to their new places? For whatever reason, as soon as this thought came to mind, she'd recall her older brother who'd long ago migrated westward. When her brother had come to help them move, first of all he'd looked into every last corner of the house and even searched through Zeynep's drawers thinking that she wouldn't notice; then he gave them a pocket-full of money and took Zeynep aside, whispering: "Take all of this, but please, when you move Mom to the new place, don't ask me to be here. You handle that sort of thing much better than I." Zeynep couldn't say a word.

And as the weeks passed by without even enough time to pray that the waters would be down when they awoke the next morning, Zeynep felt the need to knock on her mother's door and wake her up to make the final preparations. Something prompted her, shivering, to walk straight into this room where she hadn't been for months. Her eyes were first of all dazzled, sparks flashed in them, her stomach quailed, she was angry and felt like crying; as an indescribable weight settled on her shoulders, she sank into the corner. A bridal bed that her mother had secretly been preparing was now spinning around Zeynep as if poking fun at her.

While Zeynep—after each petition—had been picturing her mother falling peacefully asleep with the comfort of having done her best, her mother had been pouring all her strength and hope into this bed, minutely embroidering the cushions and the quilt that she'd covered in satin, decking the entire bed in tulle, decorating the canopy with ribbons and hiding the cold blue iron bed-frame under a colorful carrousel. Only with difficulty could Zeynep hear her mother telling her how the new place would bring her luck and that she'd be able to educate her children better there; she couldn't comprehend what it all meant, she just sat there.

Two hours later, while the men they'd hired with the money from her elder brother were carrying the bridal bed into their new home, dozens of *üzerlik*s were floating rapidly down the surface of the Euphrates towards the dam.

The Street Leading into the Water

Once this was a lovely street: right next to the mosque, and lined on either side with pomegranates. Cobbled, you know, like those nostalgic streets in old Istanbul we love to stroll on or those we lay anew.

Strangely enough, while I was wandering among the last few surviving orphan cobblestones of the street, I came across an application for the university entrance exam. Name, surname, exam number, everything complete—signed and sealed by an official, all ready to be sent off. What in the world was it doing there, what winds had blown it there? Since it had been so carefully filled out, why hadn't it been sent in? I suddenly remembered my own university applications, those first filled out in pencil, afterwards checked by each member of the family, then written over in ink, but which—checked over again and again because I was never comfortable—entered my dreams and ruined my peace of mind... Those forms had captured the focus of my life so completely that I could not possibly understand how these could be crawling on the wet ground now.

What kind of a youngster was this? A scrubby child from the East or the son of a father rich in pistachio groves and orchards who could afford to send him off to study in Istanbul? One old man told me that if they had just waited for another twenty days, we villagers could have gathered the harvest and lived comfortably for the next two years. Maybe that's why this application form was now crawling on the ground and—with the waves pounding and pounding upon the street—would soon mingle in the Euphrates.

Uprooting

The trees were tightly embracing the soil. Then came a machine to wrest them from the soil and carry them away, roots and all, with the best means of technology.

Yet this uprooting machine wasn't yet perfect because stripping the roots from the soil one by one was a very difficult job. In certain places it was scarcely possible to tell where the roots left off and the soil began. At such times they would plunge the machine downward, salvaging whatever might come out. No one would ever know how many roots were left in the soil.

Our folk became very happy when they saw green shoots sprouting under the rooted tree. I didn't want to spoil their fun, but there was really nothing to be happy about. These new shoots—when they wanted to mingle with the soil—what would they find instead? Because another old man had told me that no matter how much soil, layer after layer, dump as you would on the rock, it never did any good. A tree can't strike roots into rock.

Life Written in Petitions

Everyone who sees us invites us into the house; at least have a cup of tea, they say. There's especially this one villager, if he could only go to town and hand in a petition, he'd get his money from the government and before the water reaches his ankles could get a house built. But because he's sacrificed his trees to the waters, he doesn't have enough money to go to town and get his petition written. Because he is telling all this as calmly as can be with a smile on his face, because he's willing to invite nine people into his house of two cubicles, we can't really understand how he can stake his life on a petition; nothing comes to our minds except the disrespectful sour-faced officials; we all go tsk-tsk and shake our heads. Our whole trip passed with our going tsk-tsk, anyway. If he'd shouted, if he'd cursed or cried, then we could have comforted him, immediately collected the money among us, stuffed it in his hand for his travel and petition, and could have felt useful; this man, however, is so calm and smiley that I can't look him in the face anymore; I scorn and resent him. No, we can't write your petition, we know that's what you, like the others, expect from us, but we don't write petitions, we only write stories. When we get back to Istanbul, each of us will go to our own rooms and write pages and pages of stories for you. Do you know what a story is, Uncle? Have you ever read a story? If you haven't, we'll send you our stories, okay? Besides, everybody knows that writing a story is more difficult than writing a petition.

The Bottomless Euphrates

One can't see the bottom of the Euphrates. We've just boarded the boat, we aren't yet far from the shore, but the bottom isn't visible; we can't tell if it's 30 centimeters or two meters deep. And I, like an idiot, had been hoping to look down into the water and give my mind a rest even before reaching the banks of the Euphrates. What did I expect to see under the water, fish? Now I'm absolutely positive that if I fall into this water, I'll drown immediately.

Flowing as if to defy the postcards, the Euphrates has continuously brought civilization, allowing no other option. It's because of this, because of civilization, that Belkis' home and the industriously whining and roaring dam are now staring face to face at one another. Are they spewing anger at each other or, because they're children of the same mother, do they understand each other much better than all the rest of us do? Is Belkis asking those whining and roaring machines, the turbines, "Is it your turn now?" in a soft voice? Is this why such a beautiful woman as she is can no longer force her rosy cheeks to smile?

The moment I saw Auntie Hatice's bed, I was so taken by astonishment that laughing didn't even come to mind. No one's ever told me, however, whether eighty-year-old Auntie Hatice made this bed for herself, or when she made it: whether she made it years ago before they moved to their new place or whether she'd started on this bed as soon as she arrived, or whether she's ever thrown herself down upon those white sheets to try and ease her heart... What was going through her mind while she was decorating this bed with red satins, tulle, and even shiny paper from the stationer's? No one's said a word. While looking at Auntie's bed, I realized she was one of those women whose picture can never be taken—like Belkis.

Translated by Zeynep Tüfekçioğlu and Jean Carpenter Efe
"Bereket Tanrıçası," *Fırat'a Karışan Öyküler* (2003).
Istanbul: Can Yayınları, pp. 99-106.

Biographical Notes
(in alphabetical order according to last name)

Nalan Barbarosoğlu (b. 1961) graduated from the Philosophy Department at Istanbul University. Often featuring intricate plots, her short fiction focuses upon unfulfilled romance, on the lives of losers. Short story collections: *Ne Kadar da Güzeldir Gitmek* (Leaving Is So Wonderful / 1996), *Her Ses Bir Ezgi* (Every Voice a Melody / 2001) and *Gümüş Gece* (The Silver Night / 2004).

Habib Bektaş (b. 1951) saw minimal formal education. In 1972 he migrated to Germany as a worker. He has written and published novels and short stories in German as well as Turkish. Prize-winning novels in Turkish: *Gölge Kokusu* (The Smell of the Shade—winner of the 1997 İnkılap Novel Award) and *Cennetin Arka Bahçesi* (The Backyard of Heaven—recipient of the Ömer Asım Aksoy Award in 2000). Short story collections: *Meyhane Dedikleri* (What They Call a Meyhane / 1999) and *Ben Öykülere İnanırım* (I Believe in Stories / 2001).

Sibel Bilgin (b. 1956) has lived in Holland since 1979, where she has done research at Leiden University and directed many documentary films in collaboration with her husband Floor Kooij. Her highly acclaimed short story collection entitled *Bana Bir Harf Söyle* (Give Me One Letter / 1993) reflects a very private world. It is presented in an exquisite style highly reflective of the Turkish oral story-telling tradition.

Gaye Boralıoğlu (b. 1963) studied philosophy at Istanbul University. A journalist and copywriter, she has also done scriptwriting for several popular TV series. She has published one novel, *Meçhul* (Anonymous / 2004), and has one collection of short stories to her name: *Hepsi Hikâye* (It's All Fiction / 2001).

Contemporary Turkish Short Fiction: A Selection

İnan Çetin (b. 1966) has worked both as a librarian and a publisher. A fictional world laden with mysterious elements marks his work. *İblisname: Bir Hayalin Gerçek Tarihi* (Praise to Satan: The Real History of a Dream / 2007) is a surrealistic novel in which inmates of the "House of Compassion" endeavor to cleanse their souls. *İçimizdeki Şato* (The Chateau Within Us) is a collection of short stories Çetin published in 2005.

Mehmet Çetin (b. 1955) served a long prison term after the 1980 military coup. His poetry collections include *Rüzgâr ve Gül İklimi* (Season of Winds and Roses / 1988), *Birağızdan* (In Unison / 1989), *Eylül Çiçekleri* (September Blossoms / 1990), *Hatıradır, Yak Bu Fotoğrafı* (Burn This Photo, It's a Keepsake / 1995), *Aşkkıran* (Love-Breaker / 1997). Çetin is the recipient of the 1988 Enver Gökçe Poetry Award. He published his short fiction in a collection entitled *Asmin* (1997).

Feride Çiçekoğlu (b. 1951) holds a Ph.D. in architecture and is a professor at a private university. Arrested as a militant, she served time in prison; much of her fiction reflects the sorrows, joys and hopes of her fellow inmates. As well as oppression and torture, destruction of the physical environment and loss of historical and cultural values constitute her major themes. A simple style—at times cinematographic—and subtle humor characterize her work. Her novel *Uçurtmayı Vurmasınlar* (Don't Let Them Shoot the Kite / 1986) was made into a successful film. Her novella *Suyun Öte Yanı* (The Other Side of the Water / 1991) has been filmed as well. She collected her short stories in *Sizin Hiç Babanız Öldü Mü?* (Did You Ever Have A Father Die? / 1990) and *100'lük Ülkeden Mektuplar* (Letters from a 100-ASA Country / 1996).

Aslı Erdoğan (b. 1967) holds an MS degree in physics from Boğaziçi University. Anthropology and American Indian culture are among her areas of interest. Her fiction foregrounds both biographical and fantastic elements. A widely-traveled writer, Erdoğan published her first novel *Kabuk Adam* (Crust Man) in 1994; set in Rio, *Kırmızı Pelerinli Kent* (City in a Red Cape / 1998) is her second novel. *Mucizevi Mandarin* (The Miraculous Mandarin / 1996) is a series of interconnected short stories. Her short story entitled "Tahta Kuşlar" ("Wooden Birds") received first prize in a competition opened by Deutsche Welle Radio in 1997. Her poetic short prose has been collected in *Hayatın Sessizliğinde* (In the Silence of Life / 2005).

Cezmi Ersöz (b. 1959) graduated from the Faculty of Political Science in Ankara. He is a popular and prolific writer of fiction who started out as a poet and critic. Poetry collections: *Şehirden Bir Çocuk Sevdin Yine* (Again You're Infatuated with a City Boy

Biographical Notes

/ 1992), *Hayallerini Yak Evi Isıt* (Burn Your Dreams to Heat the House / 1998). His most recent short story collection is *Şizofren Bir Aşka Mektup* (Letter to a Schizophrenic Love / 2001).

Murat Gülsoy (b. 1967) graduated from the Department of Electrical Engineering at Boğaziçi University, where he now teaches. He was the founding editor (1992-2002) of the on-line literary bi-monthly *Hayalet Gemi* (Ghost Ship). He is a program producer for *Açık Radyo*. Black humor, irony, and remarkable characters often pervade his intricately-woven works, where reality and fiction intertwine. His novels include *Bu Filmin Kötü Adamı Benim* (I'm the Bad Guy in This Movie—winner of the 2004 Yunus Nadi Novel Award) and *Sevgilinin Geciken Ölümü* (The Delayed Death of the Beloved / 2005). His short story collections include *Oysa Herkes Kendisiyle Meşgul* (However They're All Tied Up in Themselves / 1999), *Bu Kitabı Çalın* (Steal This Book—winner of the 2001 Sait Faik Short Story Award), *Alemlerin Sürekliliği* (The Continuity of the Realms / 2002), *Binbir Gece Mektupları* (Letters of A Thousand and One Nights / 2003) and *Bu An'ı Daha Önce Yaşamıştım* (I've Lived This Moment Once Before / 2004).

Feyza Hepçilingirler (b. 1948) graduated from the Department of Turkish Language and Literature at Istanbul University in 1970. From 1981 to 1984 she taught literature at various schools. Her book entitled *Türkce Off!* (Turkish Off! / 1997), composed of her critical essays on the misuse of Turkish led to heated debates on the future of the language. Novels: *Kırmızı Karanfil Ne Renk Solar?* (To What Color Does a Red Carnation Fade? / 1993), *Savrulmalar* (Drifting / 1997) and *Tanrıkadın* (Godwoman / 2002). Short story collections: *Sabah Yolcuları* (Morning Voyagers / 1981), *Eski Bir Balerin* (An Aging Ballerina / 1984—winner of the 1985 Sait Faik Short Story Award), *Ürkek Kuşlar* (Timorous Birds / 1987), *Kırlangıçsız Geçti Yaz* (A Summer Without Swallows / 1990).

Selim İleri (b. 1949) left Law School in Istanbul without completing his studies there. A prolific writer, İleri has produced plays, film scripts, essays, and literary criticism in addition to novels and short fiction. He received critical acclaim for his first work, *Cumartesi Yalnızlığı* (Saturday Loneliness), published when he was only nineteen. In most of his writing he continued to treat the loneliness and sorrows of the middle class vis-à-vis the sharp upheavals in society. A melodramatic vein pervades much of his fiction. His widely read novels include *Her Gece Bodrum* (Every Night at Bodrum—recipient of the 1977 Turkish Language Association Novel Award), *Cehennem Kraliçesi* (Queen of Hell / 1980), *Yaşarken ve Ölürken* (As We Live and Die / 1981), *Bu Yaz Ayrılığın İlk Yazı Olacak* (This Summer Will Be the First Summer of Separation—winner of the 2001 Orhan Kemal Novel Award), *Uzak Hep Uzak*

(Distant Always Distant—winner of the 2003 Sedat Simavi Literature Award) and *Kafes* (The Cage / 2005).

Müge İplikci (b. 1966) graduated from the Department of English Language and Literature at Istanbul University. She pursued further education in popular culture and women's studies. Her subject matter reflects her avowed stance as a feminist, and her intricate narrative structure is a clear extension of her post-modernist approach. Her novel *Kül ve Yel* (Ash and Wind) was published in 2004, followed by *Cemre* (Harbinger) in 2006. Her short story collections include *Perende* (Somersaults /1998), *Columbus'un Kadınları* (The Women of Columbus / 2000), *Arkası Yarın* (To Be Continued / 2001) and *Transit Yolcular* (Transit Passengers / 2004).

Şebnem İşigüzel (b. 1973) won the prestigious Yunus Nadi Short Story Award in 1993 with her first book, *Hanene Ay Doğacak* (Bliss Will Befall Your Household). Her fiction explores the drama of the man on the street with a plain yet warm style. İşigüzel's second collection of short stories entitled *Öykümü Kim Anlatacak?* (Who's Going to Tell My Story?) appeared in 1994, followed by her first novel *Eski Dostum Kertenkele* (My Old Friend the Lizard) in 1999. Her other novels are *Sarmaşık* (Ivy / 2002) and *Çöplük* (Garbage Dump / 2004). Another collection of short stories appeared in 2001?*Kaderimin Efendisi* (Master of My Fate), and that same year she also brought out *Neşeli Kadınlar Arasında* (Among Merry Women / 2001), a compilation of articles she had written for the daily *Radikal*.

Karin Karakaşlı (b. 1972) graduated from the Department of Translation and Interpreting Studies at Boğaziçi University. She worked briefly as a simultaneous interpreter and then several years for the Turkish Armenian daily *Agos*. Her fiction deals mainly with the trials and tribulations of the ordinary man, the brute force of society and the resistant struggle of the helpless individual. Her first novel appeared in 2005: *Müsait Bir Yerde İnebilir Miyim?* (May I Get Off at a Convenient Place?). Her short story collections include *Başka Dillerin Şarkısı* (The Song of Other Languages / 1999) and *Can Kırıkları* (Shards of Soul / 2005).

Cemil Kavukçu (b. 1951) graduated from Istanbul University in Geophysical Engineering. Written in a poetic impressionistic style, Kavukçu's prose reads smoothly and quickly, but creates effective visual images and supernatural circumstances that leave a lasting impression. Novels: *Dönüş* (The Return / 1998), *Suda Bulanık Oyunlar* (Murky Games in the Water / 2004) and *Gamba* / 2006. Major short story collections: *Patika* (The Path / 1987), *Uzak Noktalara Doğru* (Towards Distant Points—winner of the 1996 Sait Faik Short Story Award), *Yalnız Uyuyanlar İçin* (For Those Sleeping Alone / 1996), *Bilinen Bir Sokakta Kaybolmak* (Getting Lost on a Familiar Street / 1997), *Gemiler de Ağlarmış* (Ships Also Cry /2001) and *Başkasının Rüyaları* (The Dreams of Another / 2003).

Ümit Kıvanç (b. 1956) has been employed by many dailies and periodicals and is presently working at İletişim Publishing House. An accomplished musician, he performed several years with the Group Mosaic. Aside from his short story collection entitled *Erkek Hikâyeleri* (Men's Stories / 1990), he has also published novels, among them *Aşkım Benim Resimaltı* (My Love is My Caption / 1985), *Bekle Dedim Gölgeye* (Wait, I Told the Shadow / 1989) and *Yalnız Olmuyor* (It's Tough to Be Alone / 1995).

Perihan Mağden (b. 1960) graduated from the Psychology Department at Boğaziçi University and is now a widely-read columnist for a leading Turkish daily. Her well-known poetry collection *Mutfak Kazaları* (Kitchen Accidents) was published in 1995. Her prose fiction often verges on black humor. She has two novels to her credit: *Refakatçi* (The Escort / 1994) and *İki Genç Kızın Romanı* (The Novel of Two Girls / 2002)—the latter was made into a film in 2005. Her novella *Haberci Çocuk Cinayetleri* (The Messenger-Boy Murders) appeared in 1991.

Murathan Mungan (b. 1955) holds a degree in drama from Ankara University and has worked for the State Theatre as a dramaturge. Drawing on folk tales, fairy tales and myth, his poems, plays and fiction problematize the human condition. Major poetry collections: *Osmanlıya Dair Hikâyat* (Stories of the Ottomans / 1980), *Kum Saati* (The Hourglass / 1984*)*, *Eski 45'likler* (Old 45's / 1989), *Yaz Sinemaları* (Outdoor Summer Cinemas / 1989), *Mırıldandıklarım* (My Mumblings / 1990), *Oyunlar İntiharlar Şarkılar* (Games Suicides Songs / 1997), and *Başkalarının Gecesi* (The Night of Others / 1997). Plays: *Mahmut ile Yezida* (Mahmut and Yezida / 1980), *Taziye* (Condolences / 1982) and *Geyikler Lanetler* (Deer and Curses / 1992) His novels include *Yüksek Topuklar* (High Heels / 2002) and *Çador* (Chador / 2004). Short story collections: *Son İstanbul* (The Last Istanbul / 1985), *Cenk Hikâyeleri* (Combat Stories / 1986), *Kırk Oda* (Forty Rooms / 1987), *Lâl Masallar* (Mute Fairy Tales / 1989) and *Üç Aynalı Kırk Oda* (Forty Rooms with Three Mirrors / 1999).

Halil İbrahim Özcan (b. 1957) graduated from the Kayseri Teachers' Training Institute and taught for three years. He was incarcerated on political grounds for ten years, an excruciating experience that is reflected in his works, some of which—written while he was still in detention—are extremely cryptic. His poetry and short fiction have appeared in various literary journals. Among his published volumes are the poetry collection *Kavgalı Küçük Fener* (The Controversial Little Lighthouse / 2005), his novel *Ejderha Yılları* (Years of the Dragon / 2001), and a short story collection entitled *Randevu Hazırlığı* (Preparing for a Rendezvous / 1993).

Contemporary Turkish Short Fiction: A Selection

Almila Özdek (b. 1972) graduated from the Department of English Language and Literature at Istanbul University, and did her MA on post-modern and feminist literature. She presently teaches in the Communications Faculty of a private university. Her short stories have appeared in various literary journals.

Işıl Özgentürk (b. 1948) holds a degree in economics from Istanbul University. She has written plays, film scripts, articles for magazines and newspapers, novels and fairy tales for children. Major short story collections: *Dünyaya Masallar* (Stories for the World / 1979), *Hançer* (The Dagger / 1981), *Alevin ve Acının İçinden* (Through Flame and Pain / 1986—short stories and interviews), *Geniş Mavi Bir Gök* (A Wide Blue Sky / 1996), *Yokuşu Tırmanır Hayat* (Life Climbs the Slope / 1999) and *Sessizlik ve Sırdır Ötesi* (Beyond Is Silence and Secrecy / 2004).

Mehmet Zaman Saçlıoğlu (b. 1955) is a professor of fine arts, a poet and a short story writer. In his innovative short fiction Saçlıoğlu forces the limits of traditional form. He uses humor most dexterously. Poetry collection: *Günden Önce* (Before Day Breaks / 1985). Short story collections: *Yaz Evi* (Summer House—winner of the 1994 Sait Faik Short Story Award), *Beş Ada* (Five Islands / 1997), and *Sarkaç* (The Pendulum / 2003).

Suzan Samancı (b. 1962) is a housewife who lives in Diyarbakır. In her poignant stories she reflects upon social issues in the politically sensitive geography that is home to her. She has written one novel entitled *Korkunun Irmağında* (In the River of Fear / 2004). Short story collections: *Eriyip Gidiyor Gece* (The Night Melts Away / 1991), *Reçine Kokuyordu Helin* (Helin Smelled of Resin / 1993), *Kıraç Dağlar Kar Tuttu* (Snowbound Mountains / 1998), and *Suskunun Gölgesinde* (In the Shadow of Silence / 2001).

Murat Sohtorik (b. 1969) is a graduate of the Department of Business Administration at Marmara University. He is presently working as a copywriter. In 1995 his stories began to appear in literary journals. *Kısa Çöp* (The Short End of the Matchstick / 2002) represents his first collection of short stories.

Deniz Spatar (b. 1967) graduated from the Sociology Department at Istanbul University. She has been working for Turkish dailies, publishing houses, and the radio station *Açık Radyo*. Her first story appeared in *Adam Öykü*, and since then she has compiled a collection of her short stories under the title *Kopya Kadınlar* (Duplicate Women / 2003). Women's issues dominate her subject matter.

Biographical Notes

Hakan Şenocak (b. 1961) graduated from the Drama Department at Ankara University. He is a poet, short story writer, and essayist. Love and death are among his favorite themes—these he handles on the borderline between fantasy and reality. His short story collections include *Karanfilsiz* (Bereft of Carnations / 1988) and *Naj* / 1998.

Ayfer Tunç (b. 1964) graduated from the School of Political Science in Istanbul. She worked in various departments of several periodicals and dailies. Presently she works as an editor for a prominent publisher. Short story collections: *Saklı* (Concealed—recipient of the 1989 Yunus Nadi Short Story Award), *Mağara Arkadaşları* (Cave Friends / 1996), *Aziz Bey Hadisesi* (The Aziz Bey Affair / 2000). Her more recent book *Bir Maniniz Yoksa Annemler Size Gelecek* (Mom and Dad Will Pay You a Visit at Your Convenience / 2001) is a best-selling volume of recollections.

Özen Yula (b. 1965) studied economics at Hacettepe Univesity in Ankara and did an MA in the Drama Department at Ankara University. He is predominantly a writer of both fiction and drama although he directs plays as well. Violence, sexuality, death, betrayal, and obsession—as well as a quest for God recur among his themes. Ordinary folk with surprisingly extraordinary character people his fiction in settings that include not only the cities, towns and rural areas within Turkey, but reach to America and the Far East—not to mention ancient Mesopotamia. In addition to a novel, Yula has published his collected plays in three volumes—among them *Gayri Resmi Hurrem* (Unofficial Hurrem), which has received several prestigious drama awards. His short story collections include *Öbür Dünya Bilgisi* (Knowledge of a World Beyond / 1993), *Kayıpkent Üçlemesi* (Trilogy of a Lost City / 1995), *Buğuevi* (Mistinesshouse / 1998), *Arızalı Kalpler* (Malfunctioning Hearts / 2002) and *Tanrı Kimseyi Duymuyor* (God Doesn't Hear Anyone / 2005).

Hür Yumer (1955-1994) studied business administration at Grenoble University. He was an acclaimed translator of French fiction. A collection of his own short stories was published posthumously under the title *Ahdımvar* (I Vow / 1995).